THE
DIRTY WORK
OF
DEMOCRACY

For Jackie and Mia

THE
DIRTY WORK
OF
DEMOCRACY

*A year on the streets
with the SAPS*

ANTONY ALTBEKER

JONATHAN BALL PUBLISHERS
JOHANNESBURG & CAPE TOWN

© Anthony Altbeker, 2005

Published in 2005 in trade paperback by
JONATHAN BALL PUBLISHERS (PTY) LTD
PO Box 33977
Jeppestown
2043

ISBN 1 86842 230 5

Cover design and reproduction by
Flame Design, Cape Town
Typesetting and reproduction of text by Alinea Studio, Cape Town
Set in 11.5 on 14.5 Bembo
Printed and bound by CTP Book Printers, Duminy Street, Parow, Cape

'In Moulmein, in Lower Burma, I was hated by large numbers
of people – the only time in my life that I was important enough
for this to happen to me. I was sub-divisional police officer of the
town ... In a job like that, you see the dirty work of Empire at
close quarters.'

GEORGE ORWELL: 'Shooting an Elephant'

CONTENTS

ACKNOWLEDGEMENTS

This book owes its existence to a lot of people, some of whom I can thank by name.

The first is Graeme Simpson. Graeme ran the Centre for the Study of Violence and Reconciliation with more dedication, inspiration and intelligence than did the director of any comparable non-governmental organisation in the country. I say this not because he liked the idea of this book when I first proposed it to him and then went off and secured funding for it, or because he is a friend, but because this is the widely held view of anyone who knows anything about civil society's engagement with crime and policing. He is now in New York, stretching other muscles and learning other skills, but he has left the sector much enriched.

There are others at the Centre whom I must thank. Amanda Dissel tolerated (but only just) the missing of more deadlines than I had any right to expect. She and her team – Bilkees, David, Gareth, Jonny, Kindiza, Lulama, Sasha and Themba – created an enormously stimulating environment in which to work.

A number of people helped me to get the final manuscript into shape. The lovely Jackie May read and savaged my first drafts. Ivan Vladislavic, my editor, was kinder and gave me the assistance I needed to get over the numerous humps and hurdles I encountered. A number of readers – Jonny Steinberg, Elrena van der Spuy, Jo Stein, Paul Levy and Phillip Altbeker – offered me both encouragement and advice. Naturally, whatever help I have been offered does not diminish my personal responsibility for any errors or omissions in the text.

All of Graeme's backing, all the stimulation offered by CSVR, and all the help with the manuscript would have counted for nothing if the police had turned down my request to do this work. Two of the South African Police Service's deputy national commissioners, Louis Eloff and Mala Singh, looked kindly on my request, and without their support my research could not have happened. Beneath them there are any number of officers whose cooperation and assistance helped enormously. I cannot name all as many requested anonymity, but the station commissioners at Barberton, Elsies River, Galeshewe, Ivory Park, Maluti, Parkview, Rosebank, Sea Point, Thokoza, Wynberg and Yeoville gave me access to their staff. Each also helped me think through the challenges they face.

Finally, it is the scores of uniformed cops in their patrol vans, and detectives in their clapped-out Mazdas, with whom I passed endless hours, and who fielded thousands of questions with mostly good grace, who are owed my biggest thanks of all. Theirs is not an enviable lot, but despite the added burden of having me tag along, I found them welcoming, helpful and interesting. I can honestly say that without them, this book could not have happened. I hope they find in it an account of themselves, their institution and the society in which they work, that does justice to the complexity of the problems they face.

*

The researching and writing of this book was supported financially by a grant made to the Centre for the Study of Violence and Reconciliation by the Ford Foundation. The views expressed are not necessarily those of either of the two institutions. My deep gratitude to them, however, ought to be reiterated.

PREFACE

During 2003 I spent time at eleven police stations around the country, observing police officers going about their duties and asking them thousands of annoying questions. I'd been granted the privilege of access to the organisation on the basis that I would provide the South African Police Service with a series of case studies to be used in their management training programmes. The *quid* for that *quo* is this book.

My intention was to write a book about the challenge of policing South Africa and, in so doing, to explore the nature and temperament of South Africa's police officers: a kind of travel book that took as its subject police stations and their denizens. The execution is, no doubt, flawed and incomplete in any number of ways. It is also, I fear, going to disappoint those who would have police officers portrayed as men and women of faultless judgment, indomitable bravery and the strictest moral fortitude. That kind of sugared overpraise may be thought by some to be essential to raise the organisation's morale, but it is also sentimental nonsense and burdens police officers with standards that are hopelessly unattainable. I have, therefore, tried to write about police officers as real human beings doing work that is usually unpleasant and often traumatic, and that almost always consists of an endless series of insoluble dilemmas. That is the consequence of having to do a society's dirty work, and I hope that any policeman who reads this book will recognise in it some of the complexity – moral and practical – which he must confront every day.

One problem with an approach that is not governed by the laws of hero-worship, however, is that what is reported here may not please everyone in the Service, particularly some in its higher ranks. This has meant that I have not been able to adopt the approach taken by Kurt Vonnegut in his novel *The Sirens of Titan* when he assures his readers that the people and places depicted in the novel are real, adding: 'No names have been changed to protect the innocent since God Almighty protects the innocent as a matter of heavenly routine.'

I could not put pen to paper with the same assurance as Mr Vonnegut that no consequences would flow for those I describe, since the Police Service, an organisation which I studied for more than two years in writing this book and with which I have been professionally associated for more than a decade, is less dependable in its treatment of its members, innocent or otherwise, than is the Good Lord of his flock. Police officers know this well, of course, and the result was that many of the men and women with whom I worked asked that their names never appear in a published text. Having agreed to do this for some, it seemed impossible to justify identifying those who had not thought to ask for the shield of anonymity simply because they had failed to realise that an outsider, with his outsider's eyes, might not see things the way they do. For that reason, the majority of names in this book have been changed. Those that have not belong to people who did not request anonymity and whose designation would, in any event, make their identity perfectly obvious to anyone who wished to discover it. There is, for example, only one station commissioner at the Sea Point police station, so the gesture of giving the man a pseudonym would be meaningless.

Apart from this unavoidable concession to the constraints of writing about an organisation as notoriously bashful as is the Police Service, the people, places and events recounted here are all real and are reported as accurately as my memory and note-taking skills would allow. The only exceptions to this are that, in a few instances, hybrid characters have been created, drawing together the views of a few individuals, to render the narrative more readable. In addition, in a few other places some facts have been changed in order to misdirect those who would peer behind the cloak of anonymity. In chapter seven, for instance, some of the words I have attributed to the men I call Constable Morena and

Sergeant Twala were, in fact, spoken by other officers in similar circumstances. Bringing in more names and more characters would have need-
lessly burdened my limited skills, especially given the consistency of
their views with those of their colleagues. Another example: the central
character in chapter twelve, Inspector Makaye, does not work in Ivory
Park but, given the man's idiosyncrasies, if all I had done was change his
name without also changing the station at which I found him, his
identity would have been all too easily unmasked. For the interested
reader, more detail about all such modifications is contained in an
author's note at the end of the book.

★

It is customary in this kind of work for the writer to say at the outset
that in working with the police he encountered enormously impressive men and women devoting their lives to vital work in conditions
which he, with his middle-class sensibilities, could barely tolerate for
a moment. The expression of these sentiments is often intended to
reflect as well on the writer and as on his subjects, and is seldom
offered except as a kind of fee paid to purchase the moral space to
criticise some – but not all – of the people described.

This is not a convention I would want to overturn for the simple
reason that the Police Service really is filled with men and women of
courage, integrity and determination, people who spend their lives in
an organisation whose ethos might quickly render me fit only for the
asylum, and in conditions that are horribly frightening and depressing by turn. Though they are seldom uncomplaining, they live for
their work, do it largely for others, and would not change it for anything.

Having said that, I must also say that the more time I spent with
the organisation, the more I realised that these are ordinary men and
women. They are not superheroes. All are fallible and some are worse:
ignorant, lazy, brutal and even corrupt. The humbling thing about
spending time with policemen and -women, however, is that even the
worst among them, the ones who spend large portions of every day

working the angles and pocketing what they find on people they search, will, in the course of a typical year, do more good for people who are strangers to them than will the average researcher/writer throughout his life. Policemen, it transpires, don't have to be supermen to do good. All they have to do is turn up for work.

CHAPTER ONE

THE DIRTY WORK OF DEMOCRACY: GALESHEWE, JANUARY 2003

It's around 7pm. The sun is low in the sky, and shadows, their work done for the day, are stretching out for the evening. Some of the oppressive heat of the day is beginning to lift, pushed away by a dry breeze. Crowds of people are making their way to their homes or to local watering holes, as taste and temperament dictate. In the street outside the police station, women in short skirts are carrying crates of beer. Loosely clothed men shout greetings to one another. One drags at a foul-smelling hand-rolled cigarette, and the thick smoke of his breath obscures his features before dissipating in the wind. Taxis ferrying people from town swerve through the streets, just about avoiding pedestrians and hooting angrily when someone ambles a little too deliberately in front of them. Music, a discordant blend of whiny American R&B and bass-heavy kwaito, moves with the dust and smoke of the sunset. On the horizon, a hint of storm clouds glows red and orange in the setting sun.

The entrance of the Galeshewe police station is humming as police officers in blue and soldiers in their browns come on duty. The station stands next to one of the main roads leading into the township. The cops, most in their late thirties and early forties, flirt with pedestrians. The soldiers, grimmer than the policemen, mill around their personnel carrier, their R4 automatic rifles and stiff body armour making their movements awkward and ungainly, insect-like. The bush-camouflage they wear doesn't work in the city. But it does what it must do: it carries an aura of authority and potential violence.

The shift commander is Inspector Malete, a solid, reliable man with a tired, wise smile. He laughs when I point to some of the soldiers and tell him that I've always had a thing for girls with guns. He is six foot tall, strong and fit. He talks slowly but with command, and it's clear that there is respect for his authority even if the logjam in promotions means that he outranks few of the men and women on the shift.

The police officers are tired. They were on duty all of last night, and the day has been a scorcher. At home in their tin-roofed, air-conditioner-less homes, none had found any sleep. It is the last weekend of the month, the first after payday, and the night promises to be a long one.

I shrug when Malete tells me confidently, but not dismissively, that I won't make it through the night: 'Two night shifts is hard work. You need to get used to it.' I agree with him and remark that there is time enough in every twelve-hour shift for me to drive from my home in Johannesburg to the green sea of Cape Town. It is a long time to spend in a car driving in circles.

Inspector Zele, the one woman on the shift, tells me that she'll be working in the charge office tonight and that she seldom goes on patrol. 'It's too dangerous. Men try to take advantage of women police,' she says. When I ask, she tells me that she has never used her firearm and doesn't want to. She is a short woman who somehow seems larger than she is. Her loud, flirtatious manner, willing laugh, and the side-arm on her hip all make her more imposing than you might guess. She is stubbornly trying to arrange a transfer to East London where her boyfriend lives. But in order to do so, she needs to find a cop working there who is willing to swap posts with her and move to Kimberley. 'But who,' she asks with more than a hint of bitterness, 'would want to come to this dry place?'

Our conversation is cut off by a woman's scream. It is a real scream. A scream of terror and pain. And it's nearby, just on the other side of the chain-link fence that surrounds the station. Soldiers gathered around their vehicle and police chatting at the entrance of the station, bristle. Then a heartbeat later they react, rushing out in a flurry of arms and legs towards a man and woman fighting in the street. He has his arms around her, wrestling with her, grabbing at the bag she is holding. She is wailing in fright, trying to stretch the bag away from his grasping hands.

The first to reach the two is an enormous officer. He's from the earlier shift and we haven't met. Heavyset, he stands well over six foot and looks a real bruiser. Putting the man in a choke-hold, he rips him off the woman. The attacker, in his mid-twenties and with a wild afro, staggers backwards, fighting to keep his balance. He stumbles, falling into a crowd of four or five on-rushing cops and soldiers. Fists fly at his head and body, one or two glancing off him, the rest missing their mark altogether. He falls at their feet, more from loss of balance than from the impact of the blows. He lies there a moment prone, then the original cop, burly and vicious, launches a ferocious kick to his abdomen. The sound, a dull, meaty thud, brings the action to a sudden stop. Movements freeze. Breath is drawn in. Hot blood cools instantly. It sounds like something irreparable has been done: a man can die of a blow like that.

Cops and soldiers, everyone in the circle has the same reaction. As a life might flash before a dying man's eyes, each imagines the consequences: the investigation and the cover-up; the disciplinary hearing and the lies; the delay in promotions due, and the stain on careers.

Shamefully, my first thought is for me. What, exactly, is my responsibility here? What if the beating continues? Do I help the man? Do I call the cops off and threaten to report them? If I try, would it make a difference or will the powerlessness of the outsider be exposed? But if I don't do anything, will people say that I should have? Am I brave enough to confront these men if I must? This is dangerous ethical ground. I don't want to be implicated in police wrong-doing, but nor do I want my work to come to a grinding halt almost before it has begun. If this goes on, if the man dies, I think to myself, I will be in a serious pickle.

Slowly the man begins to stir, groaning. Visibly, the men and women standing over him relax. Relief floods over me too. Whatever ethical crisis the kick has evoked has not been compounded by the death of this drunk moron, so stupid he attacked a woman in front of a police station.

Two of the women soldiers haul him to his feet, prop him up and begin to lead him to the station's holding cell. Initially he is limp and moves with them, offering no resistance, but as they approach the building he struggles weakly, grabbing onto the fence. The soldiers, almost but not quite entirely uninterested in him now that the action is over, karate-chop his arm. One, a rifle draped over her shoulder, steps back and gives him a half-hearted kick in the thigh. Behind them, the other cops and soldiers are adrenalised, they stalk each other and the pavement, predators pissing the signs of their presence, their existence, into the night air, telling the world that whatever happens in other places, no-one should disrespect them in this way. This does not happen here. It cannot happen here. It must not happen here. Certainly not in the very mouth of their den.

★

In 1974, one of the world's leading students of policing, Egon Bittner, proposed an unusual definition of the subject. Unlike the policy-makers and pundits who argued that the police should be understood in terms of the goals they claimed to pursue – the prevention of crime and the capture of criminals – Bittner insisted that a proper understanding of the police had to begin with the means they use. In particular, he argued that the police can be understood only if one grasps what is unique about them: they alone are empowered to use force to resolve the innumerable conflicts, disturbances, disasters and, yes, crimes that arise from the simple fact that people with different interests and passions have to share a common social space. They are not, therefore, to be thought of solely as crime fighters. Yes, they deal with crime. But they do so only because crime falls into a wider category of incidents which he described as 'something-ought-not-to-be-happening-and-about-which-something-ought-to-be-done-now! situations.' There are literally millions of these incidents. Many, perhaps most, are not criminal, and a large proportion of those that are technically crimes will, in the cold light of day, seem trivial and, therefore, wasteful of police time and resources.

Where a serious crime has been committed, it will be obvious how a cop should use his powers and what he should seek to achieve: he should leave no stone unturned until the wrongdoer is brought to justice. In other cases, however, precisely what ought to be done when the police are called out is unclear. A police officer's warning might quell the anger of a tenant being evicted or get a noisy neighbour to turn down his music. The arrival of a large, uniformed, nightstick-wielding representative of the law can get a car that has been blocking a driveway for two hours moved. The same man standing in the living-room of a family whose members were, a moment before, on the point of tearing out one another's throats, can offer the would-be pugilists the chance to step back from the brink and go to bed without any loss of face. Cops, in other words, use their authority to use force, particularly the implicit threat of arrest, to do much more than fight the crimes and criminals that haunt the middle-class imagination.

But why call the police in these circumstances? Why not call a social worker or a neighbour or, heaven help us, a lawyer? Why turn to a government agency, the members of which are armed, uniformed and supposedly engaged in the never-ending hunt for criminals, to help resolve these petty clashes of interest?

Bittner's answer was deceptively simple: you call the police when this kind of unpleasantness rears its head because you think that there is a chance, remote or otherwise, that resolution of the problem may require the non-negotiable use of coercive force. That might mean that one or both of the parties may have to be arrested in order to prevent their making any more trouble. But, whether an arrest is required or the officer's presence alone is sufficient to resolve the problem, what is decisive is the right of the policeman to bring an unpleasant situation to a close with the measured use of legally sanctioned, but nonetheless coercive, force, and to use the threat of this to impose a solution, how-ever temporary, fragile and imperfect it may be. Without the certain knowledge that the police retain arrest as a final option, tensions between the protagonists might explode and cycles of pre-emption and revenge could easily take hold. That is also why, except in cases of self-defence, the right to use force legitimately is supposed to be enjoyed exclusively by the police. It is an exclusivity that is prized and which must be guarded jealously for, in its absence, society could revert to a war of all against all.

5

From this point of view, policing is best understood as a means – the allocation by society to certain designated people of the right to threaten or actually to use coercive force to resolve an unpleasant situation. The police don't exist, in other words, to control crime. They exist as a means of dealing with situations which need immediate handling and which might require force, or its threat, for resolution. Crimes are perhaps the most important of these moments, and, because those who handle criminals need sometimes to be allowed to use coercive force, the pursuit of them will always be a police matter. But crime is not a stable category of activities and it does not exhaust the universe of situations in which the police and their powers might be needed: disasters are unpleasant, and may require for their handling that some people are empowered by law to move gawkers along; traffic accidents are unpleasant and can lead to horrible acrimony necessitating police attention; a drunken argument can quickly escalate into something even more unpleasant, as can the presence of squatters on a piece of land the owner might want to sell. The list is endless, and the result is that societies rely on their police for a whole lot more than dealing with the crime and violence that television shows suggest are the police officer's standard fare.

Because clashes of interests and passions are inevitable, giving somebody – by convention, a police officer – the exclusive right to use force legitimately is a precondition for a viable society. But the precise tasks that each society sets its officers can tell us a great deal about its *zeitgeist*. Police officers in the People's Republic of China, for instance, don't do the same things, or do them the same way, as the Metropolitan Police in London. The English bobbies' approach, in turn, differs from that of their colleagues across the Irish Sea in the Royal Ulster Constabulary. These differences spring from two distinct but connected sources. There are, on the one hand, differences that emerge out of the society itself. What sorts of situations demand police attention? What kind of crime is committed, and how often? What kind of unpleasant situations arise, and how frequently? But differences also arise from the character of the police themselves and the state they represent. Do they demonstrate in word and deed a commitment to helping the little guy, the vulnerable

6

victim, or are they the bodyguards of the rich and the socially powerful? Do they routinely violate the rights of suspects? Do people actually turn to them for solutions, and do they respond when called, or are people, for whatever reason, more inclined to sort matters out for themselves? Are their judgments trusted and respected?

In a country as obsessed with crime as ours, all of these are interesting and important questions. Yet these are not the only questions rewarded by the study of the police, for police officers are more than just street-corner politicians negotiating an end to petty disputes, crime preventers and investigating officers. They are also an indispensable building block for any society. They are not separate from their society, and the nature of a police force and its work reflects the society of which they are part. The result: their successes and their failures are the successes and failures of the whole social order.

This was a point well made by George Orwell, who spent a few years as a police officer in Burma in the 1920s. It was, he wrote, a hateful job. He loathed the Empire of which he was a minion, the community in which he worked, and, above all, the duties of a police officer. These, he wrote, brought him into close contact with 'the dirty work of Empire'. Now Orwell was an arch anti-imperialist, and by describing policing as part of the Empire's dirty work he was probably drawing attention to the fact that the British police in Burma were part of the oppressive machinery of colonialism. But he might also have meant something else. He might have meant that policing, by its nature, is usually done after the milk has been spilt and the shit has hit the fan. Its primary purpose, after all, is to respond when things have fallen apart. His hatred of policing notwithstanding, therefore, the observation that police officers do a society's dirty work would be as true of newly democratic South Africa as it was of the British Empire because, in both cases, it is police officers who are called in when something that ought not to be happening nevertheless is happening or has happened. It is to them that we turn when our society has failed in some way, and as a result they spend much of their day poking through our nation's viscera, examining its half-digested excreta. They deal with a South Africa that cannot even be seen from any other vantage point.

Of course, in exploring the underbelly, cops are more than mere tourists, heading off to take in one sight after another. No society, much less one in the midst of a transformation as profound as our own, emerges fully formed from the welter of paper – the constitutions and laws and social compacts – that give it birth. Were high-minded documents enough to create a well-ordered, graciously polite society, we would have one. In the real world, it falls to men and women to breathe life into these promises and to turn the common decencies envisaged by our law into reality. This takes boots on the ground, and it requires those who wear them to take assertive, sometimes confrontational, action to push the recalcitrant into line. This is the essence of policework and police officers, and this is why cops are active participants in the building of our civilisation. Their actions or inactions, the choices they make and the habits of mind from which these spring: all of these help to shape the world in which we live. Whether for good or ill, their presence, even their gaze, can affect the outcome of events that shape people's lives. As Orwell might have been pointing out, cops will need to get their hands dirty. But that does not mean that a society could do without their efforts. The work may be dirty, but it is also noble, and, if we wish to understand our world and how it works, we must understand our police officers if only because they play so important a role in shaping it.

Thinking about policing as part of the process of civilisation-building raises issues that are quite different from the usual run of questions posed about law enforcement and crime prevention in South Africa. These questions tend to revolve almost exclusively around the level of recorded crime, with inferences about the performance of the police drawn from the slope of the trend line. But using these lines as the basis on which to assess the police does a disservice to them. It is analogous to using the trajectory cut by HIV/Aids through the population as a measure of the performance of the country's doctors and nurses. Doctors, like the police, generally step in only after the event. They, like the police in relation to criminality, have a role to play in reconfiguring the behaviour that determines whether the epidemic grows or contracts. Still, it would be quite odd to think that doctors and nurses are responsible for the epidemic and for the conduct in which it thrives. Policing, like medicine in the face of HIV/Aids, is primarily reactive. And, as importantly, it is but one tool among others through which the underlying human behaviour might be altered. Thinking about the role of the police in this way suggests that there are important gaps in any assessment of the police – favourable or otherwise – which relies exclusively on changes to the level of recorded crime, for, whatever the implicit claims of populist politicians calling for more patrolmen and better-trained detectives, our crime levels are simply not the fault of the police. They may haul an assailant off his victim, but they are not responsible for the attack.

There is, however, a price to be paid for doing society's dirty work, and cops are often put in terrible situations. Some of these are physically dangerous. Many, many more threaten their souls. Few cops stay bright-eyed idealists for long: their work breeds cynicism and disenchantment. One reason for this is the long-term exposure to society's sewers that officers must endure. Another is that much of what police officers do usually has a scrappy, lesser-of-two-evils feel to it. Policing's solutions to the problems with which they deal are always partial, often cosmetic and seldom more than temporary. Worse still, doing a society's dirty work involves a great deal of in-your-face, up-your-nose, standing-on-toes confrontations. No-one could police South Africa's streets otherwise. One result is that even apparent solutions, when looked at through another prism, can be made to look like failures. If aggressive policing works, someone is bound to ask whether it was necessary to be so aggressive. Others will point out that aggressive policing often seems to be directed at society's most vulnerable groups. Yet, if the police are too passive, if they allow wrong-doers to slip through their net, they're sure to get hammered for that too.

Theirs is a no-win contest between themselves and the innumerable conflicting values our society purports to hold dear. It is a dirty business and there are no perfect solutions, certainly none that will please everyone. Because of that, watching them at work can tell us something important about ourselves.

CHAPTER TWO

A SOCIAL WORKER AND A POLICEMAN: INSPECTOR MOLEFE, GALESHEWE

Laurel and Hardy.

That's what I thought when first introduced to the well-rounded and soft-faced Inspector Molefe and his angular partner, Inspector Jansen, 'They look like Laurel and Hardy.' But the physical similarities between them and the comic actors belied the officers' world-weariness and the humourlessness with which they approached their appointed tasks. Dyspeptic and bitter, neither would have made a merry drinking buddy. But, with nearly forty years of police experience between them, both knew the job and its demands inside out and, like the actors they so resembled, they could slip into character whenever they had to. It was clear, however, that neither relished the performance, and I wondered if either ever really had.

Jansen, phlegmatic as a stone, was not a man easily drawn into conversation. Once Molefe got going, on the other hand, he could barely contain the sour resentment that boiled inside him, and after one particularly frustrating domestic disturbance he turned to me to complain. 'You've seen what the job is. They want me to be a social worker, a doctor, a magistrate, and a policeman. This job is very bad. I'll tell you frankly, I'm very negative. If they want me to do this shit, they must pay me more.'

'How much do you get?' I asked.

'R82 200 a year,' he replied sourly. It was no fortune, but it was a figure which, together with overtime and medical and pension contributions, put Molefe squarely in the middle of South Africa's middle class. How much, I wondered, would satisfy him?

'Think about those people in parliament. All they do is sit on their arses behind their desks. They don't do 12-hour shifts. They sleep nicely at home while I am out here getting R1,33 per hour for night duty. My wife has no job and I have four kids. I want what those politicians get. If the government wants me to do all these jobs, it must pay me what I want. Otherwise they must give me a package and let me fuck off. I tell you, I am very negative. They have promoted all these people from the street to being officers. Just because they were in the struggle. I'm an inspector with 20 years, but I must still drive a van all night and deal with all this rubbish.' He gestured vaguely at the houses around him. Lit by the pylon lighting erected in the 1980s to help the police keep an eye out for late-night sedition, each was no more than a shadow in the orange light. Every one of them, or so it seemed to Molefe, had its own maddening history of domestic strife to which he'd been called at least half-a-dozen times.

'It's bullshit,' he muttered, almost to himself. 'All of it.'

Against this kind of disillusionment there is no satisfactory response. It was, therefore, hardly surprising that both Molefe and Jansen went AWOL for most of the following night's shift. Before then, however, I learned that a surprisingly large proportion of policework is done in the intimacy of strangers' living-rooms and bedrooms, and that going into these places meant penetrating the veils with which people seek to close off their private worlds from the gaze of others. It was an uncomfortable experience, one that left me feeling compromised, as if the smells of paraffin-heating which accompanied these forays left a dirty residue on my being. This was a feeling, and a smell, which I came to associate with policing.

From Jansen and Molefe, I also learned the standard operating procedure of the South African policeman when called to sort out one of these domestic something-that-ought-not-to-be-happening situations. Once on the scene, they'd quieten everyone down, warn people not to shout or swear, listen to all sides, and then tell them all that there is nothing much that anyone can do for them so they'd best learn to get on with one another. For the most part, this was done with a solemn authority, without resort to shouting or to any unnecessary aggression.

Nevertheless, criminal cases were seldom opened and arrests were almost never made unless the violence that accompanied the dispute went beyond the pushing and shoving, slapping and punching which, in South African policing, is barely considered violence at all.

★

The Northern Cape is notorious for having some of the highest per capita levels of family violence in the world, and I'd come to endure Galeshewe's dry heat because I wanted to see how South Africa's constabulary handle these calls. It didn't take long for a call to come in: there was a list of six addresses waiting for my humourless Laurel and Hardy immediately after they'd booked on duty. It wasn't long, therefore, before we were on a dusty street on the edge of the township lined with cramped houses of brick and zinc.

Galeshewe was not a pretty place. Trees were at a premium and, during the baking daylight hours, so too was shade. Parklands were few and far between. There were no sights to see, and one can safely say that people did not live there for the view. There wasn't one. At the same time, in comparison to the destitution of some townships, particularly those surrounded by vast seas of shacks and shanties, most of Galeshewe seemed less desperately poor. Houses and gardens were well established and consistently maintained. Many were bordered by well-manicured hedges and flowerbeds. Even the dire hostels, in which migrant miners had once lived their prisoner-like lives, had been turned into family units and seemed reasonable places to live. Their reconstruction had made a big difference to the community, Molefe told me as we drove past them: 'In the past, the hostels had no toilets, you see. The people who lived here used the bucket system, and at night some of them would throw their buckets over people in the streets.'

The first complaint was on a street that was deep in shadow. The officers had been called because a man had been attacking his wife, a woman of indeterminable age in a dark dress that had been only half-heartedly buttoned. The top of a bra appeared in the V between her breasts.

As was almost always the case, the cops had arrived after the fighting was over. The woman, who was otherwise unscathed, was bleeding from a knife wound in the palm. She was remarkably calm as she told the cops that her husband had gotten drunk and that they had fought. She didn't say what the fight was about and neither officer asked, but she kept pointing to the blood seeping from her hand, telling us that she wanted him arrested, specifying that the charge would be attempted murder.

She was not entirely sober, but she knew her law.

'And where is your husband now?' Molefe asked, barely trying to conceal his boredom. She didn't know. 'Drinking somewhere,' she sneered, making her answer drip fiercely. 'With his friends.'

While she spoke, three dusty children gathered around her, and one of her neighbours was walking to and fro behind us, filling an endless series of buckets from a tap at the end of the road. One lascivious eye on the young woman with her buckets, Molefe asked the bleeding complainant what she would do with the children if they took her to the station to lay a charge against her husband. There was no-one with whom they could be left; they would have to come along.

The kids were small and brittle-looking, their eyes glassy with wary anxiety and worry. One, a boy of four or five, was crying brokenly. It must be hard, I thought, to see children's faces like this every shift.

Molefe sighed, leaving no-one in any doubt that he could have done without all this: opening the case would take a good half hour at least, and he had other complaints to attend to. Who knew what was going on at those places? He turned to open the back of the van and was in the process of directing her and the kids into its dark interior when the woman's calm shattered and she launched a furious volley at a shambling, dog-eared man who could only have been her husband.

'Where have you been, you fucker?' she screamed in Afrikaans. 'I've got the police with me now. Let's see you fight now, big man. They're going to take you to court. You fuck. You bastard.' Spittle sprayed as she rushed at him, swearing at the top of her lungs. 'They're going to arrest you for attempted murder.'

The man's reaction was unexpected. He spoke to the police, almost shouting, as he walked past them towards his house, pointedly ignoring his wife. 'I don't care what you do. Arrest me if you want. I just want my fucking shoes and we can go.'

He blustered his way into his house, a mostly-zinc affair barely big enough to contain his anger. A dog, abject and anxious, was tied to a pole outside the structure. He was pulling this way and that at a short chain, his shoulders hunched against the strain. The ructions in his family were agonising. He wanted someone, anyone to show him some love, to tell him things were OK. But he'd been forgotten as the family tried to sort out their problems and, unable to sense what to do to be of most help, he barked uncertainly at the police, frequently looking to his master for some confirmation that this was the right course of action.

After a few moments the man emerged from the house and, standing at his doorway, called the police. 'Come have a look at this,' he shouted. 'Look at how the bitch hides my beer away from me.'

Neither Molefe nor Jansen was having any of it. 'No. Get your shoes,' Jansen yelled. 'We're not your friends. We don't want to see your house.'

The man shrugged a fuck-you-too at them. 'Where have you hidden my shoes?' he shouted at his wife. 'I can't find the fucking things.'

Getting him into the van proved no easy task: he was drunk and, with the single-mindedness that some drunks cultivate, he was determined that he would not leave the place shoeless. Even after he got in the back and the door had been closed after him, he called out repeatedly for his wife to find and bring his shoes. For some mysterious reason of her own, she fought through her anger and pain and hatred, and did so. Then she, the shoes and the three children were bundled into the back of the van with her husband so that she could ride uncomfortably to the station to open a case.

This was not a joyous family outing.

At the station, the charge office was full of people and the atmosphere was charged with the bitter anger of victims now made to wait for police attention.

The arrested man was taken to the holding cell while the woman began to swear out a statement to Jansen. Soldiers, complainants and assorted wretches sat on benches, eyes glued to a television perched high above the charge office counter.

The Galeshewe police station had only temporary holding cells and could not accommodate prisoners overnight. Before they were taken elsewhere, and while paperwork was being completed, they were kept in a makeshift holding pen behind the charge office counter. Although those inside it couldn't be seen from the civilian side of the desk, they could be heard. Knowing this, the arrested man began to call for his son. The boy's tears had left him with the worn, aged look of poor children everywhere, and his father's calling, rhythmic and repetitive, cut straight to his heart. He began to roam around the charge office, looking for a way to get to his father, becoming more and more anxious and distressed. His mother, on the other hand, appeared all but entirely unmoved as she told and retold her story to Jansen, pausing only to measure out her lines of snuff.

Next to her, a man bleeding from a small wound in his back was trying to get the attention of the officers on duty. He didn't seem all that insistent, and the cops, for their part, weren't treating him with any excess of urgency either. Next to me a soldier, part of a contingent deployed to the township to help with cordon-and-search operations, was working himself into a bit of a temper.

'Look how they dress,' he said to me, his sour beer-breath all but melting my skin. I didn't think he meant the woman Molefe and Jansen had brought to the station: she'd buttoned up her dress in the van. 'Look at them. Little girls! And this is how they come to a police station.' Becoming more cozy, he added, 'I don't want to be ugly, but I don't think that these blacks know how to behave. At least we Coloureds don't act like that.' To illustrate his point, he went into an incomprehensible tale about an incident that appeared to involve three people, a knife and a case of beer stolen from a shebeen. When he finished, I told him that I didn't have a clue what he was talking about. At this he nodded in sage agreement.

I noted with some relief that one of his colleagues had taken his rifle away from him.

In the meantime, Jansen was advising the woman with the bleeding hand to start the process of applying for a protection order against her husband. But her son had by now found his father and, returning to his mother with a message from him, he began to plead with her not to do anything that might harm the man who'd brought him into the world.

★

Galeshewe is named for a nineteenth-century Tswana chief who led the Langeberg Rebellion in 1896. The celebration of colonial history that is the MacGregor Museum in Kimberley tells you that the rebellion was sparked by a police officer's killing rinderpest-infected cattle belonging to the chief, and paints the rebellion as unreasonable resistance to harsh but necessary controls needed for the good of all. There is, however, another version of this story. In this one, a Tswana rebellion was actively pursued by some of the area's colonial settlers who were looking for a pretext on which to seize what good land still belonged to the indigenous community. They saw the plague as a likely spark for rebellion, and were more than a little put out when most Tswana chiefs chose to cooperate with the authorities. Chief Galeshewe and his people, however, had no tradition of cooperation. They believed that the rinderpest had been introduced by the government in order to reduce Africans to servitude, and refused to go along with some of the regulations imposed on them. Just as the settlers had hoped, when the government decided to clamp down on what was now regarded as an incipient rebellion, it offered large rewards of land and cattle to volunteers to march on Galeshewe. The chief and some of his followers escaped the initial slaughter – as many as two hundred people died – and fled to the mountains of the Langeberg. There, aided by the difficult terrain and the presence of infectious cattle diseases which deterred his pursuers, he resisted a force of 2 000 regular and irregular troops for nine months.

When the troops did eventually march into the mountains they attacked both Galeshewe's followers and the local residents, many of whom had actively cooperated with the militia. But this appears to have made little difference to government forces, and somewhere between twelve hundred and fifteen hundred people were killed, while thousands more were shipped off to the Cape as indentured labour. A local priest reported that the general approach of the colonial army 'seems to be that they are out to shoot kaffirs, and that it is difficult, if not pedantic, to make such distinctions as that between loyals and rebels.'

After the rebellion had been put down, Galeshewe's land was confiscated and sold off as 120 farms.

I saw no memorial to Chief Galeshewe in the eponymous township. On the grounds of the present police station, however, stood a monument to those who died selflessly in the struggle to liberate South Africa. Poor design had meant that, rather than the sombre up-raised fist that was presumably intended, the statue looked like a large, inappropriately jaunty thumbs-up. It was a memorial that irritated some of the station's officers. 'It's a political thing,' Jansen said to me in what was, for him, a burst of hearty long-windedness. 'They have no business putting it up at a police station.'

He may have been right, of course, except that this wasn't really a police station, and the police were operating out of a building that had once housed the quislings of the black local authority. Before 1994, Galeshewe, despite its estimated one hundred and forty thousand people, was deemed unworthy of an actual police station. This was for the same reason that innumerable other black residential areas had no charge office, patrol cars or holding cells: policing the townships then was not about preventing crime and solving petty disputes, it was about defending the social structure from the rebellion that was smouldering through the country. Besides, cops saw townships as enemy territory, the sort of place they didn't enter except when they absolutely had to, places where beat-walking policing was an utterly unrealistic ambition.

That was also why few of the older cops who worked this area had grown up here. 'I moved here from Johannesburg in 1982,' Molefe told me. 'In those days, if you were a black police, you couldn't work where you had family. You'll come home one day to find them dead.'

'And you?' I asked Jansen. 'Where did you come from?'

'I'm from the Cape,' he replied. 'But I worked in kwaZulu.'

17

'What did you do when you were there?'

'In kwaZulu?' he sneered scornfully. 'I did what everyone else did. I dodged bullets. Lots and lots of bullets.'

★

After dealing with the stabbing victim and her shoeless husband, who would spend the night in jail, but whose case would be withdrawn by his wife the following Tuesday, Molefe and Jansen hit the streets again, trekking from one domestic dispute to the next.

Molefe, who was driving while Jansen and I shared the passenger seat, was telling me once again about how unhappy he was with the way the Police Service treated him, when he was waved down by a young boy. Anxiously, the boy told us that there were problems down the road, that a man had been throwing stones at a house where a sick woman lived, and that the stone-thrower had threatened to kill everyone inside.

We were in the delightfully named suburb of Vergenoeg Uitbreiding 2, literally 'Far enough, extension 2', and, while the van was stopped, I could hear music pouring out of at least four or five shebeens. The noise, the heat, the dusty streets and the orange light of the pylons created an atmosphere more like a juvenile beach party than one in which thousands of families would soon be trying to sleep.

The child's anxiety attracted a few passers-by who'd stopped to listen. One, an old woman, was puffing on a joint, and the sweet smell of marijuana filled the air. 'Go get them,' she called after us as Molefe executed a difficult three-point turn. 'Lock all the bastards up.' She laughed heartily at what she plainly thought was evidence of a wacky sense of humour.

The house was at the end of the street with open ground both in front and behind. The plot on which it stood was a bit larger than most in Galeshewe, with enough room for two large trees. But the garden, an island of weeds in a sea of hard-baked ground, was a mess, a chronicle of inattention and neglect. A rusty gate was bound shut, and scraped against stones poking through the path as Jansen pushed it open.

Two women were in the yard, bathed in the yellow light cast by one of the township's floodlights, while a man, sitting on a stump, skulked in the shadows of one of the trees. From under the brim of a ragged hat, he looked at us and through us. He was obviously *daggadronk*.

As they entered the yard, Jansen and Molefe were hit full bore by a verbal barrage from one of the women. She was sitting in a doorway, her back against the jamb, and despite the violence of her tirade she didn't stand up. Being yelled at by someone who couldn't bother to raise herself was strangely degrading, and I sensed that Molefe took some offence. In the odd moments when the woman wasn't yelling, she puffed on a cigarette so hard you might have thought she blamed it for her woes. The other woman, skeletal and quiet, sat on a blanket, her legs curled beneath her. She seemed to be in the last stages of a wasting disease, and barely moved throughout the exchange.

Slurring her words, the woman in the doorway shouted, verging on the hysterical, that a man had been at the house earlier and had threatened to kill them. 'It's an injustice,' she kept repeating, tears of frustration forming above a self-righteous pout.

'Who was the man?' Molefe asked with studied calmness.

'How the hell should I know?' she began to explain helpfully before being cut off by the woman on the blanket, who said simply: 'It was her boyfriend.'

This seemed to fire up the man under the tree. 'Fucking slut,' he muttered, before recovering his equanimity and going back to his appointed task of staring into space.

'*He's* also her boyfriend,' the woman on the blanket offered in a tone that almost masked her exasperation.

This infuriated the first woman. 'Keep your stupid nose out of my business. Who gives you the right to speak about my life? This is my house. You stay because there is no-one else to look after you. Who the hell are you to talk to the police about me? It's an injustice.'

Molefe was getting annoyed, and, if only because he knew it would irritate the banshee by the doorway, he turned to the woman on the blanket and asked what had happened. She told him that her sister had two boyfriends. Earlier in the evening the other one had arrived unexpectedly only to find this one – she pointed at the man ensconced

19

under the tree – at the house. The new arrival had flown into a rage and, as we already knew, threatened to kill everyone. The tone of her recitation, like her body language, suggested that this behaviour was not altogether unexpected.

By now Molefe was rapidly losing whatever vestiges of sympathy with the ostensible victim he might once have had. He had clearly decided that the main reason for the disturbance of the peace was the loose morals of the woman with two boyfriends. 'You can't have two boyfriends,' Molefe lectured her. 'There is always trouble when there are two bulls in one kraal.'

'Who the hell are you to tell me what to do?' she yelled at him. But Molefe took no offence because, in truth, he really didn't care how she lived her life. He was merely making a gesture, offering the sort of conventional advice that he hoped would end as quickly as possible this little expedition into the mess of another's life.

The shouting had brought two young girls out of the house. Apparently convinced that the police were about to cart their mother off, they began begging her to be quiet, their voices straining with growing desperation as she continued to throw volleys of indiscretions at the cops, glaring malevolently at them all the while.

Molefe turned to the man under the tree: 'And you. Who are you?' he asked with a hint of irritation.

'Ag. No. No-one, man.' The man mumbled his response, barely looking at Molefe.

'Then get the hell out of here. You're making the problem worse for everyone.'

'Me? What did I do?' he asked. His voice broke with an unlikely innocence.

'Just get out. I want this thing sorted out before we leave. If you're still here and the other one comes back, then there'll be problems. So just go.'

But still the man was reluctant to leave and the reason soon became clear: 'How can you make me go?' he asked. 'All my *zol* is here.'

I didn't think that a terribly politic thing to say, and Molefe, who had gone bug-eyed, couldn't believe what he was hearing. 'Move now or

I'm going to arrest you,' he shouted. Then, in quieter, more sarcastic, tones: 'I'm sure you can get more dagga at your own place.'

The man considered his options for a moment and then asked if the cops could give him a ride. This infuriated Molefe. 'Do I look like a taxi? Get out of here!' He took a menacing step towards the irritant who, realising that the game was up, stood unsteadily, dragging himself from the stump on which he'd been seated, and looked around for whatever goods and chattels he may have left behind. Having established that he had everything, he wandered over to the house and started to edge his way past his girlfriend who was kicking at the ground between her feet, fury seeping from her pores.

Molefe grabbed him by the shoulder. 'I thought I told you to go. You can't go in to get your *zol* in front of me! Are you totally mad?'

'Relax, Sarge. I wasn't going to fetch *zol*,' he placated. 'I just want my rolling papers.'

Molefe's eyes were popping out of his head. He looked like he might throw the man into the street, draw his sidearm and shoot the obstreperous hophead. But he regained his composure quickly, and turning back to the woman, the source of all his troubles, Molefe began a lecture the broad thrust of which I was to hear again and again in these sorts of circumstances. He told her that she was bringing all these problems on herself, that she would be better off with one man, that she should stop drinking, that she was a bad example to her daughters.

To this, the woman was both indignant and indifferent: not unreasonably, she said that it was her life to live and that no-one had any business telling her how to go about it. But Molefe, out of anger more than any great concern for her well-being, was insistent, and his badge gave him an irresistible authority. It was an implied threat that was picked up by the two young girls, who begged their mother to be quiet and listen rather than provoke the policeman into making an arrest. But her anger couldn't be contained, and, spying a bossy-looking woman peering over the fence, she turned her sights on her. 'And you, you *poes*, get your nose out of my yard. Who asked for you here? Do you think nothing bad happens in your yard?'

With a final warning to the woman to sort her life out and not to bother the police or her neighbours, Molefe and Jansen left the property. The man, recently evicted from his hidey-hole under the tree, was still in the street, and the cops made a lukewarm effort to tell him to bugger off. Then off we went, leaving two women, one dying and the other drunk, to care for the kids.

It was after we left them that Molefe told me about how negative he was, and how he wanted to earn what parliamentarians earned. He was fuming from the sheer futility of it all. What, he wondered, was the point of going into people's homes time after time only to learn that they were fighting for reasons which were beyond both his desire and his power to fix? If people got their lives into grief, if they drank and fought, if they couldn't bear their spouses and their needs, if they couldn't stomach another day of hard slog just to put food on the table, why the hell should anyone expect him to be able to solve their problems?

★

Back at the police station, Molefe went to write up his crew's activities from the past few hours, while I sat in the charge office making some notes. It being a weekend, I was not alone.

Soldiers were sitting on the hard benches, watching the badly lit tits and bums that are the late-night weekend fare of some television channels flash across the screen above the charge office counter. These had turned the charge office into a moral quagmire, titillating and scandalising by turn. Beneath the TV, the counter cops wrote out statements from people reporting crimes. One was from a woman, insistently waving a protection order under the nose of the inspector behind the desk.

'When are you going to arrest him?' she was demanding. 'He isn't allowed to do this to me. The court says so. Look at me,' she said, pointing to cuts and bruises on her face. 'Do you think I did this to myself? I'm not fucking stupid. He can't do this.'

She was dressed in a skirt that may once have been white. She was small-built, and her face looked as if wind and sun had made it shrivel further. Wiry hair had been tied into tight, short knots, creating a patch-work of squares between which her pinkish scalp shone through. It was a hairstyle created in anger. To calm her, her teenaged son – hair in a large afro, a small backpack hanging between bony shoulder blades – lit a cigarette to bounce between them, telling her to calm herself, trying to pull her back to the benches where she too could watch indescrib-ably bad pornography. 'All I want is that you arrest him. I've got a pro-tection order,' she said weakly, retreating to the bench against the wall to sit next to a badly beaten woman whose husband had been arrested. He was a real charmer who had sought to garner some official sympa-thy by allowing her to lean on his shoulder as she walked into the police station accompanied by the officers who'd saved her. Look how I sup-port my wife, he seemed to advertise, ignoring the fact that it was he who'd inflicted the injuries in the first place.

Watching them, I reflected that when middle-class South Africans talk about the police, the image they usually have in their heads is of uniformed men and women mustered against the armed robbers, rapists and murderers who are intent on depriving their victims of goods, dignity and even life itself. Theirs is the quintessential image of police officers as a thin blue line, men and women whose task it is to guard the boundary between good and evil, keeping innocent people safe by keeping evildoers out. Most police officers share this conception of policing. They too see their job as patrolling some perimeter, working to prevent the carnivores on one side from attacking their prey on the other.

But there is a problem with this metaphor, the animating idea of which is that criminals are different from their victims, that they come from a different walk of life, and that they can be stopped as they cross from one world to another. Men like Molefe and Jansen know better than that. They know that police officers spend a great deal of their time far from whatever frontiers exist, working instead in the intimacy of people's lives, dealing with the fallout from failed marriages, unravelling romances and troubled friendships. Many are petty cases – minor assaults, *crimen injuria*, and the crime that cops inelegantly call 'malicious injury to property'. But others result in the stabbings and rapes and murders that drive South Africa's crime statistics relentlessly upward. In these cases the image of a thin blue line is completely misleading because in none does the wrongdoer have a boundary to cross: he lives within the perimeter, sleeping beside or drinking with his eventual victim. Anyone posted on a frontier looking for an assault launched from the other side would be looking the wrong way.

Because of their intimacy with their attacker, and because many of the victims are drunk when they're attacked, Molefe, like millions of cops around the world, couldn't bring himself to see the victimised as entirely blameless. They may suffer a crime committed against them, but none was the proverbial 'innocent victim'. 'Weren't you drinking?' he'd ask them. 'Isn't it wrong to have two boyfriends? Aren't you also to blame for this problem between you?'

Cops resent being dragged into these things. They would infinitely prefer to be out trying to prevent crimes in which one party is unambiguously guilty and the other is equally unambiguously innocent, rather than helping to counsel two equally damaged people who now bitterly regret having committed their lives to each other. They would infinitely prefer to hunt criminals who prey on strangers rather than ex-boyfriends with anger-management problems. But the reality is that interpersonal problems generate a huge proportion of the calls to police emergency lines, and, instead of spending every waking minute chasing bad guys in stolen cars, policemen spend their days acting as emergency couple-counsellors or as what one criminologist famously called 'street-corner politicians,' two roles for which their training offers no real preparation.

It is this as much as anything else that accounts for the typical cop's disenchantment. The constant entanglement in the debris of other people's lives has drained him of whatever sympathy he might once have had for the people who think they need his help. He's become indifferent to them, contemptuous of the mess they've made of their lives, and angry that it has all somehow become his problem. His resentment is as much about his deep dislike of the people who call for his help as it is about his inadequate pay. He doesn't like being made to feel the voyeur poking around behind the curtains that should shield people's private lives. It is not what he signed on for. And yet, day after day, week after week, year after year, cops are called into situations in which those veils have been torn apart, revealing the people behind them as they really are, *in extremis*, without their masks, and, often enough, desperately drunk to boot. Pity might be one response to this. But with constant repetition and familiarity, pity is impossible to sustain, and soon enough it is replaced with its near-cousin, contempt. Stripped of their dignity, those who have called the police into these situations are no longer seen as victims but as 'losers'.

This then is the job. This is what it means to have to do society's dirty work. It is what the police do, and it is little wonder that many do it without relish.

CHAPTER THREE

AN OUTPOST OF PROGRESS: NIGHT PATROLS IN THE DRAKENSBERG, FEBRUARY 2003

Inspector Luyanda Thembeka went to bed drunk. He'd been drinking quarts solidly for three hours. Sitting in the thinning sunshine, he'd watched evening spread across the sky in obdurate silence: a man with things on his mind. Eventually, after the sun sank behind the mountains, he tipped the last of his beer onto the dust in front of him and stood up. He looked over at his partner, the teetotalling Sergeant Samuel Sibi, stretched out his back, and turned towards the room in which we were to sleep. He took in the four bare walls that supported the corrugated-iron roof, looked at the military style cots arrayed around the gas stove, frowned at the depressing pile of provisions, and offered the world a heart-felt grunt. He seemed suddenly to remember that his bladder was full and he turned away from the room, walked to the end of the wall and relieved himself into the patch of weeds that grew there.

Above the one-roomed building, the stars were coming out, casting their thin veil of dust above hills that rose plumply around us. In the gloom, the silence that enveloped the village, a tiny settlement with no electricity or water or tarred roads, became primordial. I felt my ears might pick up sounds made thousands of kilometres away, but apart from the occasional whistling of a neighbour or the barking of a dog there were none to hear. The silence, like the darkness, was as thick and luxurious as a wool blanket.

Oblivious to the pleasure I took in all that silence, Thembeka switched on a battery-powered radio. We were on the very edge of the SABC's signal, the very edge, perhaps, of the world, and the choral music to which the radio was tuned hissed and crackled horribly. There was little improvement when the music was replaced by an haranguing Sunday evening preacher.

Sibi and I chatted for a while over the remains of our beans-and-bread supper. He was a small, wiry man whose hardiness was legend. On New Year's Day in 2001, when a freak storm in the Eastern Cape dumped snow on the Drakensberg in the middle of summer, he and some colleagues were stationed well above the snowline watching for cross-border stock thieves. This was summer, so they were ill-equipped for the weather, and their commanders, fearing they might die of exposure, sent a helicopter up to fetch them. 'I was surprised by this,' he assured me, a little conceitedly. 'I grew up in these mountains. I know the snow. I know the cold. It can never kill me. I walked in it with no shoes even as a small boy.' His toughness notwithstanding, the work he and his colleagues did was hard on the body, and they were plagued with persistent colds, pneumonia, TB and the flu.

Presently Sibi and I stood up. We stowed the coffee mugs we'd been drinking from, kicked the stones on which we'd sat out of the path, and followed Thembeka into the room. The day had been hot, and the atmosphere inside was choking. Already dense with the smell of hundreds of gas-cooked meals, most apparently charred to ashes, the smoky stench was now being soured by the thin steam of beer and sweat rising from Thembeka's body. There also appeared to be a lumberjack, buzz-saw and all, secreted somewhere up his nose. Sibi looked at his partner and then rolled his eyes at me. 'Good luck sleeping,' they seemed to say. 'You're going to need it.'

★

Sibi and Thembeka were members of the Drakensberg Area Stock Theft Unit. Formally a specialised detective unit, it was charged with investigating cases of stock theft in six areas along the border between Lesotho and South Africa. Investigative units generally do not do patrol work, and most detectives regard their occasional deployment on a shift or at a roadblock as somewhat unseemly. But in the Eastern Cape's mountains, catching thieves and recovering the animals they'd stolen after the fact is such a thanklessly impossible business, these detectives spent as much time walking beats through the mountains in the hope of catching cattle raiders in the act, as they did following up crimes after they had been reported. The reasoning is as simple as it is inescapable: once a thief gets away with his haul, the animals won't be seen again. By the time the case is reported, the animals will have been driven across the border into Lesotho or ferried out of the area for sale to stock speculators. They will have been slaughtered for meat, or branded by their new owners and integrated into a herd somewhere over the next mountain. Only very rarely will they be found by detective work, and even when they are, arrests that would stand up in court will be made only rarely because establishing precisely who is legally in possession of an animal in a communal field is next to impossible without willing witnesses. Nor can the animals be dusted for prints, and even the most civic-minded of sheep will be unable to identify the men who stole it. All of which is to say that it is more productive to try to catch thieves in the act than to try to arrest them later.

Yet, if investigative work was hard, the challenges posed by patrolling the region were extraordinary. The area is big. It is home to something approaching half-a-million people and twice as many animals. But it is also extremely poor, and the scores of villages that pepper the mountains, between which the land is virtually empty, are connected only by rough tracks. There are no metalled roads, no houses, no fences, no electric pylons, no telephone lines. This is wide-open communal land, thousands of square kilometres of meadows and valleys, hills and mountains, and it mocks the efforts of the handful of cops and soldiers and police reservists who walk eight- or ten-kilometre patrols on the off-chance of catching thieves making off with their four-footed loot. Summer or winter, clear skies or rain, they walk their nightlong beats through the pathless countryside, playing tag with some of the most wretched criminals imaginable.

★

Thembeka and Sibi, roused by their body-clocks, woke up at about midnight. In the dim light provided by a candle perched half-way up a wall, the two dressed in tough workmen's clothes, threw blankets over their shoulders, and, each holding a staff, headed out into the velvet darkness. I followed them. I had neither staff nor blanket, but, driven by my unreasoning horror of ticks, I was wearing a shiny pair of water-proof pants over my jeans. I also had a couple of thick-cut peanut butter sandwiches and a bottle of water in a small backpack.

Spot the city-boy, I thought.

The night was cool, and a thick dew had formed on the ground, making every step an unwanted adventure. But for the dogs barking at the unexpected tramp of feet, the village was utterly silent. Soon enough, though, we left the track that led through this settlement and struck out into the veld. We were on no path that I could see, and, because my night vision was a good deal less developed than these men's, I had to work hard to keep pace. I followed Sibi, trying to put my feet down exactly where he put his and, through this device, hoped to avoid the ankle-twisting tufts and holes and stones that assailed me every time I fell more than a step behind. I had the impression that Thembeka was irritated by this: he was the more senior man, after all, and if anyone ought to have his footsteps dogged, it was he. But Sibi's pants were lighter in colour and his legs were easier to see, and I could make no apology for following him without drawing attention to Thembeka's pettiness. So I followed Sibi and promised myself that I'd find something about which to defer to Thembeka in the morning.

We walked for about three hours through a mostly treeless terrain that was seldom flat for very long. Hills rose steeply around us as our route circled hollows and mounds. Most of the slopes were reasonably shallow, but some were so precipitous that, clambering down, I'd slide and lose my balance. When climbing them, I had to take huge, wrench-ing strides that made my thighs ache. Stones often shifted treacherous-ly, but there was never anything to grasp or to break a fall. It seemed that at the bottom of every hill there was always a little stream which had turned the earth to a gluey mud.

Naturally, I twisted my ankle painfully about half-way to our destina-

29

tion, a valley enclosed on three sides by steeply sided hills, and known for that reason as Paddock. There we climbed a large, free-standing rock and found comfortable spots to sit or lie while we listened to the stillness. Above us, the odd shooting star danced with man-made satellites that glinted in a sun we couldn't see. Inside the plastic sheaths of the water-proofs, my jeans were soaked through with sweat that could now not dry. The light summer breeze, which on another night might have been fra-grant and cooling, seemed crisp and raw against my legs. 'Be quiet,' Sibi whispered unnecessarily. 'If thieves come, they mustn't hear us.'

I knew enough not to make a noise, though. The previous night two officers who'd been sitting on this very rock had recovered eight cows stolen miles away from the hillside village of Khaoue. I'd been with the investigators when the complainant had come in, and had gone with them to the crime scene. There I watched them inspect the rude kraal from which the animals had been taken. There was no evidence to gather, however. A rusting iron gate in a fence enclosing a muddy patch next to a hut had been pulled open and the animals had been led off.

'You heard nothing?' one of the investigators asked Victor Thengwa, the owner of the stolen animals.

'Nothing,' he replied. He was a shoeless subsistence farmer who spoke his high-school English well, and who kept himself curiously well-apprised about developments in Iraq by listening to national news and current affairs programmes on his radio.

'You saw nothing?'

'Nothing.'

'OK,' the cop said. Then he looked at me: 'We must go and look across the border. It might take us a few days. Are you going to come with us?'

As it turned out, we were spared a long search because the animals had already been recovered by the cops out here on this rock. We only learned this when we bumped into Victor's brother, who had gone looking for the animals at dawn, and was now returning to call off the rest of the search. It was a rare lucky break for Victor, who told me that the 88 sheep his father had once owned had all been stolen in the past few years. I could only assume that he was pleased to have his cattle back, but Victor wasn't given to displays of emotion, and took the news in with a stolid equanimity that suggested much about the way he and his family coped with the vicissitudes of luck and income that plague peasant farming. The recovery of the animals had not been accompanied by an arrest. Stock thieves are usually young, fit and agile, and those had easily eluded the older cops. 'They know we won't shoot,' one of the detectives told me later in the day as we stood over the rough, grassy bread the thieves had dumped as they fled arrest. 'They are not scared of us.'

★

Shivering on the rock next to Thembeka and Sibi, I wondered how representative was the success of the night before. Two cops had been sitting in the dark, hoping to be of use to someone, but knowing that they had no real control over events. Their organisation aspired to improve people's safety by preventing crime and catching crooks, but out in the real world there was little they could do to force the issue. If a stock thief passed by, well and good; but if none did, their efforts would seem wasted. Whatever success they did achieve had as much to do with luck as anything else. I wondered whether all policing might be a bit like that. Could it be that the lonely cop on the mountain waiting for stolen cows to pass was emblematic of policing more generally? It seemed a noble way to spend one's days, but it was also more passive and, somehow, sadder than I'd imagined policing to be.

There seemed to be few birds about, and dawn broke quietly over Paddock, the sun easing itself over a ridge, slowly smearing its pink light across the sky. We'd been sitting on the rock for about two hours, and from a law and order point of view it had been an utter waste of time. Nothing had passed us, least of all a herd of cows driven to the point of collapse by anxious thieves. 'If anything was stolen last night, it's gone by now,' Thembeka muttered. 'We can go home.'

After the exertions of the night, the early morning air was clear and bright, and, with one of my sandwiches safely scoffed, even Thembeka seemed less ill-humoured than he'd been. He talked animatedly about the plight of the stock theft unit, the future of which was uncertain because of the restructuring of all the specialised units. 'Me?' he replied

31

when I asked what would happen to him. 'They can put me anywhere. But they must tell me who is going to do this work. You need men on the mountain every night. They need to know the terrain. They need to be fit. They need to enjoy the work. If you give this work to the ordinary detectives or even the uniformed members at the police station, it won't get done. It's a lonely life, this one. They can do what they want with me, but if we stop doing this work, they must move me out of this area because the people here will be very angry. Then it will be just like 1998.'

The thought made him sigh.

★

No-one knows how many people died in Maluti in 1998, and it is doubtful if anyone ever will.

Crime statistics for the station record that about forty people were murdered in each year between 1994 and 1996, and that about thirty were killed every year between 2000 and 2004. In the three years between 1997 and 1999, however, the official statistics record, with blithe implausibility, the grand total of three murders. The anomaly is not a deliberate fraud. It is far more likely that a special task team was handling all the station's murders at the time, and that someone forgot to ask it to complete a return for the official record. Why, you might ask, would a specialised unit have been deployed out here in the sticks? Why waste precious resources on a quiet country district? The answer is that between 1997 and 1999 a war raged in these hills.

Precisely when or where the long-running problem of inter-communal cattle-raiding and stock theft turned into something nastier is uncertain, but it may have had something to do with a rise in cattle theft within Lesotho at the same time, which may then have spilled over the border. That, in its turn, may have been the result of South Africa's mines employing fewer and fewer Basutho migrants, which had exacerbated poverty. What is certain is that at some point in the mid-1990s, the age-old cycle of theft and counter-theft, which had long been integrated into communal life, was ratcheted up to a new level. Somewhere, a community, frustrated at the drip, drip, drip of its stock losses, armed itself and sent out a band of men to retrieve its stolen animals. That action, itself not wildly different from what had gone before, kicked off a rapid escalation. Perhaps the men took what did not belong to them, took more than they were owed, or used an unacceptable level of violence. Whatever it was that they did, it must have offended against a neighbouring community's code of justice and honour, and pretty soon a cycle of vengeance and violent retribution was spliced into the traditional sequence of theft and counter-theft. In the subsequent months and years, scores of people, the precise number unknown and unknowable, died as marauding bands waged war from the backs of their horses.

The failure of the state's policing apparatus to control this flare-up of communal violence can be traced back as far as heart or political whim desires. Some say that it was due to the destabilising, demoralising effects of the transformation through which policing in South Africa was going at the time. But perhaps the roots of the collapse of law and order lay in the 1980s when Transkeian policing was weakened by the ascension to power of General Holomisa, whose power base lay in the army, and who is said to have favoured them when allocating budgets. Then again, it may have been because the Transkei was one of South Africa's dumping grounds, and its institutions had been so grotesquely malformed that even by 1997, three years after the incorporation of the Transkeian Police into the SAPS, 19 of the region's 33 police stations still had no telephones and its senior officers had an average of only nine weeks of formal training in their entire careers. And even this history had a history: ever since the earliest days of colonialism, little effort had been made to build modern institutions in this part of the country, so far from the gold and diamond fields to the north and the commercial farms to the west. The result was that whatever it was that collapsed in the 1990s, it wasn't a full-blown modern police service with all the bells and whistles that implies. It was, in fact, something far less sophisticated.

However the failure is explained, the fact is that the police were unable to prevent the violence erupting and were for long periods incapable of bringing it under control. Without adequate numbers, lacking the vehicles needed to conquer the terrain, and hopelessly disorganised by the rapid restructuring of the institution itself, the cops were reduced to spectators, able only to watch as the communities they were ostensibly charged with policing went to war to protect and avenge themselves. It was as if a laboratory experiment exploring what happens when the institutions of the law wither away had been conducted. The outcome might not have surprised Thomas Hobbes: with no sovereign in play, once the informal rules of the communities of the area were violated, nothing could prevent a war of all against all from erupting.

★

On the way back from Paddock, Sibi, Thembeka and I stopped at a traditional stockpost and talked to the herdsman who lived there. His was a large kraal miles away from anyone else, and it had been, for that reason, the kind of place where dirty deeds were done during the peasant war in the late 1990s. He and three other men lived in shacks in the middle of a kraal built against the side of a small koppie. The entrance had been turned into a soupy mud where animals had churned the earth, and a rickety fence made of wire and misshapen posts was built between boulders and scrubby trees. The shacks in which the men lived were little more than a formless heap of scrap that hung precariously this side of complete collapse. To get to them, we had to walk through shin-deep mud and shit which sucked at our boots. Stupid-looking cows, so scarred from their numerous encounters with the branding iron that, but for the naivety in their eyes, they might have been a bovine prison gang, watched us pass incuriously. The wise-guy goats, clustering conspiratorially, seemed to laugh at our struggles.

I cursed them, and reminded myself how good goat meat tastes.

A swarm of flies, invasive and relentless, probed away at any exposed flesh. Perhaps they were pursuing the stench – of old rags and urine and washing left wet too long – that was penetrating my clothes (even the waterproofs!) and seeping deep into my pores. Fighting them off left me drained and depressed, but the herdsman, whose pail of morning milk throbbed with the creatures, must have reached an accommodation with them. They hovered around him like happy children.

The herdsman's was a wretched, lonely life spent watching other people's cattle for months at a time, earning little more than the meat and milk he needed to survive. Nor was his a life without danger, even five years after the war. 'The thieves will come here late at night,' Thembeka explained. 'You can see where we are, how far we are from the police station. By the time anyone comes down the mountain to tell us about the theft, the animals are already on the other side of the border. Then it's hard to find them and bring them back.'

'Are these men in danger?' I asked. 'Do the thieves ever attack them?'

'No. Usually, they use *muti* to put the men and the dogs to sleep. Then they get away without being noticed.' Perhaps I looked sceptical, so he continued more defensively. 'Sometimes the thieves shout warnings that they have guns and will kill them if they come out of the shacks. Most of the time these are young boys here, so they believe the thieves and they stay inside.'

The senior herdsman at this post was far from young, however. Wizened, strong and seemingly a little demented, he was a man to whom the cops deferred. This was a function of his age, but there was more to it: Thembeka told me later that this man had once followed stolen animals into Lesotho alone and, when he found the culprits, had attacked the kraal before waiting for support. Having survived so reckless an undertaking, he was feared by everyone in the area for his power and for the power of his ancestors.

★

The day after the mountain patrol, I was at the Maluti police station to interview Superintendent 'Buddy' Badenhorst, a round-shouldered, big-bellied, blue-clad Santa Claus of a man who commanded the seventy-odd souls that made up the local constabulary in these parts. Despite his approaching retirement, he seemed a man who, after all his years of service, still thought himself to be discovering the richness and variety of his work. His excitement could not be subdued. I suspected that it might well overwhelm his subordinates.

Buddy's police station was perched on a hill overlooking the town of Maluti. It was on the crest, and behind it the earth fell away as if into the abyss, leaving nothing but a vast expanse of sky, so pale and vacant it seemed to suck colour from the scene and made it seem as if the station house might be standing on the very edge of the world. Beautiful as it was, the landscape was strangely drained and exhausted, and the mountains in the distance were the colour of old bones. The air barely moved. But the stillness was the stillness of age more than peace, of fatigue more than serenity.

The building itself was of sharp-edged blond bricks. It had brightly painted trimmings, and was fronted by a small, well-clipped garden of aloes, leggy daisy bushes and purple agapanthuses. It was the very picture of the earnest, optimistic sincerity cultivated by the public service. Across a rutted red-mud road that was losing its struggle with the forces of nature, things were quite different. Hundreds of matchbox houses lined the slope down into the valley. Each was as ugly, as bare and as functional as the last. With their backs turned to the view, they formed a sullen, oppressive multitude.

This was Maluti, a town that General Bantu Holomisa, then the tinhorn dictator of the non-state of Transkei, had once intended to transform into the region's second city. Those ambitions had been successfully resisted, however, and modernity hung lightly on this place. The police station, magistrates' court, post office and taxi rank, together with the mobile pension payout points that rolled into town every month: these were the principal evidence that we were not in the eighteenth century after all.

Beyond the town were the villages, the residents of which were, if anything, even poorer, more detached from the modern world and more isolated from its institutions than were the townsfolk. They lived in a world of subsistence and tradition, a world in which time travellers from centuries past could have made their way without too much adjustment.

In the best of all possible worlds, the institutions of state, equipped with development plans and social safety nets, would have done something to improve conditions here. It is a cruel irony, however, that the state is always weakest precisely where it is needed most. One might be tempted to say that here, in these mountains, the institutions of the modern state – the representative assemblies, the countless bureaucracies, the service-delivering agencies – lay in ruins. But that would imply

36

that they had once been strong. The sad truth was that they have never been stronger. Nevertheless, the state's weaknesses were manifest in the crumbling roads, the absence of street lights, the shoddily built buildings and the unfenced, open land that was unfarmed but was also, paradoxically, over-grazed. The absence of institutions was also obvious in the dearth of policing. Here the number of cops per capita was less than a tenth of the national average, and it was little wonder that two-thirds of respondents to a recent regional survey said that they saw a cop less than once a month. Despite this, the per capita murder rate was something like half the national average, and less than a sixth of the rate at which South Africa's urbanites killed each other.

Sitting before the police station surveying the scenery, I wondered what the hell I was missing. I was in the depths of the old Transkei, where the state was stretched thinnest and was least able to project its authority, where the police stood the least chance of investigating, much less preventing, crime. How was it, then, that per capita crime levels were lower here than in much of the rest of the country?

There was no way, I thought, that law and order could be maintained in this wide-open countryside with only a handful of cops per shift and a couple of vehicles of dubious utility on the 95 per cent of the roads that weren't tarred. If something happened down in a *lallie* or at the stockpost I visited or on some half-forgotten goat track in the mountains, how on earth, I wondered, would the cops hear about it, much less respond in a timeous fashion? And, knowing the inevitable futility of calling them out, who would bother to walk the miles to a phone to make the call? Who would come to a police station to report an assault or a theft? I could even conceive of the occasional murder that might go unreported or unrecorded. There were thousands of square kilometres in which a body might be hidden, and it wasn't hard to imagine witness-less circumstances in which a murder might happen. It led to a Zen-like question: if a man was murdered in the depths of the countryside, would his passing ring an administrative bell or leave a statistical ripple?

Why then was the war of the late 1990s an aberration rather than the rule? For someone weaned on a diet of Hollywood cop shows, the proto-Marxism of my university political science, English theories of public administration, and American empirical research on criminal justice, it seemed quite inexplicable that blood was not flowing through this land.

When I first thought about the problem of policing places such as this, I had wondered if the isolation in which people lived meant that the moderating effects of living among a mass of people would be muted, that the restraining influence of the presence of the crowd on an individual would be diluted, and whether, as a result, individual behaviour would be that much wilder. This was one of Joseph Conrad's great themes: what happens to a man when cut off from the restraining bonds of civilisation? Kurtz, in *Heart of Darkness*, quickly forgot himself and pursued his 'abominable satisfactions' and, in *An Outpost of Progress*, a short story Conrad wrote a few years before the more famous novel and which foreshadows its themes and even its most famous lines, Conrad is even more explicit about the degeneration that sets in. There, two of the less impressive specimens of European civilisation are sent to man a trading company's outpost deep in an African jungle. The effects on them are appalling: they lose all moral compass, becoming first slavers and then murderously violent. Conrad writes that 'few men realise that their life, the very essence of their character ... are only an expression of their faith in the safety of their surroundings. The courage, the composure, the confidence; the emotions and principles; every great and every insignificant thought belongs not to the individual but to the crowd: to the crowd that believes blindly in the irresistible force of its institutions and of its morals, in the power of its police and of its opinion.' In the absence of these, for Conrad, man is a morally dubious creature, given to monstrous desires that most cannot properly restrain.

It was only months after I left Maluti that I realised that all these sources – the cop shows, the university political science, Conrad most of all – had led me astray. They reminded me of the old joke about an economist stranded on a desert island with only a can of beans. Having consumed all the coconuts, and on the point of starvation, he sets himself to open the can but has no tools. Starving and flailing about for food, he falls back on his training and constructs a theoretical model to help him open the can. The model proves intractable, however, so he decides he must make a simplifying assumption, and decides to take as a given the presence of a can-opener.

The difference between that economist and the literature I'd read was that in the books, it wasn't a can-opener that was assumed, it was the presence of an institution that looked something like a modern state. Always and everywhere in the academic and policy literature, questions of crime and justice are approached in a manner that takes for granted that the structures of government exist, and then proceeds to ask how these might be made more effective. None of this had equipped me to think about what happens when there is no state in the usual sense. I simply couldn't conceive of an orderly society without its formal ordering agencies, of a society that was organised without having organs of state. Perhaps this was why I was so rudely sceptical of the cops' account of how peace had been secured in the late 1990s.

That account, given to me by Superintendent Badenhorst and then members of the Stock Theft Unit who were around at the time, goes like this. By the end of the 1990s, it had become clear to even the most dogmatic policeman that working by themselves, the cops could not end the war. They could not watch all the flashpoints and monitor all the people who'd been drawn into the violence. They couldn't get to scenes of conflict in time to prevent violence, or even recover enough cattle to make thieving less lucrative. So, instead of trying to impose their easily evaded will, the forces of law and order pursued another course: a pact between the warring factions was worked out. In terms of this pact, each community would focus on keeping its own house in order: each would make sure that the cattle owned by its members were clearly marked, and that transactions that affected the herds were conducted through well-policed channels and were properly recorded; suspicious cattle – animals that were unmarked and unrecorded – would be brought to police attention; and peace committees would make sure that the chiefs and headmen, who were responsible for the herds of their people, fulfilled their responsibilities earnestly and honestly. In terms of the agreement, in other words, communities assumed many of the regulatory functions of the modern bureaucratic state, functions that the formal institutions, made ineffectual by under-funding and poor management, were simply unable to accomplish. But, after the police had helped broker the deal, they did all this without the formal administrative structures on which modern governance depends. Instead, they relied on local people, community leaders, and the reciprocity that came of an awareness that all would benefit if they could each come to trust the others.

All of this struck my city ears as either utterly implausible or deeply sinister, or both. How do you ensure that chiefs and headmen hand over stolen stock found in their own people's herds? How do you stop them forging records of herds and transactions? How do you prevent them from cooperating with stock thieves or condoning the thieving of members of their communities when they steal from their neighbours? With the state as weak as it was, and authority in any event having been ceded to these structures, the only plausible mechanism seemed to be some form of vigilantism.

'Tell me about the peace committees,' I said to Buddy Badenhorst as we sat in his pokey office, with its mock-up of a kraal protected by the battery-powered alarm system he wanted sponsored for his farmers, and reviewed my experiences in the area. 'How does it work? How do they relate to the police?'

'We work closely with them,' Buddy said. 'We have to. They are the ones who must handle a lot of the problems.'

'But is there a lot of vigilantism?' I pressed.

'You must understand that we have to work with these guys,' he replied carefully. 'Without them, there is no way we can keep the peace and control stock theft. But I won't lie to you. Sometimes we find bodies on the mountain, and no-one can explain who they are or what happened to them.'

I remember thinking at the time: 'Aha! The cops are supping with the devil!' Or words to that effect.

Months later I realised how simplistic my censorious response had been. It wasn't that I was wrong to worry about vigilantism, it was that I had completely failed to grasp what was interesting about the relationship between the police and the peace committees, who were, in effect, nego-tiating the position of the boundary between the modern state and some-thing else. I'm not sure precisely what this 'something else' is. And even if I had thought through the problem at the time, I doubt I'd have a very sat-isfactory answer now, because the information I would need to formulate it lies in social structures which are utterly opaque to me, unfathomable and impenetrable. I can't be sure that I would have had the words to frame the questions, much less the conceptual tools to understand the answers.

Perhaps this is why my interviews with peace committee leaders were so unsatisfactory. These were men of calluses and leather who'd spent years watching their herds and keeping order in their communities. They obviously drew on the authority of older institutions – tribal systems and feudal chieftaincies – whose power existed alongside the rickety institutions of the state, and when I expressed doubt that their approach could succeed, or voiced suspicion at their methods, I must have seemed more than a little insufferable. Who was I to doubt whether the headmen and chiefs who kept track of herds and allocated land to farmers really kept accurate records, or to suggest that they colluded with stock thieves? Who was I to question whether the members of the peace committees could be kept honest? I had nothing to offer that would replace these fuzzy, least-bad solutions cobbled together in the countryside. Communities were now relying on older institutions whose logic and principles bore little relationship to my liberal democratic notions. It was true that these institutions had set the war in motion. But then they had also brought peace. No doubt, theirs was not a model of due process justice, but a justice that would be crude, error-prone, and brutally unsentimental about how those who offended against social norms were to be treated. It would be a tit-for-tat form of justice in which checks and balances were absent, and accountability deeply flawed. I thought it ugly and a good deal less than what the constitution promised. But those aspirations were unobtainable, and in any event the same could be said of the formal system itself: it too could hardly promise to secure what the constitution promised.

In retrospect, I think there was another lesson here: although all societies need their ordering institutions, what we understand as policing in its modern guise is needed only where societies are large and anonymous. In the smaller, more settled communities of the past, the simple fact that everyone knew everyone else was enough to keep the peace. Whatever we tell ourselves about the strength of social bonds in our communities and the power and currency of *ubuntu*, those days are gone forever.

41

CHAPTER FOUR

BUSTING THE RESTAURANT ROBBERS: INSPECTOR ALIDA VAN ZYL, ROSEBANK

The patrol officers with whom I spent that Saturday night in Rosebank went on duty at 7 o'clock. Half an hour later, after all the booking-on registers had been signed and cars had been allocated to their two-man crews, I got into a police vehicle with inspectors Vilikazi and Dladla. The car was not the one they usually used: realising that the standard two-seater van would make an uncomfortable ride for three, the station commissioner had arranged for the officers to use one of the station's back-office vehicles. It was a tiny, two-door affair, the sort of car that a young secretary earning her first salary might drive. It was, in other words, underpowered and thin-skinned, hardly the ideal vehicle in which to race to the scene of a violent crime. But then, this was Rose-bank, where violent crimes are, by South African standards, pretty rare. 'You're going to be bored, bored, bored,' Constable Morena, another patrolman I'd spent time with during the week, had laughed when I told him my plans for the weekend. 'Nothing happens after 10 or 11 at night. It's dead like the desert.'

But Morena was wrong. No sooner had we closed the doors of the car than the radio, sputtering into life, anxiously announced a 2-3-alpha. A robbery was in progress. Fifteen armed men, the radio control officer said, were at that very moment robbing a restaurant. The address was barely two kilometres from where we sat.

My stomach tightened and my heart pounded painfully against the bullet-proof vest that suddenly seemed very small and inadequate.

★

When I began this project, one of the issues I had to think about was whether I wanted to put myself in situations of real, life-threatening danger. In an effort to make the decision, I did some calculations to see how much risk I was actually looking at. I knew, for instance, that about a hundred and fifty police officers were killed in 2002/3. Some back-of-the-envelope calculations suggested that even if all the deaths occurred on duty (and some police analyses suggest that as many as sixty per cent occur when officers are off duty), then, on average, one officer was killed on duty every two days. With more than seventy thousand members on duty in any given 24-hour period, the odds of my being with a crew in which an officer was killed seemed quite small.

Then I looked at it another way. If 150 officers were killed in a year, then the murder rate for South Africa's hundred and twenty thousand-odd police officers was something like two-and-a-half times higher than the national average of nearly fifty murders per hundred thousand people. It was, I thought, a surprisingly small differential. In fact, it overstated the risk differential because the national murder rate includes both men and women even though men make up about 85 per cent of all murder victims, which means that the per capita murder rate for men is itself nearly twice the national average. Being a man, in other words, the odds of my being murdered on any given day were not all that different from those of the average police officer, and hanging out with cops wasn't going to put my life more at risk than would my working with bank clerks or train drivers or street sweepers. I chose to ignore the fact that, as a white, middle-class South African, albeit a male one, my odds of being murdered were substantially less than the national average and, therefore, substantially less than the odds of a police officer's being killed. I also ignored the fact that a street-cop's odds of taking a bullet were probably a good deal higher than those of the counter-cops at the station and desk-jockeys in the rest of the organisation. Such considerations, I reasoned, would merely make me nervous. And, as everyone knows, it's nervous people who get bitten by dogs.

These rational calculations flew out of my mind when I heard the call to the restaurant robbery. And, in short, I was afraid.

I was afraid because responding to an armed robbery while it is in

43

progress is a genuinely frightening experience, even for cops, and fifteen armed robbers sounded like rather a lot. I was afraid because I knew that we were very close to the scene and had every chance of getting to it first. I was afraid because I knew that the crew I was with would be heavily outnumbered (fifteen armed men!). And I was afraid because I was in the back seat of a two-door vehicle and was suddenly aware that I wouldn't be able to get out of it quickly if I needed to.

Where the fuck would I go if the gang opened up on the approaching police car?

This was the ultimate something-that-ought-not-to-be-happening-and-about-which-something-ought-to-be-done-now situation, the *raison d'être* of policing and the reason why I was interested in the boys in blue. But I found suddenly that I didn't want to be where I was.

Acutely conscious of my fear, I admit that I was delighted when Inspector Vilikazi, the driver for the night, failed to respond in the manner cop shows on TV had led me to expect, when he failed, in other words, to hunch down over the wheel, stand on the accelerator and fly off in a cloud of burnt rubber. Instead, he calmly reached for the receiver and asked radio control for confirmation of the address. I, at least, had heard it perfectly well the first time and knew it to be a popular complex of restaurants and bars. But apparently Vilikazi, a man who presumably knew the precinct a whole lot better than I, needed to hear it again.

VILIKAZI: Control, could you confirm that address?

RADIO CONTROL OFFICER: The address is corner Long and South streets.

VILIKAZI: Could you repeat that?

RCO: That's corner Long and South.

VILIKAZI: Again?

RCO (getting short): Long and South! Long and South!

VILIKAZI (sounding like the consummate professional, as if he was writing himself a careful note which, in fact, he was not doing): OK, that's Long and South. What is the complainant's name?

RCO (exasperated): I don't have those details. There are fifteen men there, you can't expect me to have all the details and you don't need them now. Just go there.

VILIKAZI (musing, playing for time and looking over at his crew for support): Ja, Control? That address. It's not our area. Try papa-victor (Parkview police station) or bravo-lima (Bramley).

RCO (angry and frustrated now): I'm not going to discuss whose area it's in. I need vehicles. I need back-up at the scene. I need you to move now. Now!

VILIKAZI (beginning to act, but reluctantly, his eyes rolling): That's a papa (positive), Control.

What with the delays between question and answer, the interaction had probably taken the best part of two minutes. These were two minutes that had reduced our chances of getting to the crime scene first. They were two minutes that reduced the crew's chances of having to confront a horde of armed men without support. In the back of the car, I didn't regret the two minutes. But there were others, I knew, who would not have seen things in quite the same way. In those same two minutes, after all, the bad guys could get away. Worse still, innocent people might be injured or killed.

Having successfully delayed our departure, the driver now put the car in gear and called a cheery farewell to a pair of officers standing on the pavement in front of the station, and, still without any undue haste, steered the car towards the address of the robbery. He took the scenic route, but eventually we got to the main road. There Vilikazi could see other police vehicles and hear sirens up ahead of us, and, relieved, he put on his own siren and began, at last, to gun the motor, dear thing that it was.

We were, by then, barely half a kilometre away.

When we finally arrived, we found three police vehicles and two more from a local armed response company on the scene. They were parked at crazy angles in the parking lot. It was a scene of vehicular chaos lit by blue and yellow strobe lights, and it was clear that, despite what radio control had said, the gang was long gone.

As is often the case, initial information provided to responding officers was flat wrong.

I shouldn't have been surprised that the gang was gone, however, because I knew one of policing's darkest secrets. I knew that apart from brawls, riots and extended domestic disputes when neighbours intervene, cops are almost never able to get to the scene of a crime while it is still in progress. Almost without exception, by the time the cops are called to a robbery or a burglary, the bad guys are long gone. There are exceptions, of course, but, whatever the public's obsession with reaction times, all the empirical evidence ever accumulated on this subject confirms that quicker responses make next to no difference to arrest rates. Nor do they seem to help prevent death or injury. The reason is obvious when you think about it: however quickly cops respond to a call, that call is seldom made until well after the criminals have left, and, especially in an urban environment, that gives them plenty of time to lose themselves. Indeed, in all the hours I logged with the police, the only time a criminal was caught on the scene of a crime was on a rainy night in Cape Town when police, responding to a burglary call, found the suspect in the garden standing next to a broken window and a hi-fi system. His partner was long gone. He, however, had been left to wait for the police because, in breaking the window, he'd cut his arm badly and could now not climb back over the garden wall. Large patches of blood on the walls testified to what must have been desperate efforts to get out.

The restaurant that had been hit was one of those up-market franchise bistros that serve good pizzas and heavy pastas, thrive by generating a bubbly atmosphere, and from which no-one ever leaves feeling that he's been under-charged. It was a Saturday night in the middle of winter, and Johannesburg's diners were out looking for high-fat meals accompanied by lots of red wine. Because it was relatively early, the place hadn't been completely full. Even so, there must have been twenty or thirty people seated at the tables when the gang rushed in. Now, half an hour later, the gunmen were gone and the restaurant's patrons and employees were in shock. One young woman, ashen-faced and wobbly on thin, skirted legs, was the only casualty. She'd been pistol-whipped and had blood pouring from a wound on her forehead. The others seemed shattered: outwardly calm, but on the lip of hysteria. I knew the sensation because something similar had happened to me about six years before. Just as I had been when it was my turn, they were horrified at how close had been their brush with death, how randomly it had come at them, and how vanishingly thin and permeable was the boundary between safety and mortality.

46

Apart from the bleeding woman who was being taken to hospital, the owner-manager, a tall man in his late twenties, seemed to have borne the brunt of the robbers' aggression. He'd bravely taken charge when the men burst in, trying to calm both his patrons and the robbers, while getting his staff and customers to cooperate with them. He'd made himself a focal point, a target, and was now keeping himself occupied, filling the time so that he couldn't dwell on all the ways in which things could have gone horribly wrong. His parents arrived shortly after we did. His father, taking in my bullet-proof vest, told me that what this country needed more than anything else was the reinstatement of the death penalty. He was shaking with shock, horrified that he might have lost his son that night, and kept insisting that a disgruntled ex-employee might have been behind the crime. He was looking for someone to blame, some way to make sense of what was, in all likelihood, a random act of violence, just another in a string of restaurant robberies in Johannesburg's northern suburbs.

In the meantime, the officers from the security company's armed reaction unit were being excoriated by the restaurant's own security guard who said he'd been pushing his panic button for thirty minutes before anyone arrived. The men from the armed response, in their turn, had leaped into action and were busily trying to establish that it was not their company's responsibility to respond when that particular panic button was pressed. Official-looking forms were appearing like hankies from a magician's top coat. Their company was contracted by the building, another company was responsible for the restaurant; the security guard's panic button summoned cars from the other company. Why its cars had not arrived was anyone's guess. Perhaps they had not received the signal. Perhaps they had had no vehicles available. Perhaps the security guards who were supposed to respond when a panic alarm was activated had found their own reasons to dawdle.

I asked Vilikazi and Dladla whether they thought the robbery might have been timed to coincide with the change of shifts, reasoning that if the gang had attacked later, the restaurant would have been fuller and their haul would have been bigger. 'Maybe,' Vilikazi offered. 'Maybe that is also why they came here, to our border with both Parkview and with Bramley. They knew that it would confuse us.'

I thought that this probably gave the gang's leaders too much credit, and that Vilikazi was trying to rationalise his sluggish response to the initial call. He was trying, I suspect, to explain away actions that I might otherwise interpret as signs of his cowardice.

★

It is easy to be critical of Vilikazi and Dladla's drag-ass response to the emergency. It is true that even had they responded more promptly, they would not have arrived in time to confront the men or to make arrests. Nor would a more rapid reaction have made any difference to the (mercifully low) number of casualties. But there was also no way to know all this at the time. On the contrary, from the increasing anxiety in the radio control officer's voice, they could only have thought that a more rapid response might have made a potentially life-saving difference. Yet still they had delayed.

From my point of view, however, it was far harder to carp. This was the first time I'd been in a vehicle when so serious a call came through, and, to my humiliation, I found that I had been very frightened. I was exquisitely aware of the thinness of the car's outer shell, and tried to find a way to shrink into the space protected by the ceramic plates in my bullet-proof vest. I kept wondering which parts of my body were most exposed, and audited them obsessively, feeling for each with my mind to make sure it was still intact and in its place. It was a horrible sensation and led to a perverse assessment of which parts of my body would be most expendable. (For the record, the fleshy part of my thighs lost the popularity contest.)

These were macabre thoughts, and afterwards I thought about what the men sitting in the seats in front of me must have been thinking and feeling. They too had families. They too would have wanted to see morning with their bodily integrity intact. Is it any wonder that, in spite of the self-presented mythology of policing, they were unwilling to cast dice so heavily loaded against them as would have been a confrontation with fifteen armed men? Cops, after all, are human, and few human beings are so selfless as to risk everything for others. Darwinian natural selection has seen to that. So, whatever the public insistence that officers live only to serve and protect, and that they place the interests, safety and well-being of members of the public above their own, that is not the way of most of them. Like anyone else, they play the percentages, and an encounter with fifteen armed men (armed with what? radio control hadn't said) would have been far too dangerous for two cops alone.

But there is another consequence of their not rushing to the scene: once predatory criminals, strangers to the people they attack, have escaped, it is usually all but impossible to track them down. Having fled the scene successfully, there was now every chance that the gang would get away with its crime.

Consider the matter from the prospective investigator's point of view. To bring a case to court, a detective needs evidence against the person who committed the crime. There are only three kinds of evidence: witnesses, confessions and physical evidence. This is the detective's holy trinity, but predatory crimes like the raid on the bistro seldom throw up much of value.

What, for instance, would the typical witness have to offer by way of clues? He might be able to describe some or all of the attackers. He may even be able to pick them out of a line-up. But he would never have clapped eyes on the men before the robbery, and would be bound to provide only the most general information: age and race, size and gender. Nothing more. This is why 'stranger crimes' are solved much less frequently than are cases in which the victim knows the victimiser and can lead the investigator to his door.

Item two in the trinity is the confession, but at this point in the investigation, getting one was out of the question. Cops get these only after they have a suspect, and usually when arrests have already been made. It need hardly be pointed out that predatory criminals don't usually walk into police stations to clear their consciences.

The only hope, then, seemed to lie with whatever physical evidence might be found. There would be no DNA, but might one of the robbers, hopefully one with previous convictions, have left a fingerprint? And if he did, would the fingerprint expert be able to isolate it from the millions of prints left by patrons and employees? If a print had been left, could be isolated, and was then linked to a man with a previous conviction who still lived at the address he had lived at when last arrested, perhaps an arrest would be made. This type of evidence might propel the investigation towards a suspect. But the truth, confirmed by numerous pieces of research into detectives' professional craft, is that most often physical evidence, like confessions, is used by officers to corroborate existing suspicions. Only very rarely does physical evidence alone lead to the arrest of an offender against whom there are no other grounds for suspicion.

That is the reality of predatory crime: witness evidence offers little concrete information about who committed the crime, and what physical evidence exists is often next to useless in tracking down the assailants. The sad truth is that the crimes that suburbanites fear most – the whodunit crimes of robbery and hijacking and home invasion – are also the most difficult to solve. So, having fled the scene successfully, the restaurant robbers had every reason to expect that they might escape justice altogether.

And they very nearly did.

★

Inspector Alida van Zyl was not typical of her profession. She was small and blond and very pretty, and, because I first met her on a rest day when she was dressed informally, I caught a glimpse of a ring in her belly button. Hers was not standard-issue cop couture.

Van Zyl and her partner, Hybre Kirsten, were based at the Parkview police station and had been assigned the docket for the restaurant robbery. They shared a large, functional room utterly lacking in charm or glamour with another officer who was arrested within days of my meeting him for trying to sell a docket to the suspect in one of his cases. The incident upset Inspector van Zyl who, like many cops, preferred to think only the best of her colleagues. 'He is the sweetest man,' she told me after the arrest was made. 'He's got this really innocent face. I can't believe that he thought of doing this thing himself. Someone must have put the idea into his mind.'

But the thought that a corruptible cop had sat in her office for months while she and her partner tried to link eleven men to a series of serious crimes troubled her more than did her misreading of the young constable's character. 'I don't know what we'd have done if our files went missing. I know we would have been in serious trouble.'

Van Zyl was a hard woman to characterise. When I'd met her and sat across a desk asking questions about the case, she'd seemed smart and straightforward. No nonsense, just a good memory and an unusually sound ability to tell a chronological tale. It was a skill many of her colleagues lacked. Then I'd watched her flirt outrageously with her suspects, a group of young men being held awaiting trial at Diepkloof prison. She'd been coy and teasing, playfully pretending to be one of the boys to get them to cooperate. Later, a third aspect of her character was revealed: the gun-wielding, trash-talking, no-shit-taking street cop who pushed her way right into people's faces and then right up their noses.

The result was inevitable. I was smitten and lost all objectivity.

★

When the Parkview station commissioner had given the restaurant docket to Van Zyl and Kirsten, he'd told them to focus on nothing else. It was a serious crime, he'd said, a lot of people were involved. He'd promised them that if they solved it, they'd each get a week off. Generally cases such as this were pretty hopeless, but this time the cops were luckier than they usually are, and had two clues to work with. The first was a description of the man who had led the robbery, offered to them by the restaurant's owner-manager, who'd told them that the chief bandit was a young African man who was tall and skinny, bald and acne-scarred. He also said that the man wore a thick gold chain with a crucifix.

The description was about as helpful as cops generally get in these circumstances. In other words, not very.

The second clue was far more promising. The licence number of one of the getaway cars, a Ford Laser, had been noted down by an observant passer-by. Usually, that would mean very little since most professional criminals steal cars or number plates before doing the deed. But this time,

51

when Van Zyl plugged the car's licence into the vehicle registration system, she found that it was, in fact, registered to a Ford Laser, and that the car had not been reported stolen. Could it be that someone had been stupid enough to use his own car in the robbery? God bless amateurs!

Bad news followed the good, however. The car was registered to a woman whose address placed her in a building in central Johannesburg. But when officers were sent to the flat to check it out, they found no-one by that name living there. Nor was there anyone who could tell them where the woman might be.

In the usual course of events, that might have been that: with no-where else to go in pursuit of the car's driver, the detectives would have closed the docket and moved on to the next case. But Van Zyl and Kirsten had been told to focus on this case exclusively, and with nothing else in their in-trays, they decided to try to buy themselves a bit of good luck. 'Most of the people who commit crime in this area come either from Alexandra or from Hillbrow,' Van Zyl told me as she flipped through one of the many lever-arch files that the case now filled. 'The address of the car's owner was in the city, so we decided to look for the vehicle there.'

'What do you mean "look for the vehicle"?' I asked.

It was about six months after the fact, and I was sitting in Van Zyl's office. I'd tracked her down through the station commander, and I'd been expecting to be told that the case had been shelved, along with thousands of others, as unsolved. I was wrong: Van Zyl was in the process of closing a whole series of restaurant robberies for which at least nine men would be standing trial. There would have been eleven, if two of the men hadn't escaped from custody. The trial, however, wouldn't begin for another four or five months. I had a lot of catching up to do.

'I mean exactly what I said,' she answered. 'We drove up and down those streets looking for the car.'

The two women drove Hillbrow's grid for a week before the patron saint of investigators smiled on them. Waiting at a red light, they saw the car with three men inside. After all those hours driving those roads, they could only have been surprised and delighted at their good luck. But imagine the surprise and horror of the three men in the car when the vehicle that the two policewomen called for backup swung up to them, and they suddenly found themselves surrounded by police officers, their weapons drawn, yelling for them to get the fuck out of the car.

The men were brought to the Parkview police station. 'They were calm,' Van Zyl said. 'They knew what was going on. They weren't scared.'

South African law demands that arrestees be taken to court within forty-eight hours of their arrest, at which point they can apply for bail. In many cases, that is no real burden to the cops because an arrest usually either follows an investigation, in which case the officer can give the court enough information to decide whether to grant bail or not, or the suspects, having been caught at the scene, are so obviously guilty that the court will happily grant the investigating officer a little more time to find out precisely who the arrestee is and whether they are likely to abscond. This case was different, however, and the link between the men and the crime was much more tenuous. No-one had placed the men at the crime scene, and, even if the plates of the car hadn't been forged and weren't duplicates, no-one could say that these three men had been there. That, at least, was the reasoning of the prosecutor Van Zyl spoke to, who told her that without more evidence she wouldn't even dream of wasting the court's valuable time asking for an extension.

That gave the two investigators 48 hours to come up with something stronger with which to oppose bail. A confession would have been nice, but none of the men seemed inclined to offer one. That left arranging an identity parade as the only option.

In general, an identity parade is a no-lose proposition for detectives because a court will regard a positive identification as strong evidence of the suspect's guilt. It also knows, however, that victims are often too frightened to look their attackers in the face, so magistrates and judges will completely disregard any failure to pick a suspect out. In this case, however, because there was no other evidence directly linking the men to the crime, much was riding on a positive identification.

There was a problem, however. Van Zyl and Kirsten could find none of their key witnesses. The man who had noted the registration number was out of the country, and the owner-manager, a man who had phoned them every day to find out if they were making progress, now informed them that he would not take part in a line-up because he was suffering from post-traumatic stress and his shrink had told him that he needed 'closure'.

Van Zyl and Kirsten would have to try a different tack.

While the three men had been in custody, one of the cellphones that had been confiscated from them had been ringing off its hook. When asked about the numbers that appeared on the cellphone's screen, one of the men said it was a friend of theirs, one Shoes Nkomo. Having already searched the addresses the three men gave as their abodes, and with nothing better presenting itself, they told the men to take them to Shoes's place, a flat in Hillbrow. When they got there, however, they learned that Shoes didn't, in fact, stay there, although his girlfriend did. But the flat contained nothing that could definitively tie the three men to the restaurant robbery or give the police any other plausible reason to hold them for the crime – there were no stolen cellphones or drugs or unlicensed firearms that are the usual fallback options in these cases. They did, however, find something very interesting – a large, framed head-and-shoulders shot of Shoes, a man who turned out to be bald and acne-scarred, and who was the proud owner of a large gold crucifix.

He looked just like the suspect described by the manager of the restaurant.

Naturally enough, the woman of the house, who probably loved the man, denied knowing where Shoes was, claiming she hadn't seen him for weeks, but telling Van Zyl that he made his living selling fruit on the side of the road.

She had to say something.

By now the 48 hours were almost up, and the local prosecutor had to decide whether to ask the court for an extra week to investigate the case before hearing a bail application. What she had was the fact that the three men were found in a car linked to a robbery, and a photo of a man who might have been the leader of the gang. She had no witnesses who could place the three at the scene, and the detectives didn't want to show the photo of Shoes to witnesses in case that compromised any identification parade they might stage if and when Shoes was finally arrested. She decided that her chances of getting an extension were too slim, and told the investigators that the three could not be held for further investigation.

The investigation had stalled. That it had gotten this far was a tribute to the detectives' creativity, hard work and good fortune, but, even so, the well had run dry.

★

Twenty years ago, even if the thought hadn't yet occurred to him, when a case reached this point, a detective's mind would have turned to torture.

'I know that one or all of these little shits were either involved in the robbery, or know the people who were,' he might have thought. 'This is a vicious gang made up of nasty people who must have committed other crimes and who are, even now, probably planning to commit more. A little bit of pain, and I'll get my man.'

In the moral economy of the time, this sort of thing would not have seemed unreasonable, and South African law offered precious few safeguards against it. If a confession was wrung out of a suspect, it would fall to him to prove that it had been offered involuntarily. In the nature of things, this would often amount to his word against the word of a whole team of detectives. For obvious reasons, there were seldom sufficient grounds to overturn any confession, and the result was that policemen would frequently use what they euphemised as 'methods' to get the evidence they needed.

One of the most common and most powerful arguments against the infliction of pain as a means of extracting evidence is that such evidence tends to be unreliable. People in pain, so the argument goes, will say what they believe their torturer wants to hear. It is not, therefore, unreasonable to think that coerced confessions are unreliable, and that anyone convicted on the basis of one might very well be innocent.

Stated in these terms, renouncing the use of torture poses no serious moral dilemma for either cops or society. Torture is bad, but since its results are unreliable, we can get along just as easily without it. The trouble is that things are not really that simple, and the infliction of pain, used smartly, can be made much more reliable than this argument

55

would lead you to believe. The trick, for a smart torturer, is not to go for a confession, but to get the suspect to cough up some piece of corroborating evidence that proves his guilt independently of the infliction of pain. We can be certain, for instance, that a suspect who takes a cop to a stash of stolen jewellery was involved in the theft. Likewise, we can be certain that a suspect is guilty if, after a session with some heavy in a blue uniform, he takes a cop to an unrecovered murder weapon, the location of which only the killer could know.

Horrible as it sounds, torture can be made to produce reliable evidence.

I asked Inspector van Zyl about the temptations of police 'methods' in a case like this. You're pretty sure that these guys were involved in the robbery or know people who were. They were, after all, found in a car the make, model and licence number of which match those of a car seen at the crime. You are also reasonably sure that a picture found in a flat to which you've been taken shows one of the robbers described by a witness. 'Surely,' I asked, 'you thought about other ways of making these guys tell you something usable? Even if it was only an address at which you might find Shoes?'

Van Zyl had been eating the last remains of supper, a bready-looking pizza she'd bought on her way into the office, fuel for what would turn out to be an unsuccessful night out looking for one of the missing suspects. She looked at me a little coyly and smiled disarmingly.

'Sometimes you are really tempted,' she replied. 'The first murder I investigated … Jesus, I wanted to hurt those guys.'

At the time Van Zyl had been stationed at 'the hole of Hillbrow', and the murder had been impossible to solve. Even though she knew who did it. The victim had been shot, but, instead of being found where he'd been killed, he'd been brought in to the Johannesburg General Hospital by a friend. The result was that they had no murder weapon and, worse still, no crime scene. The man who brought him in said that the deceased had rung his flat's intercom already injured and dying. He had no way of knowing where the shooting had happened.

'We had nothing to work with. So I did some background checking and found out that the man who'd brought the victim to the hospital

56

had a firearm licence. But when I asked him to bring it in so that we could test it against the bullet that had been taken from the body, he told me the gun had been stolen. He said he hadn't reported it yet because the theft happened the day after the murder and he was still too upset. Then we applied to the court and we got the cellphone records of the victim and his friend. It turned out that they were both in the same area for the whole day.

'We really believed that this guy was guilty. But how do you prove it? The only way is if we could get a crime scene and find something there. All I wanted from him was that address.

'Ja. It was very tempting to use methods.'

'But you didn't?' I asked.

'No.'

'Why? What stops you in a case like that, when you know someone is guilty and it's the only way?'

'It comes down to one thing, and one thing only,' Van Zyl replied. 'Do I want to go to jail for this little shit?'

It was the practical, no-nonsense answer you'd expect from a cop. There was no angsting over the rights and wrongs of beating information out of someone, just the rational calculation that it wasn't worth it. Why risk your career and your freedom to solve a murder? If society refuses you permission to use any and all means to get the evidence you need, well, that's its problem. Fewer cases will be solved, and more bad guys will walk the streets, but that's a choice made by society, not by individual police officers.

Whether or not Van Zyl or Kirsten or any of their colleagues actually contemplated the value of torturing the three men, I cannot say. I can say that none of them made a confession and none offered information that led the detectives to Shoes. But just because the three couldn't be tied to the robbery didn't quite mean that they were free to go. One was wanted on a separate charge of fraud in Garankuwa, and was transferred to the custody of officers there, while another was charged with fraud after a search of his apartment revealed two sets of incompatible tertiary qualifications. The third, an illegal immigrant with no papers at all, was deported.

As dedicated and lucky as the investigators had been, the case had, once again, hit a brick wall. It wasn't long, however, before they were to have another lucky break.

★

Three months, almost to the day, after the original restaurant robbery, two other restaurants were attacked within an hour of each other. The *modus operandi* was exactly the same as the earlier robbery: a large gang rushed the restaurant, used some physical violence to intimidate those present, and robbed them of their cash, cellphones and jewellery. Again, they would have gotten away with the crime had a member of the public not taken it upon himself to follow the two getaway cars as they drove away slowly and carefully in order to avoid unwanted attention. It might have helped that it was a rainy night, because the gang didn't spot their tail, who was on his cellphone throughout, calling in their every movement to the 10111 emergency number.

Reacting swiftly, and coordinated through radio control, officers from the Sandton police station, the Johannesburg flying squad and the dog unit threw a net over the gang's escape route, and, when everyone was in place, the drawstring was pulled.

Eleven arrests were made.

In the intervening three months detectives from across the northern suburbs of Johannesburg had been pulled together into a task force set up to deal with a rash of restaurant robberies. They'd met a number of times and had drawn up profiles of the main suspects. They had reviewed cases dating back five years, and tasked a few informers to get them some names. But this was their first real breakthrough. In what was as close to an open-and-shut case as could be imagined, eleven men had been handed to them on a plate.

Bizarrely, the first Van Zyl heard of the arrests was not through the task force. Instead, one of the three men they'd arrested ten weeks earlier, the suspect who'd been transferred to Garankuwa to stand trial for fraud and for failing to come to court, called to tell her that the arrests had been made and that the eleven men were linked to her case. He'd been acquitted on the fraud case – the docket had gone missing – but was soon to be arrested again, this time on suspicion of bank robbery in Durban. Once again, he would be granted bail, and, once again, he would abscond. He was clearly no model citizen, yet for some reason he called Inspector van Zyl to tell her that his friends had been arrested and that they were the suspects in the Rosebank case. It could be nothing other than proof positive that he too was linked to the original crime: how else could he have known of the arrest of the men involved in a restaurant robbery and that they were involved in a previous attack? It was also proof of the value of being nice to your suspects: you never knew when they'd be in a position to return a favour.

'We didn't really know what to expect at the first interrogation,' Van Zyl told me. 'But when we walked in we knew it was our lucky day. One of the men they had arrested was our old friend, Mister Shoes Nkomo. He was much smaller then we'd imagined. Really scrawny. But we knew immediately that he was the man in the photo.'

★

Once again, the patron saint of detectives had smiled on Van Zyl and Kirsten. They called the victims from the initial robbery and told them a line-up would be arranged as soon as the task team could gather witnesses from other restaurant robberies with similar *modi operandi*. It took three weeks and an advert in the local knock-and-drop newspapers inviting people to the identity parade, but when it took place some forty-odd witnesses, each a victim of a restaurant robbery across the northern suburbs, came to peer through the one-way glass at the rows of men.

An identification parade is a serious business, governed by a strict set of rules. The line-up must, for instance, be administered by police officers with no connection to the case, so that no influence can be brought to bear on witnesses. Each witness views the parades alone, and is not allowed to communicate with the others. Defence lawyers, if there are any, sit in, and are consulted continually about their happiness with the process. If there is more than one witness, suspects can change their clothes or their place in the line between witnesses. It is worse when there is more than one suspect because, in theory at least, each line-up should contain one suspect and seven or eight decoys, each dressed in a manner similar to that of the suspect, and all of the same age, race and gender. If two suspects have to be in the identity parade, a circumstance police text books teach their readers to frown on, then the number of decoys must be raised to twelve. If there are more suspects than that, additional parades should be called. For obvious reasons, each decoy should not be used more than once in a series of line-ups. So, with forty-odd witnesses, each taking a solo turn at the one-way glass, and eleven suspects, the process could have taken weeks. For that reason, court rules are a little less demanding than those set out in the textbook, and they allow much bigger parades with more suspects and more decoys, when other approaches are unfeasible.

Nevertheless, the highly ritualised format of an identity parade revealed Inspector van Zyl in a whole new light. Coy and playful, she teased the suspects about how happy they all seemed to see her, how much healthier they looked having had three square meals a day, and how good they looked in the civilian clothes she gave them to wear during the identity parade. When I asked her about that, she told me that it was part of her method: 'If they think you like them, they some-times come to you for help. Two of those boys have already called me at the office. You never know, if they think you'll help them, maybe you get something out of them.'

The first line-up took much of the day, and some of the witnesses grew restive and left before taking their turn, but in the end all eleven were positively linked to the two Sandton robberies for which they'd been arrested, and nine were picked out by witnesses from Van Zyl's original case. Some of the men were also identified by victims from two other restaurant robberies. Nor was that the end of matters. One of the cellphones taken from the men when they were arrested was identified by a woman who'd been robbed at a coffee shop in another part of the city. Unfortunately, the chain of evidence linking it to a particular man among the eleven had been broken: on the rainy night in which the arrests had been made, all the personal property taken from the men was put in a waterproof bag before anyone thought to note which item had been taken from which man. None of the arrestees would now admit to having been in possession of it at the time.

Then, at a flat rented by the girlfriend of one of the men, a cheque book belonging to a woman who'd been robbed at yet another robbery was found, as was a credit card taken from a woman in a smash-and-grab. Unfortunately, the firearm taken at the same time was not. But nine firearms had been recovered, and all had been stolen from their lawful owners in muggings, home invasions and, in one case, a hijacking-murder. Van Zyl hoped, but doubted, that some of those victims would recognise some of these men.

Fingerprint evidence was used to link one man to the scene of a housebreaking. He'd already been arrested on that charge, but had escaped, shooting at a police officer in the process. Another man had left a print at the scene of a serious assault in Hillbrow.

In all, 22 cases had been linked to one or more of the eleven men arrested on that rainy night. It was a form of insurance: Van Zyl knew these guys were repeat offenders, wanted them off the street, and needed to avoid putting all her eggs in one basket. 'You never know,' she said to me, 'if they'll get off on one case because of some technicality or because a witness vanishes.'

It had all been good work, but there had been one devastating set-back: two of the men had escaped. They had claimed to be younger than eighteen, and had been placed in one of the juvenile care facilities in the north of the city. Four months after their arrests, the pair escaped. And, to add insult to injury, they had done so in two separate incidents within a fortnight of each other. No-one had bothered to tell the detectives about either escape, and they found out when the two failed to appear at one of the innumerable bail applications lodged by the gang's fee-greedy lawyers. Perhaps, Van Zyl suggested, that explained the brief flare-up of restaurant robberies in the area around the time of the escapes. Ironically, one of the first to be hit was the same bistro Vilikazi and Dladla had been called to six months earlier.

★

Skill, effort and, in the end, a healthy dose of dumb luck were needed to find and prosecute the men responsible for the original robbery, but the success of the investigation shows what can be achieved by committed detectives who are given the time to focus on a single case and to pursue as many avenues as present themselves. But in its own way, Van Zyl's case also shows how heavily the odds are stacked against even the most dedicated investigator, for, in truth, if Shoes and his friends had not been arrested all but in the act of robbing another restaurant, none of them might have seen the inside of a cell. It's a depressing thought, but the men were brought to justice largely because they were unlucky enough to have been followed from the scene of a robbery.

Depressing as that thought is, the experience from which it is drawn matches everything criminologists know about the way detectives work in other countries too. In the United States, for instance, empirical studies into police investigation have found that if an offender is not caught on the spot, and witnesses cannot give the cops information that specifically identifies him, arrest rates fall to well below ten per cent. Cops need information to make arrests. Names and addresses are best, but telephone or car registration numbers will do in a pinch. It really is as simple as that: if witnesses and complainants provide no evidence linking a specific individual to the crime, detectives are seldom able to make the connections themselves. Investigators, it turns out, seldom solve the genuine whodunits and are more likely to use evidence to confirm the guilt of a suspect already known to them than they are to use it to track down unknown suspects. This is why incidents of interpersonal violence, crimes committed by people known, and often related, to their victims, are solved so much more frequently than are the predatory crimes that frighten their prospective victims so much. The difference flows from the nature of the crime and of the events which surround it, events which no detective, however dedicated, can control. Anonymous, predatory crime is one of the consequences of mass society, and anonymous, predatory criminals are the hardest to track down.

If one lesson to draw from Van Zyl's case is that solving crimes committed by nameless offenders is inherently difficult, the other is that with impeccable record-keeping, flawless systems of data retrieval and clear channels of communication, once a criminal is nabbed, it is often possible to pin some of his previous crimes to him. This too is common to jurisdictions around the world where these 'secondary clearances' often make up the majority of solved crimes as witnesses are brought in to look at suspects arrested committing crimes similar to the ones committed against them, or fingerprints are used to place arrestees at the scenes of other offences, or ballistic evidence links a firearm to crimes committed at other times and in other places. In this way, one closed case can quickly spiral into twenty so long as the record-keeping is up to scratch.

There is something paradoxical about the fact that our civilisation is forced to put its trust in the power of reason to defeat eruptions of violence, that our response to the unreason that is violence is based on a faith in the power of logic and reason, and their ability to meld the scraps of information that collect around every person like iron filings round a magnet into a coherent account of what happened. Perhaps these are silly, speculative thoughts, too philosophical by half, but they lead to another. As I thought about the ways Van Zyl had linked the eleven men she had in custody to all those cases, it struck me that any detective – real or fictional – who moans about the burdens of paperwork, misunderstands the nature of his work. On some fundamental level, a great deal of an investigator's work is nothing but paperwork.

Terrifying as the thought is to anyone who has ever dealt with a South African bureaucracy, it struck me that when it comes to hunting predators, much of the dirty work of a society has to be done with pen, paper and a pair of reading glasses.

★

A couple of months after the first identification parades, inspectors Van Zyl and Kirsten went to look for one of the suspects who'd escaped from custody. They had an address in Brixton for him, one that he'd given when he was first arrested and which their colleagues had checked out in the course of organising the opposing of bail for the suspect. They hadn't gone to look immediately after the escape because escapees who aren't thick as building sand don't go back to their homes unless and until they feel that they've been forgotten.

On the way to the house, Van Zyl and I talked about our baby daughters, both of whom were sick and sleeping badly. We discovered that we had clubbed in the same places in the 1990s. It was vaguely flirtatious, and I was quite shocked when at last we got to the house and she started waving a gun the size of a small tractor around and ordering the two dozen or so squatters we found on the premises where to move and how quickly. But she settled back into her buddy-buddy charm with the building's unwelcome guests when it became clear that her suspect wasn't there and hadn't visited the place for months. The woman who took the rent said she might remember the boy, but wasn't sure. People come, people go, she seemed to say. Who can remember those the police take away?

After we left the house, I asked her if her work ever got her down at all. 'Sometimes,' she said. 'You don't win them all, and there's a lot of rubbish you have to live with. But then I think about people like the captain, and how dedicated he is, and I know that you must do this job for your colleagues. That's what keeps you going.'

Even as we spoke, her captain, the man she was talking about, was in the car behind us. He'd been shot ten years before while working a case in Hillbrow. He was in a wheelchair and would never walk again. But there he was, in his car in the middle of the night, giving his officers guidance and, when they weren't actually inside people's houses, holding up a light to help them see.

That, I thought, is real detective work.

CHAPTER FIVE

TAKING DOWN THE HIGH FLIERS: ELSIES RIVER, SEPTEMBER 2003

Let me tell you about the closest I came to an early death while working on this book.

I was with a squad of eight uniformed cops who worked their beat
harder than any others I met. Unusually for street-cops, they were led
by a captain, a stocky man in his forties called Captain 'Cappy' Roets
whose approach to his work was as quirky as it was intense. 'Let's pay a
little visit to Moeradien,' he would say to his driver, Constable Daniels,
a six-foot-four giant whom I could only think of as The Terminator. As
he said this, Cappy would point in the general direction in which he
wished to go with a pipe which he held in a leather-begloved left hand.
He worked that pipe incessantly, and he would point it in a vaguely
threatening manner at pedestrians he didn't like the look of. When his
team bust shebeens or, as happened twice, when they chanced upon
drunken brawls in the street, he would reach between his legs and haul
out an old-fashioned, *Chips*-style motorbike helmet that sported a
police badge. Plonked on his head, the metallic blue of the helmet and
the gold of the badge created an effect that was comically camp. But
they would have made encounters with Cappy memorable. Even for the
most inebriated.

The officers under his command loved Cappy Roets, who was a
man who still relished his work despite his decades of service, who was
still thrilled by the street-work. He would not allow himself to express
his exuberance, suppressing it beneath a veneer of hardened street-
cynicism. It was, nevertheless, there. And it was something that nour-
ished his troops.

The rest of Cappy's team was made up of cops who ranged from the greenest, migraine-suffering constable fresh out of police college, to a hard-boiled inspector with spiked hair and a bulldog's temperament who started one shift by asking the only woman on the squad whether she preferred to spit or swallow. This must have been a routine between them because she responded instantly: '*Ek hou van gorrel.*'

She preferred to gargle.

These cops policed the streets of Elsies River, the beating heart of the ganglands that surround the Mother City, a place where anyone who is anyone has their own gang, their own uniforms, and their own capacity to deploy coercive force. In this, it bears no resemblance to the promises made when its tenements were built in the mid-1970s. Then, the local council pledged that the neighbourhoods it was building would be arranged around attractive public spaces and that all the 'existing trees, as well as the larger hillocks and dunes', would be retained so that residents could 'enjoy a walk through the open space'. In fact, the area looks post-apocalyptic, a dystopian set out of *A Clockwork Orange* in which cinderblock buildings that freeze in winter and steam in summer loom over unforgivingly concrete yards. People live in bald, grey project housing which is so unpleasant that it forces them out of doors where they are exposed to gangsters. With all the people on the street, Elsies feels like a slum, a place in which too many human beings live in too small a space. This is a world of street-level drug-dealing, of dilapidated playgrounds and basketball courts from which even the hoops have been stolen, of tattooed corner gangs that fight for territory and rob their neighbours. It is a world of sudden, sometimes ritualised, violence in which a young man lying spreadeagled on a pavement sleeping off his Monday morning white-pipe will go unremarked by the cops.

★

The night I came close to death – that may be an exaggeration born of poetic licence: it could have been no more than a bloody nose – had begun like the other nights I worked in Elsies: it had rained. But, inured to the weather, Cappy's team spent the twilit hours of evening cruising the streets, stopping frequently to roust people who lived in alleys or in the open veld next to an industrial area to the south-west of Elsies River. These they suspected of criminality largely because they were poor and desperate, but also because some were known to them as drug dealers. When they did so, they would tip out the meagre possessions of those they searched, looking for the usual incriminating items: weapons, drugs or the paraphernalia of the addict, goods that may have been stolen. This was cheerless work, and, although I could see the reasons why open liquor bottles were emptied onto the pavement, it struck me that the state's power, exercised on this level, in this way, could only seem cruel and arbitrary to the muted, unwelcoming crowds that would gather around during these actions.

At one point Cappy had the van stop next to a group of teenaged boys, one of whom dropped something guiltily into the grass through which they were walking. It turned out to be the broken neck of a beer bottle, something that later that night would have been filled with dagga and ground-up Mandrax. That sort of thing is not acceptable, so the boy was made to place the glass neck on the pavement, jagged edges point- ed skywards, and was told to stamp on it. This was a poor boy, and he was wearing nothing but cheap, cardboard-soled shoes. Stamping on broken glass must have hurt. Badly. But this is Elsies River, a place where showing pain is no way to get ahead. So he didn't. As we drove off, however, I watched him limp heavily, putting his weight on a friend's shoulder.

Much later that night, Cappy's squad was sent to a shebeen from which, so it was claimed, dagga was being sold. The information had come in the form of an anonymous tip phoned into the police station. It was the sort of allegation which was usually made by a competitor who wanted a shebeen closed for a night or longer. But that didn't mean it was untrue. Unusually, none of the unit's members had heard that a shebeen was operating at the address they'd been given, and this piqued Cappy's interest. He thought that this might be the new site from which one of the 'high fliers' – career criminals, most of whom were involved in gang activities and had received repeated attention from the police over the past six months – might be operating. One of his men was interested for other reasons: 'A *lekker* new place,' he said in the faux-excited huckster tones of an infomercial, using his voice to rev up his colleagues. 'Hot *poes* and cold beer.'

The cops got out of the van a couple of blocks away, and, seeking to take it by surprise, approached on foot hunched down behind the walls of nearby houses. It turned out to be a middle-tier operation, catering to about forty or fifty people in a roofed yard behind the house. It sold only beer and the strong, cheap wine that is the *bête noire* of preachers of temperance in the Cape Flats. Two hopelessly tattered pool tables and a booming music system offered cheap entertainment to a crowd that ranged in age from teenager to pensioner. Most were in no state to operate heavy machinery, but some must have been pursuing oblivion since early in the evening. They had now reached the point where they could no longer lie face down on the floor without clutching onto the leg of a nearby table.

The first moments of any shebeen raid are bizarre. A platoon of heavily armed, truncheon-wielding men and women, some in bullet-proof vests, enter a room full of people in varying stages of intoxication. They have the clear intention of bringing proceedings to an abrupt close, and begin by getting people to stand up and endure a brief but intimate frisking. They move people around and look under chairs and tables for drugs, guns and knives. All of this activity, however, is greeted with a display of utter indifference. Everyone is aware that the cops are there and what they intend doing, but, very deliberately, they are also determined to ignore them. There is a discernible hardening of faces, but patrons continue their revelry with a new, grim resolution: those who are playing pool continue to play, but their knuckles tighten and their banter becomes forced; those who are dancing continue to dance, but their movements become angry and arrhythmic. The most obvious change in behaviour is among those with open bottles before them who start to drink more deeply and more quickly: there is no point in leaving anything in the bottle.

As I'd seen him do perhaps a half-dozen times already, Cappy quickly established who was in charge and asked the man to accompany his officers while they seized a couple of cases of beer and the board on which the prices of his drinks were advertised. This was the evidence the cops would need to prove that he was selling liquor without a licence if he inexplicably chose to contest the charge in court. The shebeener, a quiet, friendly man, told Cappy he'd been operating for a couple of weeks and had never been arrested. It may have been true that the place had only begun to operate recently, but I thought he must have been arrested previously: the prospect fazed him not at all. He was completely obliging, smilingly professional.

His clientele, on the other hand, were getting restive.

Terminator had been exchanging eyefuck for eyefuck with the men in the crowd, and was getting into an increasingly foul-mouthed shouting match with a group of three of the shebeen's younger drinkers whom he'd roughly searched and who were now aggressively displaying their offended machismo. Having provoked a reaction, the three were refusing to beat a polite, territorial retreat or to make the gestures of face and body that would imply submission. I thought the giant officer would soon swing his baton. The other cops were shepherding drinkers out of the shebeen and spilling what unfinished drinks remained into a drain. One old woman, emaciated, toothless and, licensed by her age and gender to rage at the cops with impunity, was screaming blue murder at them, cursing them and the 'law of the *larnie*' – the white man's law – they were enforcing. '*Daar is altyd een ou teef wat kak wil stook,*' one of the cops muttered to me, making sure she would hear. It was a description of an empirical regularity which I, as a scientifically trained, independent observer, can confirm, even if I might use less pejorative language. Otherwise, it was perfectly true: there really always was one old – ahem! – 'woman' looking to stir shit.

Having finally emptied the room, pushed all the shebeen's patrons onto the street, and stacked up the evidence they needed, Cappy began to explain to the owner what would happen. He'd be arrested and taken to the station where, if he had the money, he'd pay an admission-of-guilt fine and would then be released. 'Can you get R1 000 together?' Cappy asked.

The man seemed doubtful: 'Maybe,' he replied. 'I will have to call my brother.'

'Well, if he can get R1 000, tell him to bring R400 of it to the station. That's what the admission-of-guilt will be.'

The man grinned, taken in by Cappy, glinting helmet, leather gloves and all. There was going to be no trouble from him. Just as the handcuffs appeared, however, the arrestee's mother, a huge woman overflowing out of the sleeves of her floral blouse and over the top of her skintight pants, flew into the group of cops who were standing around her son. '*D-jy gaat nie my babatjie neem!*' she raged at their attempts to take her son, trying to pummel the nearest cop with her soft, flabby arms.

Her 'baby' handled the situation like the forty-something he was, pacifying her quickly, telling her not to worry and assuring her that he'd be back before morning, sooner, even, if she could arrange for a car to pick him up from the station. Then the ten of us – the cops, the arrestee and I – squeezed into the eight-seat van, and Terminator began the tricky business of turning the vehicle around.

It was then that I was nearly killed. Or at least had my nose bloodied.

We were packed very tight inside the van, and my face was pressed up close to a window. The cops were loudly cursing the reception they'd had. Their blood was up, filling the air with testosterone. As Terminator began to pull away from the curb, the shebeener's mother ran down the driveway, through the people so recently evacuated from the shebeen who were now standing in the street muttering about the police, and hurled a half-brick at the van. It crashed into the top of the window frame inches above my head. A little lower, and it would have shattered the glass and slammed into my head. It wouldn't have been pretty.

Terminator stood on the brakes. Apart from the fact that the woman had just committed a crime, the cops knew instinctively that there was no way they could drive away now, not without making an arrest. It would have looked as if they were retreating under fire.

The van lurched to a halt, and in one movement all eight cops flew out of it. Cappy and two others charged after the woman who was huffing her way back to the safety of her house. The other five, led by Terminator, tried to set up a perimeter as the crowd, angry once more, closed in on the van. The three who'd chased the woman caught up with her as she got to her kitchen door, grabbed her by the arms and began to frogmarch her back to the van. She was quiet at first, but as she neared the vehicle the consequences of her action started to dawn on her and she began to panic.

This was a huge woman, well over a hundred kilograms. There was obviously no way she could outrun even the oldest pencil-pusher in the Police Service. She could, however, make life very difficult for Cappy's squad just by sitting down. This she started to do, and, like a great tent subsiding around a broken central pole, she pulled herself and the three officers who were holding her to the ground. Recovering their balance quickly, the cops tried to haul her to her feet. Simple physics meant that to do that, they had to pull on her arms with great force. Their efforts were soon causing her to cry out loudly in pain.

This looked bad. Especially to the dozens of people who were now coming out of the neighbouring houses and joining the intoxicated patrons of the shebeen. From their perspective, it would have appeared that an old woman was being beaten by three policemen. They reacted as any good neighbour would in similar circumstances – they attacked the police lines.

The five cops who were trying to form a perimeter around their colleagues and the van were faring badly. Heavily outnumbered and ill-trained for the manoeuvre, they couldn't prevent enraged spectators pushing through their cordon and getting close to the woman and the officers struggling with her. Terminator had become isolated. He had followed the three youths who'd been provoking him earlier and who were the targets of a baton that he was swinging with all his might. He missed a lot. He was probably in no great danger, but his was the unit's most commanding presence and his absence was soon felt as the crowd surged in among the other officers. One of these, the greenest, was barely twenty years old, and was way out of his depth. He was small and young and white, and he was getting a little panicked by the crowd. Sensing his jumpiness, perhaps, some of the more aggressive of the mob rounded on him, taunting him mercilessly. Behind his back, one mimicked the sound of a firearm being cocked: 'ching, ching'. Barely two months before, this same cop had almost had his head shot off while chasing a suspect. Now he flipped. Wheeling around, he started yelling

71

at the man who'd made the sound, warning him that he'd fuck him up and that he should get his 'fucking ass out of my fucking sight'. There was something comical about this because the man was a good foot taller than the cop, was twenty years older and, tempered by a life in these ganglands, was completely unable to take a backward step. 'Fuck you, laaitie!' he kept yelling, 'Come and get me.' The confrontation would quickly have degenerated further if some of the man's friends hadn't taken it upon themselves to drag him away from the enraged officer.

I could understand the cop's nervousness. If someone came out of this crowd with a gun or a knife, it would have been hard to prevent their getting close enough to use it. Nor would the presence of so many potential witnesses have been much of a deterrent: in places like Elsies, a street full of eyewitnesses doesn't translate into an arrest.

The fat woman was by now screaming in pain as her ill-conditioned arms were being forced to support the vastness of her mass. At some point her pants had been pulled down as she was dragged along the ground. This had caused one of the officers, a conservative man from deep in the Transkei, to back modestly away from the sight. He had left Cappy and another officer to drag-carry her themselves. It was slow, noisy going. She was kicking out at them and biting their hands. But she was also losing the fight and was being inched towards the van. Eventually, with a final heave, countered by a last flailing foot that connected squarely with Cappy's jaw, she was deposited into the van. The cops, delighted at being able to leave and a little shocked at how a routine raid had so quickly become dangerous, clambered in after her. Terminator climbed in last, fired up the engine and drove off.

The van was now bursting at its seams, and the woman, sounding desperately close to cardiac arrest, was heaving breathlessly. 'We don't give a shit if you die,' Terminator offered soothingly. 'So shut the fuck up.'

These words seemed to do the trick, and her breathing quickly returned to normal.

When we got back to the station, Cappy and Terminator dropped off the six other officers, the two arrestees and me. Then they disappeared.

I had visions of them returning to the scene of the scuffle and meting out some instant justice. I thought they might be off to crack a few skulls. It made me anxious. In fact they only went to a local service station where, in the oasis of light around the petrol pumps, they tried to see what damage the brick had done. They really wanted to charge the woman with malicious damage to property, and hoped that she'd dented the roof or, better still, broken a police light. In this, they were to be disappointed. The brick had hit a hardened steel bracket holding the lights, and there was little more than a scratch. They were obviously cheered by the thought that she could still be charged with assault: Cappy had taken a boot to the face, and that certainly qualified.

The woman's son, arrested for running the shebeen that may have been hers, paid a R400 admission-of-guilt. He and his sister, who had by now arrived to take him home, were thoroughly amused by their mother's behaviour. In truth, though, her intemperate actions were going to cost his business far more than the fine he was now paying. Police officers don't tend to withdraw assault charges, and she was going to need a lawyer to stay out of jail.

★

Of all the gin joints in all the world, the shebeen must be the most criminogenic.

On weekends, township police stations are awash with people who have spent the earlier parts of the evening at shebeens. Many have been beaten or worse after wine-fortified arguments with friends or strangers, arguments which escalated as fists were used or weapons were drawn. Others, drunk themselves, have been robbed going home by people who were not quite ready to call it a night. In either case, the victims are an unsympathetic lot, and the facts they describe are obscure, their stories confused. It is clear, nevertheless, that shebeens are the backdrop against which a large proportion of all common law crime is committed.

That is only one aspect of the problems they generate, however. Another part is the contribution that these unlicensed watering-holes make to the ambient sense of lawlessness in a precinct and the extent to which that atmosphere encourages criminality. Not all shebeens, it is true, are wild, unruly places in which wildness and unruliness are celebrated. Not all throb with boisterous, sometimes manic, revelry or burst their seams into the surrounding streets, spilling impossibly distorted music and noisy beer-breathing crowds out into the open air to obstruct traffic, keep neighbours awake, and create an almost tangible aura of ungovernability. But even those that cater to an older crowd, those at which patrons might determinedly drink themselves to a standstill in the quiet of the shebeener's living-room, even they are brazenly, flagrantly illegal. Their ethos, their very existence, mocks the law. To patrons, owners, cops and Joe Public, the law is made to look either feeble or corrupt, and with every beer sold the police's claim to having 'zero tolerance' for offending is made to look like so much humbug. There are a multitude of these places – in the Cape Flats alone, estimates of the number of shebeens run well into the thousands – and the effect is cumulative, each adding to the sense of lawlessness generated by the others, widening the zones of disorder which surround each of them.

The raid on the fat lady's shebeen was by far the most eventful I saw. All the others took one of two forms: either the cops would go in, empty the place, searching everyone as they left, and then look around for any contraband that patrons might have hidden once they saw the cops enter the room (though they seldom found much). Then they'd leave. Or, as on this occasion, that arrive-search-leave routine would be followed by the hauling off of the shebeener and his being charged under the relevant legislation. I could never work out a legal or practical reason why some shebeeners were arrested and others weren't, and mostly it looked like different stations had just adopted different approaches. In Elsies River, for reasons which will be clear later, the pattern favoured arrest. In Ivory Park, on the other hand, cops were more content just to search the premises, telling me that that way they got better cooperation from the shebeeners who, in return for less draconian handling, would provide information about any crimes and criminals they became aware of.

Neither of these approaches dealt with the fundamental problem, though: one of the most conspicuous and popular institutions in township life operates in a legal blind spot. They cannot be condoned, but nor can they be put out of business.

You might think that since shebeens are illegal – and even the recently licensed establishments now known as 'taverns' operate only on the very fringes of legality – they can and should all just be closed down. But only the most cack-handed of station commissioners would try to do something this foolish. In the first place the average station commissioner has better things to do than focus all his resources – and it would take *all* his resources – on enforcing the arcane legislation governing the retailing of alcohol. From a crime perspective, the bottom line is that unless he is policing a small town in the Karoo and the worst crime is spitting on the pavements, he can't afford to waste his time, men and money locking up the pillars of the local business community just for selling booze. Not unless he is able to close all illegal establishments at once. If he cannot do that, then all he'd end up doing is pushing one set of customers into the arms of the equally obliging shebeener down the street, and the level of serious crime would go more-or-less unchanged. Police action against individual shebeens will be – and will seem to be – both arbitrary and futile.

But even if the resources were available to close all shebeens, the tools available to the local constabulary are hopelessly inadequate to the job. The only power they have is to arrest a shebeener for selling liquor without a licence. Most simply pay the admission-of-guilt and go home to recoup the loss which, for even the smallest shebeens, is little more than an annoying overhead. The exercise achieves little of lasting value. Nor is there much to be gained by raising the value of the fine: down that route lies only the increased incentive to bribe police officers. Making matters worse, any station commissioner who embarked on a zero-tolerance enforcement strategy would not be sure that his men would obey his instructions. Are they, he'd have to ask himself, more disciplined than the Irish-American cops to whom it fell to enforce Prohibition in 1920s Chicago, and who, thinking the policy unjust, unworkable and anti-Irish, preferred to turn a (usually well-rewarded) blind eye to the speakeasies on their beats?

Our ambitious station commissioner would also have to consider what the closing of all shebeens would mean to their patrons. He would, after all, be depriving them of one of the few consolations they have, and would be doing so using laws that discriminate against black drinkers and black businessmen. Closing shebeens under these conditions would seem to their patrons an unwarranted assault on an aspect of their lifestyle.

This, I think, partly explains the reaction of the woman who threw the rock at the cops, as well as the reaction of her neighbours when she was arrested: to them, the closure of their shebeen seemed an inexplicable, gratuitous assault on an institution which they saw as harmless. Of course they knew the law, and that the cops were only enforcing it. It was just that this was a law that spoke right past them, having been conceived in and for a world that was not theirs.

Shebeens are central to township life. The satisfactions they offer, which sound vulgar and dangerous when described on the page, are indeed neither subtle nor edifying. Nevertheless the rituals of solidarity and friendship, even when alcohol-soaked, meet precious human needs. Besides, zero-tolerance policing can only succeed if it meets minimal standards of legitimacy. The laws governing the sale of alcohol don't, as evidenced by the fact that so many people spend long hours in shebeens.

It seems unlikely that this market can now be highly regulated after all the years of lax enforcement, years in which non-compliance has been woven deep into the industry's culture, years in which the whole idea of regulation has been more or less abandoned. This is true across the country. In the Flats, however, the problem is even more ineradicable because of the symbiotic relationship between shebeens and gangs.

Since shebeening is one of only a handful of ventures in which it is possible for a township entrepreneur to make real money, it has attracted the attention of the gangs. The trouble for shebeeners is that because they operate beyond the boundaries of the law, theirs is a world peopled by all sorts of shady characters: untrustworthy business partners, thugs who demand protection money, cops on the make, and scavenging bands of thugs who rob patrons, owners and anyone else connected with the business. True, they pay no taxes, have low overheads and often employ antediluvian labour practices, all of which bring down costs; but, with their legal status making them vulnerable to sharks of all sorts, it is a tribute to the entrepreneurial spirit of their owners that they survive at all. In this neck of the woods, it takes more than just a flair for business to survive and prosper. It takes a relationship with a gang.

★

The Elsies River police station was about twenty kilometres from the ocean-view apartment I had rented in Green Point. Driving against the traffic, it took less than half an hour to get there even during morning rush hour. Despite its proximity, however, it might as well have been a foreign country, the border of which lay somewhere below Devil's Peak, over the spur of which I would drive every morning. At the highest point of the drive, before the road dived down to the ancient sea bed that is the Cape Flats, I was presented with a panoramic view of the sprawl of slums that surrounds Cape Town. With only the power station next to the highway below giving any sense of scale at all, the miles of project housing and shacks seemed to extend all the way to the Helderberg mountains in the distance.

The erection of the Flats' ghettos began in the 1950s after a half-century during which city government had dithered while population pressure mounted, too few houses were built, and far too few jobs were created. The response, when it came, was drenched in the icy cynicism of apartheid and its out-of-sight-out-of-mind ethos: Cape Town would be made a whites-only city, and the Coloured communities that were in the way would simply be resettled to new, soulless, sullenly feature-less neighbourhoods out in the Flats; and by the late 1960s hundreds of thousands of people had been forcibly removed from the city proper.

The move shattered communities, broke up families, and wrecked much of the commercial life of Cape Town's Coloured community. Worse, it consigned at least the next three generations to growing up in buildings and yards which, with their easily dominated spaces and their narrow staircases, might well have been custom-built for the nascent turf gangs which, even then, were a feature of these communities. It was a 'solution' that could only serve to store up, reinforce and multiply the social problems of the city. But that, as a National Party member of parliament once told Helen Suzman of apartheid in general, was irrelevant: 'We can hold the situation for my generation and my children's generation,' he said, uttering a sentiment that I imagine never appeared on an election poster: 'After that, who cares?'

The effects of that kind of breathtaking cynicism are apparent in Elsies today.

Picture regimented lines of bare, cinderblock buildings. Each is a series of cells, grey and cold. Built of the cheapest materials, they are piled two, three or four stories high. Access to apartments above the ground floor is up steep flights of stairs in front of the buildings and along short passages that branch away from them. There is no wall protecting the passages or the staircase from the elements, and the heavily gated apartments are small, cramped and gloomy. They are more often penitential than homey. The ground before the buildings is bare and hard, and is surrounded by more project housing of the same sort. These are the tenements of Elsies River, and they are as raw and exposed as a wound.

It is, I suppose, conceivable that places such as this might be home to healthy communities, neighbourhoods in which people are peaceable, where prim norms and civilities are respected by all. It is conceivable that even though the apartments are overcrowded, that even though their residents freeze in winter and broil in summer and that they have, as a result, high levels of anger and frustration, that even though there is little by way of recreation here and people have no money to find it elsewhere, that despite all of this, the open spaces in Elsies would be soothing and safe.

In reality, they are anything but.

'You see them,' Terminator said to me once, pointing at a group of young toughs propped against a broken wall, staring malevolently back at the police van. 'I grew up around people like that. *Hulle is vullis vir my.*' They were rubbish to him.

The feeling, I thought, looked mutual.

The group he was referring to was a local gang aligned to one of the region's super-gangs, the Firm. He didn't know what they called themselves here, but he knew that Firm-aligned gangs dominated the area, and assumed that they too must be members of that cartel. 'In one place,' he smiled, 'there was a gang that called themselves the Taliban because they were always fighting the Americans.' He paused for the punch-line: 'We used to call that section "Afghanistan".'

Corner gangs of this sort proliferated in Elsies and across the Cape Flats. They were the most visible manifestation of the way in which the local economy functioned, raw evidence that the rules of economic endeavour pretended to be nothing but what they were: predation without any veneer. They also showed something else. They showed that when the modern institutions needed to guarantee rule-bound, regulated norms of commerce and civility are absent, others will emerge. These *hoekstaanders*, men and boys standing on corners, were the local expression of these substitute institutions. They were premised on the rough order of a different world, an order that dictates that the strong survive and the weak perish. They based their self-concepts on mixed-up notions of clan and fief, bound together with local interpretations of the ideals of strength, of group solidarity and of honour. However twisted their interpretation of these values, the values themselves are noble and their emergence in this form, as others who have studied the gangs have argued, reflects on the failure of formal governance, on the failure of the law.

But, looking at these young men as they determinedly ignored the police, I reflected that all of this worked the other way too: where this interpretation of these ideals had flourished, where these institutions had become entrenched, there could be no law. The two could not exist together.

★

Elsies River was a target-rich environment for the jump-out policing that was Cappy's squad's specialty, and they spent most of their shifts hounding these *hoekstaanders*. They would drive down the township's streets weaving their way into the tenement complexes and, with their game-drive-sharp eyes, they would look for, and frequently spot, anomalies. Kids who were too close to the storm-water drains in which addicts were known to fire up their pipes got the treatment (if they could be caught). So did men who made suspicious movements of hands or face as the van went by. I could never see what it was about

79

these men's actions that had attracted the officers' attention, but, almost without fail, when the van stopped, the appointed target would run, dropping or throwing something away as he did so. This would usually turn out to be a small, tight bundle of dagga or Mandrax. The runners would be chased down and arrested. At that point, while still on the street, arrestees would often be quite combative, swearing at the officers and making a great display of their defiance. In the quiet of Cappy's office at the police station, things were usually different. There, the arrestees, so proud when in view of their neighbours, would quietly comply with all police requests and hope for a gap in conversation in which they might plead to be let off.

At other times the squad would just throw a group of *skollies* up against a wall, frisk them roughly and tell them to get their arses off the street, pushing them along and reinforcing the point by aiming their nightsticks at soft-looking spots. Half of those they encountered this way were *dofgerook*, stupid from smoking, but even they got the message: 'This street is ours. It belongs to us, the gang in blue. Get off it.'

The cops knew, of course, that they were up against it. In the first place, the terrain was a tactical nightmare, perfect for anyone who wanted to hide a stash of drugs. More importantly, they also knew that they ruled only where they stood, and that as soon as their backs were turned the street would once again play host to the local heavies. It was a game they had to play, half-heartedly pretending that it was one they might one day win.

They also spent some of their shift time visiting people they knew to be selling drugs, in the more-or-less forlorn hope that they might catch one of them with his stash. One was a vegetable *smous*, selling his legal wares from a table in the commercial district. Another worked a shebeen from a battered brick house. In the open plot next to it, one of the cops found a bag full of pills. 'That's Piet,' Cappy said of the man who found them. 'He's our dog.' To maximise the return on his officers' time, Cappy took the bag over to a group of suspicious onlookers. Picking out the smallest and weakest of the bunch, he held out his hand. 'Thank you,' he said, seeking only to make trouble for the boy. 'The stuff was just where you said it would be.'

When the bag was opened at the police station, the cops counted nearly three thousand pills. That caused a great deal of excitement until it was established that, despite the obvious pains that had been taken to hide the package, it nonetheless contained only cheap, knock-off painkillers, pills which almost certainly violated the rules of intellectual property but which were not narcotics.

On another occasion, Cappy's squad paid a visit to a high flier they'd been harassing for months. His house and what must once have been a shebeen in the yard was a veritable fortress of solid security gates and watchful lackeys. The man, tall with dark eyes, toothless in a Cape way, greeted the cops at his kitchen door holding a daughter in his arms. He knew the routine as well as they and, over the months that Cappy had been visiting, the cops had developed something of a rapport with him even as they'd put him out of business. From these premises at least.

'Come here,' Piet the dog said to the little girl as he eased her gently out of her father's arms. 'Tell me,' he said to her in Afrikaans, 'where does your daddy hide his dagga?'

Her father laughed and recovered his daughter as Cappy opened one of the industrial-sized fridges that dominated the room. 'Aha!' he exclaimed, his eyes lighting up. 'I'm going to arrest you for planning to sell chocolate without a licence.'

This was all taken in good spirit, but later Cappy told me how their constant attention had disrupted this man's shebeening, adding that because his shebeen was the base of operations for the local gang which the man led, the disruption of its operations had cost him much of his status. 'It's the only way,' he said. 'You have to hit them and hit them and hit them. If you let up for a while, they start again. Like weeds. There must be no rest for them. No rest for the wicked.'

That was also the view of Cappy's boss, Superintendent Jeremy Vearey, the station commissioner at Elsies River, who saw all of these elements, all the disruptive tactics used by Cappy and his men, as part of a grand strategy for combating gangs and gang violence in the area. Its centrepiece was an assault on the gangs' conception of themselves as the masters, in a very feudal sense, of their turfs.

★

When I asked Superintendent Vearey about the gangs in Elsies, he leaned across his desk, his dark eyes scorching mine, and told me that the thing I had to understand about the gangs was that, as far as they were concerned, they owned this place. 'Everyone who lives here, everyone who works here: as far as the gangsters are concerned, all of them owe tribute to the gangs. The gangs believe – really believe – that they have fought for their territory and that as long as they can hold it, it is theirs. Everyone who lives here must pay the gangs for the privilege. That is what they believe deep in their bones. For them, non-gangsters have no rights. That is inconceivable for them.'

Vearey was another intense man, another man full of enthusiasm, another man who relished his work, work that was for him also a game the rules of which he knew well. He grew up on these streets and, as a teenager, he was a member of a gang. He imbibed their ethos and fought in their fights. His own cousin was killed and gutted in a fight that launched a gang war in Elsies. Later, his sense of group solidarity turned political: he joined Umkhonto we Sizwe and was jailed for terrorism. Now he was station commissioner of the Elsies River police. 'The thing you learn in Elsies, especially in the gangs, but not only there, is to be confrontational,' he told me. 'People must know that you can stand your ground, that you won't back off. Whenever you meet people from Elsies, that is what they are like. I am the same. And the gangs know that.'

Turf as dominion, residents as serfs, gangsters as sovereigns: such is the world as conceived by the gangs. They live with the conviction that the boldest of the people around them could rise to be no more than prey. The rest are nothing but herds to be fleeced. Wages, or the household goods they buy, are stolen; taxi owners pay tribute for crossing a gang's turf; shopkeepers pay protection money; barbers cut gangster hair for free. Their income accumulates, tribute paid upon tribute paid, rand upon rand, each extracted from the poorest of the poor simply because they live in the wrong place. 'You know what happens when they start to spend development money here?' an analyst from a local NGO asked me rhetorically. 'Government thinks that by building houses and basketball courts they will defeat gangsterism. Instead the gangsters get their fingers in the construction companies and the workers. The whole thing winds up making them even richer.'

Although the numbers are soft and there are differences in definition of who qualifies as a gangster and who does not, some estimates put the number of gangsters in the Western Cape in the six-figure range. The vast majority of these are '*hoekstaanders*', who stand around on street corners and make a wretched living through petty theft, robbery and drug sales. These are local men who grew up in the buildings which are now their piece of turf, and played together as children, bringing one another up in packs.

The ethos of these groups fosters drug use and encourages multiple forms of criminality, but it rests on a ragbag of fantasies about warrior codes and brotherhood, about dominance and self-assertion. Their identities, their ideas about themselves, are premised on their ability to defend their turf from those who would seek to usurp them. This is what happens when men have no other way of proving themselves.

If only because it brings scale to these small-time operations and creates the potential to bring greater force to bear on those who belong to other gangs and who work neighbouring patches, many of these local gangs form alliances with others. Over time two grand alliances have emerged, the Firm and the Americans. Between them they have carved up most of the Cape Flats' ghettos into rival territories, consolidating their brands even as they have consolidated their monopoly over the region's underground economy.

There are differences in the professional literature about precisely how these super-gangs work, but it is wrong to think of them as organised, hierarchical drug distribution rings or to assume that they have the organisational coherence to govern a vertically integrated supply chain. It might well be more fruitful, in fact, to think of them as organised cartels of drug users who support their habits and lifestyles through other forms of criminality, rather than as a wholly integrated drug-dealing enterprise. It is the same *hoekstaanders*, after all, who make up a sizeable proportion of the addict population.

Although the gangs are responsible for a lot of the crime and violence in the Cape Flats, surprisingly little of it is now driven by turf wars. The rise of the super-gangs has led to there being more stability to boundaries, more respect for their location. The bigger problems arise from the fact that ganging fosters a culture of criminality in which violence is, to use the technical language, expressive: violence happens because that is what being a gangster is about. It is part of his nature.

At the heart of most corner gangs lies a shebeen. It is their headquarters. It is the hub of economic activity in their area. It is their lair.

Liquor, drugs, stolen goods and money-lending: a well-run shebeen allows fingers to be inserted into many a pie, and as a result the relationship between gang and shebeen is symbiotic. The gang needs the income from alcohol sales and the rest; the shebeen needs muscle to secure its market, to protect itself from other gang-supported operators, and to rough-up competitors' patrons to encourage them to move. If the shebeener is not himself a gangster, he must hire them or give them a stake in his operations. And then hope to God that they don't turn on him.

That was part of the reason why Cappy's interest in the fat lady's shebeen had been piqued. A new shebeen was a sign of something. It reflected a shift in the balance of forces, a hint of change in the wind. Who was running the shebeen, and to whose benefit? What were the implications for local gang politics? Did it represent one group's victory over another, and if so, who was it would be out looking for revenge in the near future? Was this a new outpost of one of the high fliers, or just a response to the start of the summer drinking season? If Cappy asked the arrestee about these matters, I didn't hear either the question or the answer. But, after he charged him and the admission-of-guilt was paid, he took great care in filling in a gang card with the man's details. It was news that the station's intelligence might want to follow up.

*

Vearey's approach to the gangs was premised on his understanding of their psychology, the semi-feudal conception they had of themselves and their relationship with their fiefs. He wanted Cappy and his squad on the offensive, engaging the enemy on their turf. It was policing, but it was also psychological warfare; law enforcement that engaged both with real people and with the image they had of themselves and which they sought to project into the minds of those among whom they lived. And part of it was based on a strategic weakness Vearey had identified.

Although the corner gangs don't literally patrol the boundaries of their turf, they must make their presence felt, they must be seen. 'The problem that they have,' Vearey explained, 'is that you can't be a gangster and be secret about it. You must manifest yourself in the community. They must see you on the streets. They must see you on your turf and around your assets. If you can't do that, then it looks like you are hiding. Why must someone respect you if you are hiding? Fear makes you vulnerable to other gangs.'

In response to this, he wanted to demonstrate to all gangsters, from the lowliest *hoekstaanders* to those who occupied the higher reaches of the super-gangs, that the gangs couldn't really control the territory they claimed. 'This is very important to us,' Vearey told me. 'If we can come in and arrest them for carrying drugs or for being drunk in public, close down their shebeens and pour the alcohol down a drain, if we can walk into their area and push them up against a wall to search them, then it says that they are not the ones who govern these streets. That's very damaging for them.' Nailing the shebeens was also an assault on the gang's finances. 'These are their most valuable assets,' he told me. 'They make much more money from alcohol than they do from drugs and prostitution. So when we hit the shebeens, we are hitting them in the pocket. But we are also hitting them in public, showing them that they don't rule these streets, that they don't own them.'

Perhaps that explained the response of the fat lady's patrons. They were the shebeen's defence gang, its muscle, and the fact that the police had marched in and hauled off the person they were supposed to pro-tect felt like an assault on their self-concept. Perhaps also they were responding to the police, reacting with fists and mouth, because if they did otherwise they would not be able to look at themselves in the mirror in the morning.

What of the neighbours, though? Or the old woman, raging at the cops for enforcing the law of the *larnie*? What were they up to?

Forests have been felled writing about the relationship between gangs and the communities in which they operate, and, while the general picture painted by Vearey of predatory packs of criminals extracting a living from the efforts of others is part of the story, that is not all there is to it. Gangs and the charismatic men who lead them, it turns out, are not seen by the community as foreign invaders. Parasitic they may be, but they are also part of the community and can enjoy a surprising degree of legitimacy and respect from the people whose vices they feed and on whose hard-earned incomes they live. This is sometimes explained by the way in which some of the leading figures in the super-gangs have laid claim to the heritage of Robin Hood. They give or loan money to the poor, they pay for uniforms for bands in the unfortunately named 'Coon Carnival', they sponsor local soccer teams, and provide, believe it or not, funds for golf lessons.

The Robin Hood-ism is nonsense, of course. The gangs' incomes are derived largely from the poor, not the rich, and whatever they hand back, it bears little resemblance to what they take away. Nevertheless, because the state is weak and people are poor, the welfare they offer does buy them some support.

But I always thought it inadequate as an explanation of the relationship between community and gangsters, that there had to be something more interesting going on, because this account seemed to reduce community members to silly, sweets-obsessed children who could be easily and cheaply bought off. I had no alternative account to offer, however, until I read something VS Naipaul had written about the relationship between the people of his native West Indies and the first generation of leaders after independence. They had more than adulation for their leaders, he wrote. What they wanted was that their leaders would represent them, and not just in 'a parliamentary way'. Instead, they wanted their leaders, who had once been as poor as they, to be rich and powerful and glorious. Precisely how leaders became rich was irrelevant. All that mattered to them was that their glory would also be the glory of their people, so that the latter could live vicariously through the former. If the leader was grand, larger than life, his people too would be grand. Did it matter how those leaders got rich? No. 'Ordinary ideas of morality and propriety didn't apply,' Naipaul wrote. 'Those were the virtues of another world.'

★

On my last night in Elsies I went out with Cappy's squad. Cappy had taken the night off, and his absence could be felt. There was less direction, less passion in the car. In Cappy's absence Constable Daniels, The Terminator, by virtue of the fact that he was the driver, became the *de facto* leader. Daniels worked the streets with something approaching fury. He had cold, dead eyes, and used them to get people to do as he said. He refused to wear a bullet-proof jacket, saying that it made you look afraid and that he would never look afraid in front of these people.

He'd grown up in Elsies, and I wondered how he'd avoided joining a gang. I was sure his bulk would have been an asset. But when I asked him, he just looked at me curiously and repeated what he'd told me earlier in the week. 'These people,' he said. 'They're *vullis* for me.' Rubbish. 'You make your own decisions in life. And I don't want to be with them.'

How he had come to the conclusion that gangsters were *vullis*, he didn't say, and the moment passed before I thought to ask. Perhaps he had experienced what American sociologists, seeking to explain the decline of crack markets in the United States, have called the 'little brother syndrome', and had watched older siblings get sucked into the gangs and suffer the consequences. Perhaps people he loved had been killed. Perhaps he just hated what he'd seen in his neighbourhood. Whatever it was, whatever wounds he bore, there was real fury in The Terminator, and it must have been a near-run thing, the choice to go straight and join the police rather than sink into gangsterism.

I saw that fury again late that night.

We were driving through the projects at about 3am. It was cold and damp, and the streets were empty. Then, from the corner of his eye, Daniels saw two men walking through some open ground between two buildings. They were a hundred metres away, but he pressed the accelerator hard and covered the ground fast enough to be sure that the men could not run. Not that they wanted to: they were in their forties, sober and quite respectable looking. So much so that when Daniels pulled up he cast one eye over them and decided not to bother getting out of the van. He just nodded, told them that they'd be safer inside, and started to pull away. As he did so, however, one of the two said, '*Naaiers*,' in a loud stage whisper. 'Fuckers.'

Daniels's truncheon was drawn before he hit the ground. 'Who said that?' he demanded.

'Said what?' one of them asked, a picture of unlikely innocence.

'Who. Said. That.' Daniels demanded again, raising his nightstick.

'Said what? No-one said anything.'

Daniels swung, hitting the man in the chest. Not that hard, but hard enough.

The man didn't move. Didn't react. Didn't take a backward step. 'What's that for?' he demanded. 'What are you doing?'

Daniels hit him again. Again, he didn't hit him hard, but I'd have expected the man to at least acknowledge that he'd been hit. Nothing doing. He stood there, his arms wide, asking what he'd done to deserve this treatment.

This was a stand-off, and Daniels allowed the cooler heads in the van to persuade him to get back in and to take them home. Cursing the two, he got into the van and drove off into the dark streets.

That incident has come to symbolise Elsies River and the places like it for me. These were places where power, whether exercised by cops or by the gangsters, was a raw, untamed force. People had to bow before it or be crushed. The courtesies demanded by our law of our law enforcers, the legal checks and balances, the cultivated social graces embedded in our constitution, none found an echo in the social rules by which these communities lived. They simply gained no purchase. The result was that policing here was as tough and uncompromising as was the world in which it functioned.

The only question was how much it mattered.

CHAPTER SIX

MURDER, MURDER ALL ABOUT: INSPECTOR MAX MOKHOSI, IVORY PARK

Until 1998, the sprawling, spreading township of Ivory Park was served by a small police station at Rabie Ridge, an older, more established Coloured community outside the township proper. The building is still used by units in the area, but is now falling into disrepair. It stands guard-like on the edge of the township, a sentry guarding the gate; its location reflecting the philosophy guiding the machinery of law enforcement in the era in which it was built. The new station house, by contrast, sits in the centre of the township, a bright, blond focal point in the iron and brick blanket that covers the hilly swells beyond Johannesburg's northern flank. To reach it, you drive along ten kilometres of a road – enigmatically named 21st of August – lined on both flanks by impossibly small houses and shacks. They form an almost unbroken line, and, as you progress among the taxis and pedestrians, you can feel the press of people, the stifling density of their collective being, close in like a net.

Ivory Park, home to a couple of hundred thousand people, has sprung up beyond the middle-aged spread of townhouses and evangelical churches that surrounds the city of gold. A stone's throw from the hub of the sub-continent's economy, people swarm to the area from across South and southern Africa. The crowd of houses in which they live seems at first an almost undifferentiated, squalid mass, but, as with most things, they become more variegated with time and familiarity: the traditional town-ship four-roomers with plots and garden walls come to seem premium accommodation compared to the cast-iron, pre-fabricated site-and-serv-ice shacks. These, in turn, differ from the ant-lines of RDP matchboxes that march in lockstep across the hills. These matchboxes are themselves superior to the rental shacks that huddle around the water and electrical mains of the houses to which they are attached. They made me think of puppies suckling at the teat. Most depressing of all were the crowded, unbroken warrens of shacks made of mismatched bits of iron and plastic, their roofs held down by rocks and broken toilet bowls, and serviced by a handful of port-a-loos and leaky taps. Evocatively enough, these last were termed 'umzabalazo', a Zulu noun for 'struggle'.

Every time I drove into the township, I wondered what it must be like to live among all these people, among all these eyes and ears. What must it be like to hear all their noises and to have them overhear all your own? To be pinned eternally in the gaze of others? I grew up in Johannesburg's suburbs where even townhouse complexes seem wide-open planes compared to the tiny, claustrophobic living spaces in Ivory Park; and the presence of the crowd, its invasiveness, made my skin crawl. It was a feeling I had again and again while in Ivory Park, leaving me sometimes with the sensation that someone was running his fingers over my back. And not in a nice way.

Despite the press of people, there was something almost rural about Ivory Park. What the municipality unblushingly called 'streets' were unpaved, of course, and they were scarred by weather and over-use. That was neither surprising nor unusual. But the redness of the earth and the lushness of the grass in the fragments of open space between houses were unexpected. So too were the profusion of trees, many of them fruit-bearing, and the fact that muddy spaces were often home to goats or cows or horses. In some places large boulders, too heavy to move, reared out of the earth, forcing paths and roads and rows of shacks to wind themselves around the obstacle just as they might do in villages in the countryside. And, in the open fields between the township and the suburbs to the south and west, women wrapped in long skirts and using hoes designed a thousand years before turned the soil to plant potatoes and beans and spinach. Apart from the power lines that hummed incongruously in the wind above their heads, they could have been on a hillside in Mozambique or Malawi or the Congo rather than 20 minutes from the Gucci store in Sandton City.

★

Practically the first thing Inspector William 'Max' Mokhosi said to me after we'd been introduced by his commanding officer, who had asked him to let me follow him around for a few days, was, 'It's going to be a long week.' I might have been a little put out by this. It is likely, in fact, that I was supposed to be. But I consoled myself with the thought that Max was just stating the obvious: in Ivory Park, cops always have long weeks. In the end, he turned out to be an enormously considerate host, one with an extraordinary take on crime and criminals.

It was a gorgeous, fragrant Monday in the summer, and Max and I were seated on either side of a desk that bore mute testimony to the busyness of township cops. A cheap wood-and-steel affair, it was littered with brown case dockets, loose papers and a haystack of the pins Max used to secure the latter to the former. A telephone clung grimly to its shrinking corner of the table top, along the edge of which ran a rack of five trays marked '24-hour inspection', 'investigation', 'state prosecutor', 'court' and 'closure'. This was office furniture that doubled as a flow chart of the criminal justice system, and, like the institutions it mapped, each tray was very full and equally untidy. Another pile of dockets was on the floor. They seemed to be trying to climb up one of the table legs, hoping to escape the anonymity and neglect that came with their exile from the detective's workspace. Between the columns of papers on another desk against the far wall, Mokhosi's friend and partner, Inspector Setlai, could be made out. Hunched vengefully over the phone, he was a mild-featured man whose coffee-with-extra-cream skin tone was the perfect camouflage among the files with which he worked. He was making feverish notes on a yellow slip of sticky paper attached to a crisp-looking folder. Other folders, older and more weathered, proudly bore their own sticky yellow slips.

A line of complainants and witnesses from the crimes of the previous weekend stood sweating in the corridor outside Mokhosi and Setlai's office, but only the latter was dealing with them. Mokhosi, who needed to find the witnesses to a murder committed the previous Friday night, had bigger fish to fry. So, leaving the complainants and their innumerable assaults and burglaries to his docket-coloured partner, he led me to the parking lot in the rear of the building.

Max was in his early forties. Trim and neatly turned out in the only tastefully unpatterned, non-metallic shirt in the unit, he had broad features, handsome and kind. They sat placidly beneath the tight curls of grey-flecked hair. There was wisdom in his face, but tiredness too. 'I want to go to a station in the suburbs,' he confided to me a few days later. 'I'm getting old, and a man must work according to his age and his energy. It will be quieter in the suburbs, I think. Here you must work until you are exhausted. You are always fighting your body.'

The other thing with which Max had to fight was his car. It was of indeterminate age and colour, and the suspension may have been older and more exhausted than the man behind the wheel. Apart from the driver's, none of the vehicle's doors opened from the outside. The result was that every time we got into it, Max had to lean across the seat to open the passenger door for me, and each time he did so it reminded me that my presence was a burden to him. On our first morning together, however, he seemed to be relishing the opportunity to show me a professional at his work, and joked that the malfunctioning of the doors was deliberate. It was, he said, a low-tech anti-hijacking device. Having made me comfortable among the papers and dockets at my feet and above my eyes in the sun visor, Max set off making sure to hit every ridge and rut the township's streets could throw at us while seeking, as far as possible, to avoid the school kids who seemed intent on examining the underside of a police vehicle. As he did so, I asked him about murder in the township: how many there were, who was involved, why they happened. That sort of thing.

'There are many murders here,' he said. 'But there are mainly two types: the South African murder and the Mozambican murder.'

'And the difference?' I asked, intrigued.

'A South African murder is usually a shebeen thing. Alcohol is involved: people are drunk and then they fight until someone is dead. But if it is a Mozambican murder, then it is probably about business.'

'Is that all?' I asked.

'There are also robberies,' he conceded. 'Those can be South African or Mozambican.'

Reaching above his head, he pulled down the dockets he'd stuck under his sun visor and flipped through them. Finding the one he wanted, he handed it to me: 'That is a typical Ivory Park crime.'

Mokhosi had been at court when the case had come in the previous week, and the original statements had been taken badly. But with a bit of effort, I worked out that the previous Monday night, the deceased, one Brian, and his girlfriend had been woken by loud knocking on the door of their shack. Brian had asked who it was and a voice had said, 'It's me.' Brian went outside and his girlfriend, whose statement this was, heard him arguing with the man. She didn't report what Brian's interlocutor said. Nor, more importantly, did she offer anything that might help identify the man. The argument become more fevered, and then the unidentified man had shouted to Brian that he had better run. She'd heard rapidly receding footsteps. She stayed in the shack, however, too petrified to move, but later that night her daughter called her to say that something had happened to Brian: they had found him stabbed at the gate of the yard and had taken him to hospital. He died before she got there.

At the end of the statement was the sad pro forma epitaph with which such statements always end: 'And that is all I know.'

'Good luck finding the suspect,' I said when I was done. 'It sounds like the witness doesn't know who the killer was.'

'No,' Mokhosi disagreed, shaking his salt-and-pepper head. 'I think she knows. But the member who took the statement didn't ask her. She will tell me when I ask.'

'So is it a South African or a Mozambican crime?' I asked, teasingly.

'Mozambique.' He was quite definite. And, as it turned out, he was wrong.

★

The murder to which Max was driving on that Monday had taken place outside a shebeen near the municipal offices. It was one of the older sections in the township, an area of cracked brick houses, each with its litter of rental shacks. The victim had been killed while out drinking, and during the same incident two of the dead man's brothers had been shot and injured. It was a serious crime: a murder and two attempted murders, and, in a less violent country, a whole team of detectives and forensic scientists might be working it. In Ivory Park at the start of the third millennium, the community would have to make do with Max.

Mokhosi, who had attended the murder scene the previous Friday night, had nothing but the names and address of the three men who'd been shot. He had arrived on the scene well after the incident, having been called out of bed, and by the time he got there the surviving victims had been carted off to hospital. In the strobe-lit rush of the initial emergency, he had spoken to no-one who could offer him a suspect's name nor indeed any details at all about the incident. He had no motive, no useful physical evidence, and had not yet even spoken to the survivors whose names and address − they lived together − had been taken by the uniformed officers who had supervised the crime scene before Max arrived. Now, three days later, he needed something to push the case forward.

For obvious reasons, he chose to start at the three victims' home.

The house was on the elbow of a steep bend in the road. The atmosphere around it seemed heavy, mournful. This impression was accentuated by the steamy smell of mud and rotting leaves that rose as Max opened the gate, and by the drying washing draped on the tree that stood in the muddy paddock that was the front garden. The house was silent, seemingly empty, and, when Max knocked on the wooden door and announced himself, it seemed to echo hollowly. For a moment nothing happened, then the door lurched open, juddering as it scraped along the uneven floor to reveal an ancient man with a hawk-like nose and fiery eyes. In a manner that conveyed to Max and me that he spoke no English, he gestured to someone within and was soon joined by a boy in his teens who became a bit player in the part-Xitsonga, part-Portuguese conversation that ensued. When it was over, the teenager turned to Mokhosi and, semi-apologetically, told him that the old man, his father, was very angry. He was suffering because one son was dead and another two had been shot.

'Do you know what happened?' Mokhosi asked.

'They were fighting,' he replied, shrugging.

'But with who? Do you know who did this?'

'No,' he said. 'You must ask my brothers. They know him.'

Mokhosi asked if they were back from the hospital yet, but was told that they weren't and that he'd have to find them there.

★

Even on a quiet Monday morning, I could tell that the casualty ward at the Tembisa Hospital was not a place to which I would want to turn except in the direst of emergencies. It was crowded with gurneys that were parked at odd angles, clogging the entrance. Many were unoccupied, but on the rest groaning men lay with swollen limbs and eyes turned blank with pain, boredom and resignation. The atmosphere was of muddle, weariness and exasperation. Beneath that, something in the air seemed poisoned. It was as if some bitter essence had condensed from the agonies of the thousands who had passed through this space. The walls were greasy with it. Mokhosi's murder victim had died here, and I could imagine no place more lonely.

With some difficulty, Mokhosi located the duty nurse and established in which ward his injured victims were now lying, and, because he knew Tembisa Hospital well, it was not long before he was interviewing one of the two survivors of the Friday night shooting. The other, it transpired, had been sent home that morning.

The injured man lay in a high-ceilinged, mercilessly sunny room, and wore the candy-striped gown of the hospital. He'd been shot in the calf, and an enormous cast had been built to make sure he couldn't move his foot. He had to pull himself into an upright position using handles hung from the frame around his bed. Trying to accommodate me, Max asked if the man spoke English. He said that he did, but he was just being polite, and soon Max reverted to Xitsonga while I watched the other patients eat their colourless chicken and cabbage lunches.

The story, as Max related it to me, was typical of the genre. The victim-witness and his two brothers had been drinking at a shebeen where they had gotten into an argument with another man. He couldn't remember, or wouldn't say, what the dispute had been about. His interlocutor, he said, had left. Later, when the three brothers left the shebeen,

95

the man was waiting for them. The argument resumed but this time the man drew a gun in support of his point of view. The brothers turned to run, but before they got far he opened fire. As Max already knew, one brother died and the other two were injured.

'Did he give you the name of the suspect?' I asked.

'He only knew the first name – Alfred – but he says his brother knows where he lives.'

'So this case will be solved?'

Max shrugged a maybe. It was a weary gesture, one that conveyed a degree of indifference as well as a more professional desire not to commit himself.

I had noticed that the detective had jotted down scraps of information while he spoke to the man, but that he didn't get the witness to sign a formal statement. I asked him why.

'It's a trick,' he said. 'Something you learn in Ivory Park. If a murder is in a shebeen, then it means that the witnesses were drunk. No-one will remember the story properly and they will all tell you something different. So, if you want your case to be strong, you must only write statements after you can get the story from everyone. If you take the statements too soon, then you get lots of mistakes. Then you get lots of problems in court. Maybe the prosecutor will even drop the case because he doesn't understand what happened.'

Before we left the hospital, Max took me to another equally bright ward. There he spoke to a young man in his late teens or early twenties who, on the detective's request, lifted his shirt to show me some fearsome criss-cross stitching that spoke of a horrendous knife wound. Talking to Mokhosi, the kid looked skittish, and when I asked why the detective told me that it was because he was going to go to jail.

'He's not the victim?' I was surprised.

'No,' Max replied with deliberate condescension. 'He is the suspect. He beat a man with a hammer.' He fell silent.

'Was it also a shebeen thing?' I asked, thinking that he wanted to make a point about how common the type of crime he was investigating was in the township.

'This is not my case,' he said, shaking his head. 'It is one of the other detectives'. It is a funny story and it will help you to understand a lot about policing in this place.'

The story he told was complicated. The man with the crazy-paving stitching had been guarding a house occupied by his cousin. The cousin had abandoned it because a family in the area had accused him of kidnapping one of its members, a crime he was alleged to have committed after accusing the missing man of sleeping with his wife. The young man had been stabbed after a fight broke out between him and people who were looking for the alleged kidnapper.

That, at least, was his version of events.

'So he was stabbed by the family of a man who may or may not have slept with his cousin's wife?' I asked. 'And another man was beaten with a hammer in the same fight? And the woman's lover, if he was her lover, has been kidnapped and was maybe killed?'

It was as if the right to put people to death had been thoroughly democratised: now anyone could do it. It was *Days of Our Lives* on crack.

'And that isn't even the end,' Mokhosi assured me. 'After this one was stabbed,' he pointed at the youngster, 'the man who owned the house he was guarding sent a truck to fetch his things. He was scared that the other family would come back to burn the place.'

'Is this the same man? This one's cousin?'

'No. It was his kinsman. That cousin was only renting the place from him.'

Oh good, I thought, anticipating the difficulty I would have in this case's exposition: another character.

'The owner of the house sent a truck to get the furniture from the house. But while it was there, the other family came back again. They must have been waiting for him. Again there was a fight, and another man was killed. This one was shot.'

'Jesus,' I said. 'Who did it this time?'

'The owner,' he said. 'We traced him because he left the truck behind when he ran away.'

'So is it over or will more people die?' I asked.

'I don't know,' he said.

'And the man who was supposedly kidnapped? What about him? Has anyone seen him?'

'Not yet. But a body was found last week by the cemetery. It is being identified now. Perhaps it is him.'

★

It was lunch time by now, so Mokhosi took me to the local fried chicken outlet. We sat in the sun looking out on a busy street that was altogether too narrow for the traffic it carried. There was a bend in the road a short way from us, and every taxi that hurtled past us slid into the oncoming lane. Cars coming in the opposite direction would hoot or flash their lights. It was horrifying and distracting, but there was also something ritualistic about this: the hurtling and the sliding and the hooting must have all been standard operating procedure, a ballet everyone danced.

Max was an old detective, who I imagined had seen all sorts of crime and all sorts of criminals. I wanted to know how he made sense of it all, how he understood criminality and its causes. It was the sort of conversation that I'd had time and time again with cops all over the country, and it had gotten to the point that I started to think myself clairvoyant because I knew what they were going to say before they opened their mouths: 'Poverty and Unemployment,' they'd tell me, capitalising the words as they spoke them. Poverty and Unemployment. Poverty and Unemployment.

This was, of course, an intuitively plausible, politically acceptable and thoroughly reasonable account of the causes of crime. It was also, when you think about it, eye-crossingly lazy, and failed utterly to explain why some poor and unemployed people committed crimes and others didn't, why a great many crimes have little to do with putting food on the table, or why people with decent jobs commit their fair share of crimes too.

These objections apart, the poverty-causes-crime thesis is an account that finds surprisingly little empirical support in the international criminological literature. Yes, there is a lot of crime in the poorer areas of the developed world's cities – there are few really good studies in the developing world – but the question arises whether that is because poverty causes crime or because crime drives businesses (and richer folks) out of neighbourhoods and therefore lowers average incomes in the area. High levels of crime in an area, in other words, may explain why those places are poorer than others, rather than the other way around. Another possibility muddying the analytical waters is that those who are poor commit crime not because they are poor but because some constitutional factor – an inability to apply oneself, say, or weak impulse control and deficient anger-management skills – makes some people both more likely to commit crime and less likely to hold down a decent job. Crime and poverty, in other words, may both be caused by something else.

One way of getting around this is to ask what happens to crime levels over the course of the business cycle. Do they rise as people lose their jobs in recessions, or fall as they get richer during booms? Unfortunately, the evidence that has been accumulated to answer this question is also decidedly ambiguous. This is partly because governments hire more cops as tax-takes rise with expanding economic activity, and allow those numbers to fall when the economy tanks. It may be, in other words, that changes in the number of police per capita that result from increased police recruitment, rather than higher incomes, might explain any measured decline in criminality at the top of the economic cycle relative to the bottom. In any event, crime often seems to rise during booms. This might be because the increased number of cops means that more crime is reported and recorded, or, as some other evidence suggests, that crime really does rise as people get richer mainly because their consumption of alcohol increases.

All of this makes the relationship between crime and poverty uncertain, a truth that is also easily demonstrated by the fact that, even allowing for the horrible unreliability of crime data, many countries that are much poorer than South Africa have to put up with much less crime than we do.

I had mustered all these debating points, readying myself to use them against Max who I just knew would tell me that poverty causes crime, when his first response to my question disarmed me utterly: 'People,' he said. 'People are the cause of crime.'

'What do you mean?' I asked, thinking his response was either even lazier than the usual banalities about poverty and unemployment, or that I was about to hear something which might surprise me.

'Just what I said,' he replied. 'Where there are people, there is crime. It is like that everywhere. So it is easy: if you want no crime, you must get rid of all the people.'

'OK,' I responded, patiently, I thought, but perhaps I was being smarmy. 'Crime is part of the human condition. I accept that. But, for the sake of argument, let's just say that there are people in our society and that there is, therefore, some crime. Why do some places have more crime than others? Why is it worse in Ivory Park than in the suburbs or the rural areas?'

'Conditions are bad here,' he shrugged. 'There are too many people. They have got no work and they are unemployed for a long, long time. They become like people on holiday. They get out of bed when they want to. When they do get up, they sit around all day and do nothing. They have too much time and so they get bored. When it is like that, all they think about is getting drunk. But then they find that there is no money to buy alcohol. That is when they decide that they must rob someone. That's where the trouble comes, and that is why there is crime: people are poor and they are bored.' He shrugged eloquently again and took a pull on his Coke.

'People say that this crime is about poverty,' he continued. 'But I was poor and my family was poor. But now I am a policeman, not a *tsotsi*. I am telling you that it is not only the poverty that makes people do these things. There is something wrong with them.' He pointed to his head, and continued: 'Something isn't right up there. Just because you are poor doesn't mean that you are not a person, a human being. But these people …' His voice trailed off into a soft whistle at the sheer impenetrability of the human soul.

'But what is wrong with them?' I asked. 'And why? What made them like that?' I wanted to know what it was about some people that had turned them into killers, but framed like that it was an unanswerably broad, all-embracing question. Who could answer it? Who had? Still, I had the impression that if I pushed him a little, Mokhosi would go beyond the threadbare clichés of South Africa's populist criminology. 'What is the difference between killers and the people they kill?' I asked, trying to be as blunt as possible.

'There are a lot of things,' he replied. 'Maybe some people are good and some people are bad. Maybe it is their parents or the family: usually the family *is* a problem. Maybe it is because they have the wrong friends or they use drugs. I don't know. But if I must tell you one thing, then I will say it is self-esteem.

'People with no esteem think that they have nothing to lose. I am poor and unemployed. I live in a shack. I have nothing. I own nothing. What is there to stop me from doing wrong things? What will I lose if I go to jail or if I die?' He paused for a moment as another taxi veered across the solid white line in the road. It seemed to me an example of precisely the point Max was making.

'You will see how people live here. Conditions are bad. But the worst is that those conditions affect people in their heads. They think they have nothing, that they *are* nothing. People like that, they get jealous when they see other people who live in a nice house or have nice clothes. They hate people who are happy. They are jealous of them. It is something that eats them, like a worm. It makes everything bitter.

'Those are the people who kill. They are the ones who have been defeated up here.' He pointed to his head again. 'For them, life has no value. Their own life and other people's. No-one's life has value.'

Boredom, jealousy, self-esteem, bitterness, and a hatred for those happier than themselves: it was perhaps the most extraordinary account of the causes of crime I had ever heard from a police officer. I was far from certain that I accepted every word he'd uttered, but what Max was saying was so much more interesting and unsettling a thesis than the usual packhorse answers to my questions that it left me quite breathless. We'd finished our lunches, however, and it was time to look for the other injured witness to the Friday night murder.

Max was not a man to sit around gabbing to a naive researcher.

★

The atmosphere at the victims' house hadn't changed in the hours since we'd been directed to the hospital, though now there were more people in the yard; friends and family, no doubt, there to grieve with the old man. Sad and silent, the place was drenched in pain and loss; it rose with the vapour from the mud. What must it be like to enter such homes every week, I wondered. Unlike some of his colleagues, Max seemed always to operate with the perception that the people around him were human beings. He carried his familiarity with death and grief lightly. Still, I wondered about whether such intimacy tinted detectives' worlds in shades of sadness. The rituals of grief must be old, familiar friends. How could they not insinuate themselves into detectives' hearts?

Max quickly located the second injured brother who had been released that morning. He was talking quietly to his father, the man with sharp, fiery eyes. He was a young man with strangely swollen features, as if he'd never quite worked off his baby fat, and had a thin cast over one forearm, the bullet from the Friday night fracas having scraped his right hand and wrist. It was not, he said, a serious wound, but he'd had to stay in hospital until a doctor would sign papers allowing him to go home. It had taken a full day.

To Max's irritation, and just as he had predicted, the story of this victim-witness differed from that of his brother. Yes, there had been an argument in the shebeen before the shooting. But it had been with two men, only one of whom had left the shebeen. That had ended the dispute. Some time later, however, the man returned and the argument resumed. This time he pulled a firearm. No doubt reckoning that discretion was the better part of valour, the three brothers left their drinks and the shebeen. But the man with the gun followed them out and the argument resumed. At some point the gunman opened fire.

'And the argument?' I asked Max as he recounted the bones of the witness's story. 'What was that about?'

'I don't know,' he said. 'I also don't care. Money. Women. What difference does it make?'

'Won't a motive help you in court?'

'No. Not with a murder in a shebeen. No-one remembers the reasons. All that matters is that I can prove who are the suspects.'

'Did he identify the same suspect? The man named Alfred?'

'Yes,' he replied tiredly. 'But there is a problem. He says that Alfred isn't the one who fired the weapon. He says it was the other man.'

'Why is that a problem?'

'Because if this story is right, it will be hard to prove that Alfred is guilty of anything. It means Alfred must confess.'

★

It was hard to understand why rival versions of the shooting were offered by the two witness-victims, both of whom, you might have thought, were in prime positions to offer accurate accounts of what had happened. Nevertheless there were now a series of questions raised by the conflicts in their stories. Had there been one man or two? Had the gun been drawn in the shebeen, frightening the three into leaving, or had it been drawn only after the three brothers had left? Most importantly, was Alfred the shooter or, as the second witness had said, was it another man? These were the sorts of questions that could befuddle a prosecutor and confuse a court, and unless a coherent story could be made of the incident, preferably supported with a confession and the recovered firearm, the chances of convicting anyone were slim. Things would be different if it was two suspects disagreeing in their accounts of events. That is expected. Differences in eyewitness testimony, on the other hand, were far harder for courts to deal with.

Mokhosi's anticipation of precisely this sort of muddle had led him to take the precaution of not having either victim sign a formal statement until he had heard as much of the story as possible. He had said that this was to avoid having a baffled prosecutor refuse to take the case to court. In this, he was either wrong or was trying to simplify matters for a dense researcher: a former prosecutor assured me that murder is too serious a matter to drop just because of confusion in witness statements. Besides, decisions about the prosecution of murder cases don't rest with junior prosecutors who will sometimes refuse to take on cases they might lose for fear of screwing up their performance statistics. These decisions are made higher up the food chain in the Department of Justice, by people who are less likely to look for reasons to avoid prosecuting cases.

Where Mokhosi's concern was valid, however, was in relation to the trial itself where muddled, contradictory statements in the docket

103

would be meat and drink to any reasonably energetic defence attorney who would use them to cast doubt on the credibility of the testimony. But Mokhosi's approach of not taking statements created a different risk: the defence might suggest that the delay between the incident and the statement-taking was itself suspicious, and that in the interim the witnesses had been coached or had had time to collude in cobbling together a false account of events.

That being so, it is reasonable to ask whether Max was right to wait until the Monday to interview the survivors, especially given the weight of evidence in criminological studies, confirmed by the practical experience of detectives, that most crimes are solved in the first 24 hours. But any answer to that question must take into account other problems Max would have confronted.

Consider, for instance, the context in which this crime had been committed: a packed shebeen filled with revelers in various states of insobriety, and dark and noisy to boot. I saw some of these later in the week, and they were adolescent in their frenzy, crammed with people and smoke and music so loud it had become a physical presence, a pounding, thrashing wave of sound that seemed to peel back my eyelids.

Accounts of anything that happened in a place like that were bound to be confused, the subject of rival descriptions and incompatible interpretations. Everyone present would have heard and seen only slivers of the events in question, and each would have a slightly different version of what had happened. Add to that the fog of intoxication and the instinct people have unconsciously to fill in details that they have not themselves witnessed, and it was all but inevitable that incompatible testimony would emerge. Even if, as might have been the case here, the denouement was reached in the relative quiet of the street outside the shebeen, the alcohol and the darkness of the street could still combine to produce evidence so confused it would make cases unwinnable without confessions or damning physical evidence.

The context in which these events took place, in other words, made it maddeningly difficult to compile accurate, consistent evidence. That problem would exist even when people wanted to tell the truth about what they'd seen and done. The trouble was, in these sorts of cases, there was every chance that some witnesses and victims would not be telling the whole truth because a fracas in a shebeen, however violent, however one-sided the eventual outcome, is seldom between a wholly innocent victim and an unambiguously guilty attacker. This was made plain to me once by a senior officer I met on a training programme. He came from a station in the Northern Cape, where stabbings and shootings in and around shebeens made up a substantial portion of all the violent crime in the area. The trouble with these crimes, he told me, is that many people in these places have an appetite for a fight and have come there to feed it. In the end, who is the victim and who is the offender 'is just a matter of luck and timing'.

This is not just a moral question about the apportioning of blame between parties in an archetypal something-ought-not-to-be-happening-and-about-which-something-ought-to-be-done-now situation. It is also a practical question of establishing guilt in a system of justice premised on the presumption of innocence and in which defending oneself from physical attack is a legitimate defence. In the absence of independent witnesses would it be possible to assert definitively that Alfred or the other man, whoever was the shooter in Max's case, had not been defending himself from the three brothers rather than the other way around? Perhaps the argument had happened in just the manner the brothers had described, but was it inconceivable that the brothers had struck the first blows? More troublingly, it was also possible that the three brothers had launched an unprovoked attack on Alfred. Perhaps they had even attempted to mug him outside the shebeen, and the story of an argument had been cooked up, a fabrication needed to disguise their guilt. The simple fact was that with only one side of the story accessible to him, Max had no way of knowing what exactly had happened. He might have responded to the human inclination to believe the injured parties, particularly as he had spoken to them first. Nevertheless, Max and the criminal justice system were confronting the nursery school teacher's eternal question – who started it?

This was another reason why Max's failure to get statements on the

Friday night might have mattered. Not only might it have created a potentially damaging flaw in his case against Alfred which an imaginative attorney might exploit, but it was also possible that the brothers had fabricated their tale over the course of the intervening weekend. It was even possible that that was why their stories differed – under-prepared, each might have had to fill in blanks when Mokhosi asked them questions they had not anticipated.

But could Max have done anything differently? Could he have avoided this problem? Consider the matter from his point of view.

He'd arrived at the scene of the shootings some time after the incident, having been called out from his home half-way across the city. By that time the two wounded brothers had been taken away by friends or an ambulance. The uniformed officers on the scene hadn't taken statements from them, obtaining nothing more than their names and addresses before they were shipped off. Perhaps Mokhosi could have followed the two injured men to the hospital, but this too might have been difficult. I'd seen something of these difficulties the previous week in Thokoza, where I'd spent a large portion of a Friday night shift standing over a body in an open field. Together with three cops, I'd watched insects gnaw for two hours on a piece of intestine the size, shape and colour of a cocktail sausage which poked through a leaking gunshot wound, while they waited for a detective to arrive. By the time he had reached the scene, worked it for clues, conducted the photographer in his work and watched the mortuary van cart the deceased's remains away, many, many hours had passed. If anything like that had happened on the night of Max's shootings, Max would have been extremely tired by the time he'd finished working the scene. He would also have been justified in thinking that the two injured survivors might have been in surgery or that they would now be sedated, unable, at any rate, to speak sensibly and consecutively. He'd have known that whatever statements he got from them would have to be retaken anyway.

The problem was ultimately unresolvable. If Max took the statements immediately, any innocent incompatibilities in the various witnesses' accounts might have led to the unjustified acquittal of Alfred as defence counsel discredited the evidence. If he took them after the stories could be made more coherent, Alfred might be wrongly convicted.

★

That there were limits to how far a community's patience could be tested by the maddening intricacies of putting these cases together was brought home to me late the following night after a patrol with the crime prevention unit that consisted of a series of shebeen-raids, the breaking up of half-a-dozen games of dice, and the searching of the homes of young men whom informers had cast as a robbery gang. Nothing much had come of these activities, and I was sitting at a petrol station as the ultra-flash BMW two of the station's officers drove was being filled. Inspector Rabutle, the proud driver of this chariot, turned around in his seat and informed me casually that the year before he'd been shot while sitting at this service station. 'I was just sitting there, next to the pump. Then there was this man next to me. It was sudden. I didn't see where he came from. He pointed a gun down. Then he just shot. He didn't say anything. Just dwah!' He made a cracking sound by bracing the index finger of his right hand against the joint of his left hand's middle finger and snapping it against the back of his left hand. He pointed at a spot high on his chest: 'The bullet hit the vest over here, but it was going down, so it just bounced off and went into my leg.'

'Jesus!' I said. 'Why did he do it?' I assumed that most of these cases were either robberies or some form of vengeance.

'It was a funny thing,' he replied. 'No-one knew at first. Then the detectives heard that it was one of the sections in Ivory Park. They heard that the community was not happy with the police because they said that we don't go there when they need us. So, because of this, they decided that they must shoot a policeman. They wanted to teach us a lesson.'

A community protests about how bad policing is in its area by shooting one of the men they want to motivate! Rabutle's story seemed too perverse to be true, and I wondered if he was putting too much faith in the words of an informant who may simply have been taking his handler for a ride. I pressed him a little about the origins of the rumours the detectives had heard and why no-one had been arrested, but he professed to know no more than he had told me. 'Policing Ivory Park is hard,' he said by way of conclusion. 'You can't police here like you police in Sandton.'

That, I thought, is probably true.

★

A couple of days after the interviews with the victim-witnesses and my night out with Rabutle, Max called me on my phone. I was, at the time, sitting in the police station's charge office, marveling at the frenetic pace of activity in what was about as busy a piece of government real estate as I've ever seen.

All afternoon, vans had pulled up in front of its glass doors to disgorge cops and complainants and a motley collection of defiant- or defeated-looking arrestees. Desk officers had bustled about behind the charge office counter beneath the inevitable fetish-photo of the president, their handcuffs jingling metallically at their belts. The air was filled with the incessant cicada-buzz of cellphones and landlines. The latter would ring and ring until an officer had a moment to fling an all-but-incomprehensible thank-you-for-calling-Ivory-Park-Sergeant-Rasegatla-speaking-good-day in the general direction of its mouthpiece. Blink and you'd miss it.

Detectives, dockets sprouting from their armpits, barged through the throng, shouting at one another as they crossed into the station's inner sanctums. Civilians sat on long benches against the walls, waiting for their turn to report a crime or have a commissioner of oaths' signature attached to a sworn affidavit attesting to some aspect of their personal circumstances, without which the welfare department might withhold a grant or a pension. They chatted among themselves. They sat mournfully. They clutched papers in hands held between their knees. Above all, they waited.

It was, I thought, a humblingly democratic experience – in here, no-one's problem was special; none was as unique as its bearer thought –

and it was borne stoically by people who, being poor, were probably over-familiar with delays.

I'd been watching the charge office for half an afternoon, drinking in the atmosphere and thinking abstractly about the challenges of policing in so difficult an environment, when Max phoned. 'We're going to arrest Alfred,' he said. 'Do you want to come?'

I found Max and the pasty-faced Inspector Setlai in their office with six or seven other men, most of whom I knew to be other detectives. In among them was his second witness, the baby-fat man with a cast on his arm. He'd brought another man to whom Mokhosi was speaking when I entered the room. The new man, I was told, knew in which shack Alfred lived and would take the cops to it.

'I think you are going to be disappointed,' Mokhosi said to me after we'd gone to the cars and had completed the complicated door-opening procedures that preceded my getting into the vehicle. 'There is information that Alfred has run away. He is no longer in Ivory Park.'

'Is that what the witness says?' I asked.

'Yes. They said that they went to look for him yesterday, but they found no-one.'

'They went to look for him themselves?' I asked. I imagined the victims' fierce-looking father leading a group of men. Perhaps they had knobkerries and sticks in their hands. The image was in my head because one often came across such groups, members of an informal system of policing that was funded by apparently voluntary contributions from the community, when on night patrols in Ivory Park. 'Is that a bit of mob justice slipping into the mix?' I asked.

Mokhosi shrugged. He was wearing a gun-grey shirt with dark pants and black tie. He looked like a B-movie Chicago gangster. But an elegant one. 'Maybe,' he replied. 'Sometimes they just make an arrest. Other times it is more violent.'

The thought didn't seem to bother him, and in this he was little different to many of his colleagues who are often a bit ambivalent about vigilantism. They know it is criminal, of course. They know it is error-prone. They know it can lead to vengeance cycles. But, more viscerally, they believe that criminals put themselves in harm's way, that no-one has forced them to do the deeds for which they stand accused. They believe also that when the victims of vigilantes commit their crimes, they know, or ought to know, that confronting a wrathful community is one of the risks they are taking. If they get into trouble, an underlying, unacknowledged attitude seems to be, they ought not to come running to us.

★

Alfred's shack wasn't all that far from where the victims' family home had been, an *umzabalazo* in a small cluster of similar structures. The detectives had to walk 50 metres through the shanties from their cars that were parked at the nearest road. When they reached the shack the witness pointed to, they found a small woman sitting on a plastic box in front of the open door. She was frail-looking, and was obviously cowed by the five detectives who'd fanned out in front of her. Mokhosi greeted the woman and asked whether she knew Alfred. She did, she said. He lived with her, in this shack. But, she said, he had left. He had returned to Mozambique on Sunday.

That would have been two days after the shooting and a day before the investigation actually got moving.

'Why did he leave?' Mokhosi asked. The woman, professing not to know, speculated that perhaps it was for Christmas, adding that she thought he would be back because he had left two bags of his belongings with her for safekeeping.

Mokhosi told her that they were looking for him and asked if he could see the bags and look around the shack. The woman saw no reason to object – and probably had no reason to think that she could – and she ushered him into a shack that was barely bigger than the double bed that took up most of the floor space. The mattress was wrapped in a plastic sheet, and in the dry heat of the room just to look at it was to imagine the sweaty nights that those who lived here must endure. Above the bed, clothes hung claustrophobically from a cross-beam in the roof, their hems only a few inches from where the sleepers' heads would be. They were church robes, the kind that cannot be allowed to touch

110

other clothes. That suddenly seemed a cruel demand to make of congregants with such limited cupboard space.

The floor was concrete hard and had been swept to a defeated-looking grey. Coincidentally, that was exactly how the woman of the house looked: defeated and grey. Gaunt to the point of emaciation, her chin and elbows and wrists were all sharp angles and brittle points. She fussed around under the bed briefly and emerged with two tog bags stuffed with the goods and chattels Alfred had left behind. Mokhosi emptied them onto the bed. Clothes, interspersed with odd mementoes – photos and hand-drawn pictures – tumbled out. 'Is this Alfred?' Mokhosi asked the woman, pointing at a picture of a large man with skin so dark it was almost blue. She nodded, and Mokhosi pocketed the picture: one for the wanted posters. The search was otherwise unrewarding. The woman said she'd never seen Alfred with a firearm, and certainly had no knowledge of where he might have hidden it if he possessed one. She could offer no information about which village in which province of Mozambique Alfred hailed from, nor suggest any means of contacting him.

Alfred's trail had gone completely cold almost before anyone had begun to follow it.

None of this really surprised Mokhosi. Murderers who are known to their victims or their families will seldom hang around waiting for either the cops or, more frighteningly, the deceased's family to come and find them. The detective had, in fact, spent the previous week in the High Court giving evidence in a case in which the murderer was arrested two years after the crime. The killer had shot a man during what must have been a heated game of dice, but he had escaped when the cops bungled a stake-out of his house. He'd spent the intervening period hunkering down in some rural backwater to which he could not be traced. On his return to the township, however, a relative of his victim had spotted him and the arrest had, at last, been made. 'Many times they turn up later,' Mokhosi told me. 'You must just wait. The only thing that is a problem is that sometimes the family doesn't call you. They prefer to do mob justice when they see the man again.'

★

Mokhosi's problems – the piles of dockets (often poorly written), the unreliable witnesses, the absconding suspects – were typical of those of cops policing society's most unruly spaces. Disordered and unstructured, this was a jurisdiction that was home to every kind of potential law-breaker. Some had spent their entire lives offending, and thought little of putting a knife in someone's face and demanding he hand over the contents of his pockets. Others were different. Like volatile compounds in a poorly managed laboratory, all that was required was the right set of conditions, the right catalyst, and an explosion of unpredictable ferocity might result. In between there were chancers and opportunists of every stripe, men and women who were in a state of high alert, always on the lookout for a quick buck. All thrived in this environment in which the tolerance for disorder was, of necessity, high, and in which particular people and events about which an investigator might need reliable information could slip by invisibly.

In some ways this was ironic. The crush of people and the sense of their perpetual motion, so oppressive on one level, created just the right amount of cover for the commission of crimes which – premeditated or not – would then fade anonymously into the background. But the masses of people crowded into tiny tin cans, each on top of the other, didn't just make investigations more difficult: it was the constant friction of their interactions, the inevitable collisions and clashes as people sought to chart their way through crowded waters, that accounted for a high proportion of the crimes committed. Mokhosi, I came to reflect, was right: people *were* the cause of crime. It was not just a question of numbers, however. Just as the temperature of a gas in a pressure chamber rises as more and more is pumped in, so too did the level of crime. Where there are too many people in too small a space, the unpleasant situations which give rise to our need for policing would arise again and again and again.

CHAPTER SEVEN

BODYGUARDS OF THE POSSESSING CLASSES: POLICING THE STREETS OF ROSEBANK, JULY 2003

'It's a quiet place, this one,' Constable Morena said for the umpteenth time. 'You can drive all day and nothing will happen. You get very bored.' Morena filled the front seat of the car. He was a big man with close-set eyes that twinkled, and a garrulousness so powerful it was almost fragrant. But it was also frustrated in the suburbs: 'These streets are so empty,' he complained more than once. 'I could never live here. I would forget that there are people in this world.'

Morena's patrol took him through the minion-strewn streets of Parkwood, Rosebank, Saxonwold and Forest Town, suburbs named for the groves of trees planted in the late nineteenth century to provide lumber for the mining industry. The streets are a tangle because, a century ago, when members of Johannesburg's expanding elite started to move down the hill from Parktown to build their mansions among the trees, they did so without the benefit of an urban planner. The result is that streets seldom run straight for very long. They twist and turn, fold in on themselves like sailors' knots, creating monstrous inefficiencies in the flow of cross-town traffic. But it is their privacy that is the most compelling feature of these suburbs, and the labyrinthine streets add layers of seclusion and intimacy; their defiance of the grid's mechanical logic is refreshingly human. The trees too – the forests of oak and jacaranda, the rarer pines and blue gums – are essential to the suburbs' privacy. You are aware that there must be homes and lives on the other side of the lines of foliage and fences, but distances are exaggerated and sounds are muted by the solemn closeness of the air, its stillness amplified by the tick-tick of the electric fences.

113

This sort of privacy is the privilege of wealth. It is privilege that is shaped by the streets and trees and walls, by the size of the plots and by the mores of the residents. It is a privacy secured and protected by residents who seal themselves in their fortresses protected by alarms and point guards and armed response vehicles. These are South Africa's royal game, its most protected of species, and crime, almost always an intrusion from another world, is combated on the basis of the simplest and most ancient of crime prevention philosophies: keep the buggers out.

And the police, for once matching their actions to those implied by the metaphor of the thin blue line, play their part in this, approaching their work in a manner quite different from the methods they use elsewhere. If you were as ungenerous and bitter about the work of the constabulary as was that old Burmese flatfoot, George Orwell, you might conclude as he did that the cops were nothing but 'the bodyguards of the possessing classes'.

★

'Policing here is totally different from the locations,' Morena's boss, Captain Dietsiso told me before she was abruptly redeployed a few days later so that the station's management team, until then exclusively black, could be made more representative through the insertion of a white male. We were in her neatly appointed office, across the hall from her boss's much more lavish suite. That had been sponsored by a luxury hotel, which had used it to field-test the furniture they were putting in their best rooms. Dietsiso had to make do with standard-issue police furniture. 'There is much less violence here compared to Alexandra or Soweto,' she continued. 'Also, most of the crime is committed by outsiders, strangers who come here looking for targets. It is our job to make that difficult.'

Because crime is committed by strangers, target-hardened Rosebank has an extensive system of street-level surveillance and armed response. Most of it is privately run, paid for by residents and local businesses. But the police work with them, meeting every week to discuss crime patterns and *modi operandi*, and to pass on what information they have about the cars driven by suspects. Private security companies, community struc-tures and the police service: all of them advise people on how to look after their property, all of them are on the lookout for suspicious people, and all of them are ready to chase suspects when crimes are committed. Even the chair of the community-police forum, an engineer, was in on the act: he wanted to design a gate that would automatically slam shut behind a homeowner's car, but said that the requisite safety features (you wouldn't want it to slam shut on granny's foot, for instance), and the shock-absorbers needed to make the system viable, might both prove to be beyond his design skills.

'We even have a forum for domestic workers,' Captain Dietsiso told me.

'How does that help?' I asked.

'Those women know everybody's business. They know which cars belong to whose boyfriends. They call us when they see strangers.'

But, she told me, her members don't just sit around waiting to be called by security guards or domestic workers, adding that it was their job to be on the lookout for suspicious strangers.

'What do they look for?' I asked. 'What makes people look suspicious?'

'It's an instinct they get,' she shrugged. 'They drive around all day. If they see the same man too many times they will search him. Or maybe the same car in more than one place, then they will stop that one. Or maybe if a car has tinted windows. It depends. Sometimes we have information about a specific car, but usually it's all about the officers staying alert and looking for something.'

★

The garrulous Constable Morena and his teenage-slim partner, Con-stable Twala, were two of the station's more active friskers and rousters. The first search of the morning had been of two middle-aged African men who looked to be heading to work at a construction site. They were in layers of thick working clothes, and their skin was leathery from working outdoors. The cops pulled up next to them and politely asked them to turn around as they patted them down. Then they looked through the plastic bags they carried.

Stop-and-search tactics of this kind have two goals. The first is to find people who are actively engaged in planning a crime or who have just committed one. Picture a man with sprinkles of powdered glass on his sleeves, a crowbar on the passenger seat and a television set in the boot, and you have an idea of what the ideal post-crime target would look like. Search him before he breaks into the house, and what you're looking for are weapons and housebreaking tools. The second goal of these activities is more subtle. It is the policing equivalent of a turf gang's graffiti. It announces their presence and says, in effect, 'This is my house. I'm in charge here.' Convey this message well, and criminals will think twice about coming to the area; convey it poorly, and the law's writ will run only when they are physically present.

In theory, South African law doesn't really allow police officers to conduct these warrantless searches. There are, however, so many exceptions to that general principle, and judicial protection of the right not to be searched is so flimsy, that in practice there is little to prevent an officer from rousting pretty much anyone he comes across. All he need do to justify his actions in court is declare that prior to the search the target did something that aroused the officer's suspicions, or assert that the suspect consented to having a man paw through his pockets and pat him down. Unless, of course, the suspect was in a car, in which case all the I-know-my-rights bets are off: South African law allows a police officer to search pretty much any car he cares to.

The unacknowledged truth about this kind of activity, however, is that it takes an awful lot of searches before anything of any value turns up.

'How often do you find something suspicious?' I asked Morena and Twala as we drove away from the construction workers.

'Sometimes,' Twala said. 'Last week a Maxi Taxi was stopped with stolen televisions.'

I knew the story, and I also knew that the car hadn't been stopped by these cops but by reservists working in the area. 'When was the last time you personally found something?'

'It was a while ago,' he admitted. 'It doesn't happen so much.'

★

116

A couple of hours after lunch – a pizza, supplied free of charge by a civic-minded restaurant owner – things suddenly looked up for the advocates of the aggressive, boots-and-all policing which promotes the active frisking of as many suspicious-looking people as possible, all in the hope of finding guns and other contraband and deterring the criminally-minded.

We were near the War Museum, on the south-eastern flank of the station precinct, and a garishly painted older-model Ford was parked on the pavement. The car's windows were tinted to the point of opacity, but the driver's was open and two men could be seen lounging in the front seats, their backrests pushed back almost to the horizontal. The driver's hand hung out of the car, a cigarette dangling from languid fingers connected to a forearm that was heavily, but inexpertly, tattooed. It was the arm of a jailbird.

In that exclusive suburban street, with mansions on one side and parkland on the other, the pair looked as out of place as a rhino in a Rembrandt.

Morena and Twala opened their doors. Neither drew his weapon, but they approached the car warily, eyes never leaving those of the men they were nearing. They moved around the car as much as they did towards it, trying all the while to stay out of the occupants' fields of fire. Morena, the lead actor in this micro-drama, approached the driver's side, while Twala circled behind the vehicle, offering his partner cover and subtly encouraging the two men in the car to focus all their attention on the bigger cop.

'Open the doors, gents,' Morena instructed the men. He didn't use any of the TV-cop lines – 'Keep your hands where I can see them' or 'Don't make any sudden moves' – because to do so would make the men feel more distrusted and disliked than was necessary. He wanted to make this as friendly as possible, to deny the men any reason to take offence, any excuse for aggression. But the men seemed to know the drill, and, giving each other an irritated glance, they levered themselves into a more upright position and opened the doors.

As the driver's door opened, a third man, cramped on the back seat, appeared.

Morena's big shoulders tensed visibly: he hadn't seen the man in the

117

gloom of the car's interior and knew that both he and Twala could now be dead if the man had been of a violent cast of mind. 'Jesus,' he breathed when he saw that the passenger was peaceable. 'Why the hell are you hiding there from us?' Later he would tell me that he sometimes had nightmares about doing this sort of thing at night. 'In the dark, you can't see who's in the car or even how many are there. It's very frightening.'

The three men, a dubious-looking bunch in jeans and dark glasses, climbed out of the car. Morena watched them while his partner patted them down. Satisfied that none was armed, the two cops turned to the car.

'What's the problem, Sarge?' the driver asked. 'Do we look too poor to be in the *rykmansbuurt*?'

I suspected that if the cops were not themselves black, he might have framed the question differently, emphasising race rather than income. As it was, however, we all knew what he meant. And, knowing that we would know what he had meant, he had made his tone and body language teasing to convey a subtle subtext: he knew he was in the right, and he wanted the cops to know that, but he also wanted to leave them the space to act as if his words had been spoken in jest. Just in case he had caused some offence, the sting of which he now sought to draw, he turned to reassure me that he knew we were just doing our jobs. I nodded in irrelevant appreciation of the gesture.

The search of the car turned up a large, rubber-banded pile of cash and a pile of empty bankies, the plastic bank bags used by drug dealers to package their product. Each on its own would have been mildly suspicious. Together they seemed pretty damning. It was, in other words, very likely these men were up to no good. But precisely what they were up to couldn't be known. Nor was the possession of either wads of cash or empty plastic bags an offence, so Morena and Twala just looked at the men dubiously.

'What are you doing here?' Morena asked, rubbing the slippery sheen of the plastic between two meaty fingers.

'Nothing, Sarge,' the driver replied with an exaggerated nonchalance. 'Just having a rest and a smoke. Enjoying the sunshine.' Camping it up, he looked upwards and added, 'It's a beautiful day.'

'Bullshit,' Morena grunted, tossing the bankies onto the passenger's seat. 'I don't want to see you guys here. You've no business in this street, so get away from here.'

'But what have we done?' the man who'd been in the passenger seat asked. 'All we're doing is breathing the air here. We can do that, can't we? Isn't it a free country?'

The driver moved to calm his friend. 'It's OK,' he said, repeating his earlier peace offering. 'They're just doing their jobs.'

'It's not "OK",' his friend said and turned to Morena, anger tightening his features. 'We've got rights too, you know.'

'Forget about him, Sarge,' the first man said. 'We're going.'

Morena was unmoved by the inverted good-cop-bad-cop routine. 'You don't belong here and we've told you to go, so go,' he instructed. 'Don't force us to arrest you.'

'And you,' he pointed at the third man as he climbed into the darkness in the rear of the vehicle. 'Don't hide when a policeman comes up to the car. One day someone will make a mistake and you'll get shot.'

★

For generations, the primary objective of state institutions in South Africa was the protection of a white minority from the seditious goals of the never-enfranchised. Each agency had its role: the schools taught that there was a racial pecking order; constitutional engineers designed ever more elaborate ways to preserve white power under the skirts of 'self-government'; and the police went after 'agitators' who refused to accept the premises of either the schools or the constitution-makers. In amongst all this activity, town planners tried to design cities that would meet both the ideological and security needs of apartheid. Ironically, the design concept they adopted was originally inspired by the blueprint for the English Garden City, which envisaged future urban landscapes composed of interconnected hubs separated by wide stretches of green. Workers living in peripheral nodes would commute to and from the centre on broad, fast-moving highways, while their children went to school near their homes. In the afternoons, they would play and laugh in the village-like commons surrounding their dormitory towns.

Naturally, when apartheid's urban planners got hold of the Garden City idea, the pretty little dormitory towns were conceived as racially separate and homogenous. And, given the nature of the society in which they were to be built, the interconnecting highways were designed primarily to minimise the routes any hypothetical army of the oppressed might use in an attack on the lily-white heart of the metropolis. Everything, in fact, was to be designed to specifications of exclusion and defensibility; even the green spaces separating a city's nodes became 'fields of fire' and 'machine gun zones'.

This philosophy was matched term for term by the approach taken by the cops. Empowered by the pass laws, they worked to keep the residents of the whites-only suburbs safe through the blunt expedient of keeping black people out. 'In the old days,' a senior officer once told me, 'if we saw suspicious people hanging around in a park watching the houses, we moved them. We even took fingerprints and photos to scare them. You can't do that now. Everyone has the right to sit in the park.'

He was an old-fashioned cop and he seemed to regard this park-sitting business as a bad thing.

'It's true,' another told me when I asked him about this. 'When I was a young policeman and we had vagrants in the area, we'd stick them in the back of a van and dump them in Pretoria.'

This second officer was a more morally complex man, and wasn't quite so sure that this was an unequivocally good thing.

Nor are these sorts of practices entirely dead. I saw something similar in an exclusive suburb falling in the precinct of the Wynberg police station in Cape Town after a resident called the police emergency number to say she was worried about three African men who'd been in the area for most of the day. When the call came through to the patrol van, the officer at radio control made no suggestion that the men were suspected of any particular crime. He told the officers only that the caller had been concerned about their presence. If there was any basis for her suspicions other than their race, it was not apparent.

The crew I was with acknowledged the call, but thought that there was little prospect of finding the right people: the area they'd been given in which to look was large, and the only description they'd been given by radio control was that one of the three men had a gold tooth. In Cape Town, that is not a unique biometric.

As it turned out, another unit from a neighbouring station was a few minutes ahead of us and the two cops from that van, themselves both African men, had just picked up three 'suspects'. The arrestees were in their late teens, and there was something pathetic in the contrast between their slight frames and the armoured bodies of the arresting officers. I didn't see them for long, though, because the cops were in the process of locking them into the back of the van. The boys had apparently claimed to have been visiting a woman in the area, the girlfriend of one of them. But the officers were sceptical about this because the caller had said that the men had been in the area for hours: 'What business do they have here for half the day?' one of the arresting officers asked the driver of my van. 'They're just looking for trouble.'

That, however, could not account for their arrest. What the two senior officers had told me was true: in the new South Africa people do have the right to be wherever they choose. Why, then, were the three being arrested, I wondered and was about to ask, when one of the arresting officers sidled over to the vehicle I was in. 'They told us they've never been to Ratanga Junction,' he offered, unsolicited, naming a popular Cape Town theme park. 'We're going to show them the roller coaster.'

He left us and got into his van and sped off, intent, apparently, on hitting every one of the speed bumps on the road as hard as he could. Locked up in the van's low-roofed compartment, the three arrestees must have been bouncing hard against the steel ceiling and the sharp edges of the van's metal benches.

★

Morena and Twala were parked in front of one of the crassest houses I'd ever seen. The building was only half-finished, but it had more filigrees and curlicues per square metre than a medieval bible. It looked like Louis XIV had met Puff Daddy in a singles bar and they'd decided to make a home together.

Morena wondered aloud what such a place must cost. 'It must be a billion rand,' he said. Ostentatious as the house was, I thought that an over-estimate and said so. 'OK,' he conceded. 'Half a billion, then.'

As the pair wondered about the layout inside − 'It must have a lift to the second floor and gold toilets,' Twala suggested − I thought about how they felt about the people they were employed to serve and protect. Here, after all, were two cops charged with protecting one group of people, with whom they had almost nothing in common, from criminals who came from another group, one with which they probably shared a great deal of life experience. I wondered how that felt.

If you ask police officers this sort of loaded question, they will instinctively duck it, reverting to the organisational bromides of working for everyone equally, whatever their race or riches. So, instead of asking what they thought about working in Rosebank, I asked them whether there were people who irritated them in the community. At this, Sergeant Twala laughed a nervous laugh which, together with his baby eyes, put me in mind of a guilty child caught in the act. 'Of course there are people that irritate us,' he said.

'Like who? What do they do?' I asked.

'You get funny things here. It doesn't matter what the police are doing, there are some people who will complain. They are very arrogant. They think they are special. That is irritating. Then they want to tell us how to work. They say that we must drive around with our sirens on so that they can see us and so that the *tsotsis* know that we are here. Have you ever driven with a siren? It can make you mad. But that is what they want.' He clicked his tongue in irritation.

Morena was listening to this. 'You know what really irritates us?' he said. 'When people tell us that they pay our salaries. We really hate hearing that.'

'Do you get it a lot?'

'A lot,' he said with not a little bitterness. He seemed a decent man, calm and assured, confident of his skills. I thought that his being reminded who paid his salary would feel like a calculated insult, one that was designed to reduce him to the status of a menial. It was hard to believe that that would improve his performance. It was also a very stupid thing to say, being true anywhere from the post office to the High Court, from a bank to a brothel. 'We don't work for them. We work for everyone. Poor people and rich, black and white,' Morena said. 'Just because they have money and they help the police station doesn't mean that they can order us around. We are not here only for them.'

This was, of course, the right thing to say. But everything I saw around the country suggested it wasn't true. In Maluti there were almost no cops, and in urban townships, where violence was far more common than in the suburbs, there were too few. In the suburbs, on the other hand, cops had a much quieter time of it. So, however equitably officers like Morena and Twala treated people they met, the organisation as a whole appeared to treat different people differently. There was, after all, something to Orwell's aphorism about the police and the possessing classes. There was also, of course, more to it than that, but everywhere in the world police resources are prioritised in part by the status of the people they serve. Now, in post-apartheid South Africa, social status is not as tightly correlated with race as it once was. It is, however, an historical fact that, since colonial days, South African policing has sought to protect white from black. The question was how much this ethos still penetrated policing in our wealthiest suburbs.

★

It would take an improbable degree of recklessness for a South African police officer to admit that race matters in policing, to admit, in other words, that race plays a role when making decisions about which people to stop and frisk. In more-or-less racially exclusive townships like Thokoza or Elsies River or Ivory Park, race is not a factor in jump-out target-selection. But, after my time in Sea Point and Wynberg and Rosebank, I could only conclude that where races mixed, cops kept their eyes peeled for young black men.

How do I know?

In the days I spent in Rosebank, every one spent exclusively with black officers, the only time a white driver was stopped was soon after I asked why they seemed to search only black men. The white driver they stopped, young and offended at the inconvenience, was pulled over to prove me wrong.

It is entirely legitimate to object to this, and many, many people do. It offends against our sense of justice when people are subjected to the loss of privacy and the assault on their dignity that accompanies a police search solely because they are black. But that objection, cast so strongly, is silly. Not even the most vilely racist cop – and the guys I was with obviously weren't that – stops people *solely* because they are black.

Apart from anything else, he simply wouldn't have the time.

In fact, race was never the sole reason for any search I witnessed: even the white driver, pulled over only to make a point to me, had failed to stop at a stop-sign – he claimed to have been hijacked there three months before, but no-one believed him – and had, in this way, attracted the attention of the officers as an obvious law-breaker. So, even where cops were engaged in racial profiling, race was only ever a single factor in a mix of others. These ranged from the target's age and outfit, to his behaviour and mode of transport, from the location of the encounter to the time of day. Race, to repeat, was never the only reason someone was stopped.

The single exception to this rule, the only time the race of the targets was the sole and explicit reason for a stop-and-search, was when some officers from the Yeoville police station pulled over a car containing five scruffy occupants, three Coloured men and two white women. Nothing about them suggested they were members of a pair of mixed couples on a chaperoned double date in the middle of the afternoon. And, after an unsuccessful search of bags and boots and cubby-holes, I asked the officers why this car and these people had been pulled over. 'They look like a cheque-fraud syndicate,' one replied. 'They send the whites into the banks to cash the cheques because banks don't cash cheques for Coloureds.'

The police were suspicious of the white women because banks are suspicious of Coloured men. Racial profiling had doubled in on itself: banks profile Coloured men as risks, the men respond by recruiting white women, and then the cops profile white women with Coloured men. The potential variations on the theme seemed endless.

Nevertheless, even if the subject's race is only one factor among many others, the fact that it is one at all was not something that police officers would readily admit. They probably suspect that South Africans, in their typically unreflectively omniscient way, are not ready to acknowledge that in the policing of the affluent suburbs of our cities, race is, as a matter of empirical fact, one of the indicators of who is and who is not likely to be up to no good. And if South Africans aren't amenable to police officers' saying this sort of thing, the cops I was with were in no great hurry to make their views known either. They preferred to hunker down and to keep this awkward fact close to their chests. It was a reticence which, in hypersensitive South Africa, was probably justified, for it would be all too easy to jump all over the cops and declare them irredeemable racists if they spoke their minds on this subject. The family resemblance between what they were doing now and what they had done in the past was just too strong.

The question that arises, then, is whether a patrolman should use race as a factor in his assessment of the amount of risk any particular individual poses to people of his beat. Frame it this way, and the answer seems a resounding no. But what if the same question was asked another way? If you know as a matter of empirical fact that the vast bulk of street crime in a given area is committed by black men in their early twenties – not all street crime: one of the detectives I worked with in Rosebank arrested a white junkie who stole a cellphone from a domestic worker after asking to borrow it to call a friend – isn't it a waste of time and effort and resources to search old women and white teenagers? Now the answer to the earlier question seems less clear.

A white, middle-class writer, who is unlikely ever to suffer the indignity of being profiled, ought to approach this issue only with the greatest humility. Nevertheless, on the strictest criteria of efficiency, the conclusion that a bit of profiling makes policing more effective is inescapable. The trouble is that there is no room for compromise here: either race is a factor or it is not. There is no middle ground, no third way. And it is more than a little awkward, therefore, to note that there might actually be benefits to profiling.

Fortunately for the white, middle-class writer, who seeks to be honest about this issue, there is a bolt-hole into which to creep, one that comes in the form of another factor to consider. This is that, trivial as the violation of the right to privacy involved in a stop-and-search may seem to those who do not have to endure it, its practice, if directed exclusively at black men, undermines the difficult business of building respect for the law. Whatever the short-term crime prevention gains accruing when police officers accost black South Africans on the streets, in doing so they are plunging into a deep reservoir of historical anger. I think this is true even when the officers involved are black and the racial dimension is neutralised a little because the cops are seen to be repeating policing strategies of the past, the strategies of exclusion and denial and humiliation which, under apartheid, the police used to segregate and separate all white people from all black people. These strategies may have insulated white people from most black criminals, but they did so by treating all black people as criminals simply because they were black. The memories of this run deep, and ignoring them is not a sensible long-term strategy for building the legitimacy needed to do the dirty work of democracy.

But there was another way of thinking about the problem of racial profiling in South Africa's suburbs, one which casts it as a particular example of a more general problem. This is that the law, when enforced, seldom lives up to the ideals of the statutes and textbooks in which it is described.

There is in our conception of the law a sense that it is something majestic, a conviction that its vast, intricate structure somehow reflects the best of our culture, and that its enforcement can do nothing but enhance civilisation. This, after all, is why we are enjoined to respect it. But up close, street-level policing, whether it takes place in Rosebank or in Thokoza, gives the lie to this most contented of self-deceptions, and, in the act of its enforcement, the law reveals a different aspect of its nature and creates a different feeling about its character. The reason is simple: on the street, the law is neither abstract nor ideal. It is, instead, a set of institutions, a machine made of fallible men and women working insoluble problems. Inevitably, and with the best will in the world, the ideals of justice embedded in ideals of the law are eroded when they grind against the immutable realities of an unwelcoming world. This is particularly the case when the law contains within it so many potentially incompatible ideals: how can the police be both efficient in the identification of suspects and pristinely non-racial at the same time?

No doubt there are an infinite variety of ways in which the practice of law enforcement might fall short of its ideal, but in Rosebank the character of the failure of the law differed from those I encountered elsewhere. The result was that I left its streets sensing that there was more to Orwell's neologism about the police and the possessing classes than I cared to admit. There, street-level law enforcement had been stripped of some of its pretensions and had become no more refined than a scheme cooked up by polite society to secure its own protection. There was something oddly shaming about this because it was so far from law's majestic, civilisation-enhancing mythology. Instead it seemed to have been designed on the basis of nothing more admirable than fear. That doesn't mean that the policework I witnessed could not be justified on the grounds of principle or of efficiency. Nor does it mean that fear is an illegitimate basis for the design of social institutions. Nevertheless, it felt strangely humiliating to recognise that, however high-minded its principles, the law, which I felt so strongly must be respected, was coarsened and cheapened by the reality of its own enforcement.

Troubling as it is to say so, it isn't obvious that much can be done about this.

CHAPTER EIGHT

ON BEING ROUGH AND TOUGH AND TAKING NO SHIT: INSPECTOR RONNIE GOVENDER, JOHANNESBURG

When I met him, Inspector Ronnie Govender was about to be trans-ferred. A detective with fifteen years' experience in Johannesburg's decaying inner city, the townships in the east of the city and the gang-lands of Westbury, he was being moved across town to a station in the suburbs. The move was part of the Service's efforts to balance racial representation in all police stations, but, what with having to drop his wife off at work in the morning, it would add more than an hour to his daily commute. He was not best pleased. 'And do you think this fucking place will pay my fucking petrol bills?' he asked rhetorically. 'Fuck no.'

Govender wasn't sure when he'd have to start his new job, but his doom was approaching rapidly, and in response he'd initiated a one-man programme of mass action that was part passive resistance and part indus-trial sabotage. 'I'm fucked if I'm going to take on any more cases,' he told me. 'If I do, I'll have to take the new dockets with me and then try to get my new commander to give me the time to investigate them. Then I'll have to come all the way back here to do the follow-up work. Fuck that. I'll rather just stay in the office all day picking my nose.'

You could say that the prospective redeployment was involuntary.

His cause was just, his methods were peaceful, and the happy result was that he had plenty of time to take me on long tours around the city and to talk about the gentle art of policing some of the most violent streets in the world.

'The politicians and senior management want the world to think that we can be gentle when we are on duty, that we can do our work like night nurses,' Govender sneered to me one morning in Hillbrow.

128

'That's bullshit. You can't be a night nurse when you go to arrest some-one in Westbury or Hillbrow. If they think you are weak, that is when they will come after you. The only way is for them to fear us. It's as sim-ple as that: if they don't fear us, then they shoot, if they fear us, they don't.'

He was responding to a story I had told him about a night I'd spent with the SA Narcotics Bureau in the same streets in 1998. It was the only time I ever saw a policeman shoot a suspect. The man had sold crack to one of the unit's informers in a buy-bust operation, and he had run when the cops stormed round the corner. In 1998, before the changes were made to the law, that was a particularly stupid thing to do and in response, the officers had shot him in the leg.

'Those SANAB guys used to work hard,' Govender continued. 'They made a lot of enemies. If the Nigies or the gangsters thought they were soft, they'd be dead. Straight.'

★

Bittner's understanding of policing is that it is a vehicle through which a society organises the way force is deployed to resolve the unpleasant situations that are the inevitable result of a multitude of anonymous strangers, each with his or her own interests and passions, living in a common social space. In the absence of policing, those situations would still arise, of course, but parties to those disputes would soon resort to private acts of violence to try to get their own way. Naturally, civilisa-tion would regard the use of violence to resolve these situations as illegitimate. That, unfortunately, is no guarantee that it would not be done. Indeed, as no less an authority than Sigmund Freud once put it, 'it is a general principle that conflicts of interest between men are settled by the use of violence.' This, he continued, is true of the whole animal kingdom, from which men have no business to exclude themselves.

The trouble is that this could quickly get very messy with everyone with interests to defend spending large portions of their days engaging in acts of preemptive, defensive and vengeful violence. It is far more efficient and sensible, then, to centralise and regularise the legitimate use of force in a body of specially trained men and women, and declare all other violence, except that done in genuine self-defence, as illegal.

But this raises another difficulty. How can we know that those to whom this dangerous authority is entrusted will use it well? How can we be sure that they will use force vigorously when it is needed and with restraint when it is not? I saw plenty of cases in which police officers used physical force. In some of these cases, the force used seemed gratuitous. The cops who used their tonfas when people spoke back to them; the officers who kicked prone, helpless drunks when they'd passed out in charge offices and had urinated on the floor; the rough handling of suspects and non-suspects at countless police-civilian interactions: all seemed unnecessary at the time and in the circumstances in which they occurred. I had come to think of police violence, like that of criminals, as being partly instrumental (it helps achieve goals) and partly expressive (it's an act of self-expression and assertion that helps define who you are). A good deal of the violence I witnessed seemed to fall in the latter category, and I wanted to find an officer who would explain and defend it. In post-apartheid South Africa, even after Minister Steve Tshwete had made the use of force politically saleable, that was no easy task.

Eventually, however, Ronnie Govender fell into my lap. This was a man who lived by Caligula's dictum, *oderint dum metuant* – they can hate, so long as they fear. The explicitness of his embrace of this idea made him far from representative of the Service. Nevertheless, his views were suggestive of attitudes that more than a few members share.

★

Govender was a foul-mouthed, ill-humoured man who had grown up in a small town in the Natal midlands and had joined the police late in life. He was stout, having probably once been quite muscular, and wore gold-rimmed glasses on a face that sported a neatly clipped beard. Physically, it wasn't hard to imagine him as the teacher he'd been before he enlisted. 'Teacher, policeman or prison guard. That's what all our parents wanted us to be when we were growing up. We could be anything we wanted, so long as it was teacher, policeman or prison guard.'

'And you? What did you want to be?' I asked.

Govender laughed. 'You won't believe me.'

'Try me,' I said.

'When I was young, I didn't want to work at all,' he said. 'I wanted to fight the government. I was the chair of the local youth committee and of the student congress. A proper little comrade. The cops used to hate me. They'd chase me whenever they saw me. And, if they caught me, they'd give me a damn good hiding.'

How had this communist and self-confessed *daggaroker* – 'it was mob psychology' – become a member of a police force dedicated to protecting the apartheid state?

'I was asked to join by people I knew who went into exile. They phoned from Botswana and told me to join the *boere*. They said they needed someone on the inside so that they could know the plans of the enemy. Someone who could help them come into the country.' He shrugged: 'Someone to help them.'

I wasn't sure about the veracity of the story – I'd heard versions of it two or three times from other men, and its romance was wearing thin – but if Govender had been politically active in his youth, it hadn't left him yearning to be a pacifist: he told me that he and a former partner he'd worked with in the 1990s had been the 'baddest boys' in the police. 'We were rough and tough, my brother. And we took absolutely no shit.'

'How many people have you shot?' I asked him when I knew him a little better.

'Many,' he replied.

'Ten? Twenty? A hundred? What?'

'Not a hundred,' he conceded (grudgingly? I wasn't sure). 'But definitely more than twenty.' He wouldn't be more precise than that, and I wasn't sure that he knew for certain.

'And you?' I asked Govender a little later. 'Have you ever been shot?'

'Not shot,' he said. 'Shot *at*. Maybe six or seven times.' He said it matter-of-factly, as another man might sound as he talked about the number of parking fines he'd received.

'Were you afraid?'

'Not afraid really. My adrenaline was pumping too much. But the way I see it, it's part of the job. I'm not a friend to criminals. I'm their obstacle. I want them to see me as their obstacle. So when they shoot at me, it's almost like a compliment.'

★

Think for a moment about what it means when a select group of individuals, men and women like any others, are granted the authority to use coercive violence to solve other people's problems. They are given awesome responsibilities and, to fulfil them, they are granted the legal powers needed to invade the privacy of people's homes, to deprive individuals of their liberty and, where necessary, to shoot suspects. Set apart from the rest of their society by their powers and responsibilities, there are also physical indicia of their distinction from their fellows – uniforms and badges, vehicles and handcuffs. And, if that were not enough, the sense of separation is heightened by the reality of their working days: the odd hours, the risks of physical danger, the continual descent into the sewers of human life.

It is little wonder, therefore, that cops often see themselves as men apart, as standing outside and above the society they police. They look down on laypeople with a mixture of paternalism and suspicion, all the while trying to ensure the safety of a citizenry whose motives and intelligence they doubt. It is an image made manifest by the police officers' habit of referring to the rest of us as *hase*. As rabbits, we are cast as silly, scurrying creatures who are also weak and defenceless, prone to being immobilised with fright in the lights of on-coming traffic. It is an image that contrasts the power of the cop and the helplessness of the civilian, the strength of one and the dependence of the other. And it blends with another image, that of the cop who is a steadfast defender of the weak, a guardian of the vulnerable, a steely centurion whose moral resolve is backed by a credible physical threat. A cop's cop, then, is a hard man living in a hard world, an authority figure, detached, remote and, if one can give the word its original meaning, terrible. He is asked by his community to stare down the grim realities of the streets on behalf of those unable and unwilling to do so themselves. His detachment and hardness are the requisites of the job, and they must be honed, even at some cost to himself, because without them he cannot function. Without them, he may as well go home to his slippers and his tea.

This image reflects an ideal built into the self-image constructed by the world's police services and pursued by many of their members. It isn't a representation of reality, but it does have real consequences in the attitudes and actions of police officers who must live up to its demands. This isn't seen as altogether a burden, however, because cops know that having the aura of authority conjured up by this ideal makes policework much, much easier: officers who possess it are listened to, their requests are complied with, their instructions are obeyed. They get the respect and deference their office ought to command. Acquiring this aura can be difficult when the service is reputed to be corrupt and incompetent, but that is a matter for another place. For the moment, suffice it to say that establishing respect and deference helps cops get things done.

There is a nuance here that must be recognised: although the intention is to command respect, policing is not academia or medicine or gardening, and, unlike those vocations, the nature of the respect required by cops bears a striking resemblance to fear. Being feared is not, of course, the same thing as being respected. There are, nonetheless, links between them, a family resemblance, and, particularly in the places in which society's dirty work gets done, there is often no daylight between an officer's commanding respect and his just plain being feared.

That there are places in the world where a cop who is not feared is all but inviting a bullet in the chest is something that men like Govender believe in their bones. And it may well be true. But this is a troubling truth because, if cops are to be feared, they must actually do things that make them fearsome. Their roughness, their toughness, their disinclination to take shit: these things cannot merely be proclaimed. For the image to be credible, the attitude must be demonstrated. Sometimes repeatedly. Cops must, in other words, actually be the hard-arsed enforcers they proclaim themselves to be, because to create the impression that one is a ball-breaker, one actually has to behave that way.

This, perhaps, explains a well-known finding of research into incidents of police brutality. In many of these, the treatment meted out by the officers was rationalised by them as a response to some sign of the recipient's lack of respect for the cop who beats him. There is even a name for this crime: contempt of cop. The perceived disrespect could manifest itself in anything. Perhaps the recipient was unwilling to make the gestures of face and eyes that imply submission. Perhaps he answered back with a bit of thoughtless lip. Perhaps he failed to beat a polite retreat when instructed. Worst of all, perhaps he ran from an officer who wanted to search his pockets. None of these things necessitate a police beating, of course. But, in the wrong circumstances, any of them might result in one.

And the phenomenon is universal. Consider the advice an official in the Canadian ministry responsible for overseeing the Mounties once told me that he gives to his own children: 'Know your rights,' he tells them. 'But don't insist on them if you're alone.'

★

'The first time I shot someone was in the time of the struggle,' Govender told me. He was dressed in jeans and running shoes, and a wintry sun was glinting off his spectacles. In their reflection, I could see the forecourt of the busy service station, the restaurant of which had provided us with two nasty coffees and a pair of rubbery burgers. The day was bright and warm, and we had just finished a tour of Westbury, a hideous ghetto where buildings had been erected from spit and cement. Crumbling, graffiti-ed houses backed up against two- and three-storied blocks of flats made of the coldest, barest concrete imaginable. The spaces between them were filled with car wrecks and drug dealers. Cracked and stained, the buildings looked like prematurely ancient ruins and seemed ready to crumble under the weight of a passing gaze. Govender had brought me here to show me the street drug trade he'd policed about a decade earlier, and, while he was at it, to renew old acquaintances: 'Look how fat you are now,' he'd shout at men he recognised. 'Still dealing your shit?' Most took this with good humour, and there were only a few references to Govender's mother and her apparently wild ways.

'I was in the security cops in Cape Town,' Govender said of that

134

shooting. 'We were in the townships, working our subjects.' He smiled an oily grin: 'People who are in parliament now.

'It was late at night, and we had information that they were in one of the shebeens. We went in hard. You couldn't go into those shebeens soft. Not in those days. But the guys we were looking for weren't there. While we were inside, the comrades fetched some petrol bombs. When we came out, they had set my car on fire.

'I was so pissed off. So fucking angry! You won't believe that this gentle man you can see today could be so angry. We just let loose. Shooting, shooting, shooting. Bam! Bam! Bam! Then, afterwards, they told us that four people were shot.'

'What happened? Were you charged?'

'When you shoot someone, they must investigate. They have to do it. But I wasn't worried because the law was on our side.'

Govender was right. In the eighties, cops could shoot just about anyone they suspected of involvement in any but the most trivial of offences, whether political or criminal. They weren't allowed to open up on anyone, of course, not even on rioters, and they were morally and legally obliged to use the minimum force necessary to effect an arrest. But if anyone from a suspected serial killer to the proverbial apple thief gave them any trouble, resisted arrest or fled, the officer would have been well within his rights if he'd let them have both barrels. There was no requirement of proportionality, no requirement that the cop or anyone else be in any danger, and no requirement that he believe that, if left unarrested, the suspect would be a danger to anyone at some later date. The effect was that the four men outside the shebeen – rioting during the state of emergency, destroying state property and posing a direct threat to police officers' lives – would have been members of about the least protected species on the planet.

The inquest court found that there was no need to prosecute.

'And the last time you killed someone? What happened then?' I asked.

Govender looked at me, his face darker than before. 'It was in 2000 or so,' he said. 'I was living in Hillbrow and I used to shop at the Checkers there. One afternoon, after I finished my shopping, I caught someone stealing my car radio. I came out of the shops and he was sitting there, in my car. If you didn't know, you would think it was his car.'

'What did you do?'

'I watched the little fucker until he was finished. Then, when he got out of the car, I shot him.' His voice was cold but he seemed to be affecting an indifference that I wasn't sure he felt. His eyes didn't meet mine. He was quiet for a moment and the hamburger he was eating seemed to hang from fingers that had gone limp in the act of remembering. It prompted an obvious question: 'Is it hard to shoot someone? Do you regret it?'

Govender smiled another oily smile: 'I know what you want me to say. You want me to tell you that I am sorry for what I did. But I'm not. You can't regret shooting criminals. They are the criminals. Not you. If you shoot them, you are just doing your job.'

This response suggested something that had never occurred to me before: that in handing over the right to use force to a group of men and women who would, thereafter, be designated society's guardians, we also demand of them that they renounce the natural human instinct to self-doubt. How can you trust yourself to use force if you have doubts about your judgment? How can you make yourself willing to shoot someone if you allow yourself to see the world from his point of view? To be a cop, it suddenly occurred to me, you must embrace a degree of certainty about your actions or be forever paralysed. This was not a profession that admitted members with an ironic sense of themselves; you had to take yourself seriously pretty much all of the time.

I pointed at the café on the other side of the road. 'So, if a kid ran in there now and stole a packet of sweets, would you shoot him?'

'No. Not for sweets. Maybe he's stealing because he is hungry. You can't shoot someone for that.'

'And if he broke into a car and stole a radio?' I pointed at a fancy 4x4. 'Would you shoot him if he broke into that vehicle?'

'Then I will shoot him. I will try to make an arrest, but if I can't, I will shoot him.' One cop's interpretation of the doctrine of proportionality: the sweets-thief lives, the radio-thief dies.

'And you'd have no regrets?' I asked.

He was emphatic: 'No regrets.'

★

136

After I paid for lunch, Govender and I got into my car – because Govender was refusing to take more cases, he had been refused access to an official vehicle: he drove so that my hands would be free to take notes and so our conversation would not be interrupted by his giving me directions. He took me through the streets of Hillbrow, Berea and Yeoville because he wanted to show me the world as he understood it, to show me how the breakdown of authority had advanced so far that it was now written into the grimy facades of the buildings and the hardened faces of the thousands of people who worked those streets for every cent they could get. 'They'll kill you for the shoes you're wearing,' he muttered when we got there, slipping his firearm from his waistband and sliding it comfortably under a fleshy thigh.

On the way, I told Govender that I wasn't sure if I believed him about his having no regrets. Then I told him about Hannes, an ex-policeman I'd met earlier in the year.

Hannes had been in the police force in the late 1960s and early 1970s. He'd been studying to become a psychologist – in those days, as a result of the organisation's qualifications-intensive promotions policy, policemen received generous financial support for their studies – and had recently retired from a long career as a shrink to open a guest house in the Lowveld. He was also dying, having fought a long attritional war with cancer. That, combined with his being a psychologist, made him seem more open and reflective about police violence than any other officer I spoke to.

Before he'd left the police, Hannes had been involved in two shooting incidents in which men had died. The second case didn't bother him. It was, to use the stodgy Hollywood-ism he'd offered with a tired, self-deprecating smile, 'a righteous shoot'. But the first, he told me, was different. That had been part of his initiation. A man had died unnecessarily in a grotesque rite of passage, and the memory of it haunted him. 'Me and the senior men chased this guy into an alley. He was trapped against a chain-link fence and there was nowhere for him to go. But the sergeant told me to shoot anyway. He said that they were doing it for me. That was the way things were with them. You weren't regarded as a proper cop until you shot someone. It was their idea about how you blood a policeman.'

Nearly forty years later, Hannes professed to be tormented by this still. He wished he hadn't done it, and said that if he'd been older and emotionally stronger, he would have resisted his colleagues. And he didn't think he was alone. He told me how, sometime in the 1980s, he'd been in a bar in Durban. There were some cops drinking at a table – 'once you've been a cop, you can tell them a mile away' – and he got to chatting with them. 'It turned out that one of them had just been blooded. Like I had been. The other men were cheering him on, welcoming him into the brotherhood. But I just looked at him and said, "I'm sorry for you." He broke into tears.'

Inspector Govender thought about what I told him, but dismissed it: 'I think your friend Hannes wasn't supposed to be a policeman. Criminals are criminals, and if you are a policeman, it's your job to deal with them.'

'But you are also a human being,' I said. 'Can human beings really kill and not feel sorry about it?'

'Cowboys don't cry,' Govender responded with one of the Service's most overworked bromides. 'I told you before: if you are soft, then you will be killed. Hannes was right to leave the police; he would have been killed. And if he wasn't killed, maybe his partner would be. I wouldn't want to work with a man like that. How would I know if he will back me up when the shit starts to fly?'

★

Even by the free-wheeling standards of the law governing the use of deadly force that operated until 2003, the two shootings Govender had told me about were no more than arguably lawful. True, the law of the day allowed the shooting of people caught in the act of malicious damage to property (the burning of the police car) and theft (the car radio). But shooting was only permissible if less violent tactics would not have sufficed to make an arrest. For Govender, however, the legal justification for any shooting was a secondary consideration. Foremost in his mind, at the time of the shootings and when I interviewed him later, was the need to assert his authority and to demonstrate unequivocally that such things cannot be done with impunity to policemen. His view was that criminals deserve such things, and that cops should do unto them what needs to be done. What he had done was less about preventing crime or bringing a suspect to justice than it was about punishing those who had stepped out of line and, at the same time, reaffirming the intimidating authority of the policeman.

'Are you worried about the changes in the law?' I asked Govender, referring to the long-delayed amendments to section 49 of the Criminal Procedure Act. They had been promulgated a few weeks before we spoke but had been in the pipeline for almost five years before that. They were, I thought, universally detested by policemen, because they sought to reduce the authority officers had to use deadly force when trying to make arrests. Many cops had told me that the law would have a chilling effect on policework, that none of them would take any chances, and that, as a result, the bad guys would get the upper hand.

I thought that some of the anxiety cops expressed about the law was misplaced and foolish, because it was often based on a mistaken belief that the law would allow shootings only in self-defence. It is true that the new law was far from clear, perhaps dangerously so, but that it allowed shooting when attempting to make arrests of dangerous criminals was plain enough. But perhaps the officers' anxiety was not completely rational: it may have reflected a wounded sense that the change in law meant a diminution of police officers' authority. In effect, the new law meant that cops' shootings would be judged in relation to a new set of standards, standards that were not all that different from those used to judge shootings by civilians. The law brought the centurions' authority to use their weapons closer to that of the *hase*. And, whenever I had a discussion like this with a policeman, I couldn't help wondering whether the retraction of trust in existing custom and practice that was implied by the new law was driving some of the suspicion and anxiety that he professed.

Govender, however, had a different, more pragmatic, take on the issue.

'People think that the new law says we can't use force. But they are wrong,' he told me. 'You can still shoot if you want to. But you must be clever. The old section 49 never said you had the right to kill, only that you could shoot to make an arrest. You can still do that.'

'But what about the requirement that there must be some danger to someone? That's a big change, isn't it? Doesn't that make it harder to shoot?'

He was categorical: 'No. You're wrong. You can still shoot. So long as you get your statement right.'

I asked him what he meant by 'getting your statement right'.

'If you are going to shoot, then you mustn't be proud. You mustn't say in your statement that so and so did x, y and z and that that made you shoot. Don't say he did something bad and so you killed him. Then it will look like you intended to shoot, it will look like murder. And they don't give you five years for murder! You must just say that you were trying to make an arrest and that he attacked you. If you do that, then no-one will stop you from shooting. If you shoot, don't be too proud to say that you were scared, that you thought the man was going to kill you. If you say that, no-one will prosecute you.'

★

There is much to commend in the self-conception of cops as their society's hard men, the defenders of its weak and vulnerable. No doubt there is a price to pay for living up to this pared-down, truncated image of what it is to be a man – and you will see in a moment that Govender himself half-acknowledged the price he had paid for his hardness – but that such men are necessary in a society is difficult to dispute. I have said already that one of the implications of this is that cops must live their hardness. To be credible, toughness cannot be merely proclaimed, it must be demonstrated, honed and defended. If the hardness of cops is to be believed, it must also be real, and those who are asked to believe it must have some experience of it.

It must be said that not all cops are much good at this. In Barberton, for instance, I saw an obviously drunk truck driver simply refuse to be arrested and the policeman, much smaller than the drunk and radically out-muscled, was unable to do anything but let him go on his merry

140

way. In Sea Point, I saw two cops walk away from a man accused of trying to suffocate his girlfriend who had told them to 'get fucked', and who had refused to answer questions or listen to their instructions. Incidents like that left me feeling embarrassed, as if I'd just seen South African law enforcement in the nude. Nevertheless, they suggested the difficulty of policework if policemen don't command respect.

There is also another story to tell, one best described by Joan Wardop, an Australian criminologist who has worked thousands of hours with the Soweto Flying Squad. There, she argues, excessive toughness is frowned upon and the wild men who engage in it are ostracised, their colleagues refusing to work with them. This is not, it should be noted, because the Soweto cops are more rights-conscious than are men like Govender. Their reticence about displays of unwarranted violence is more pragmatic: in Soweto, you never know who is watching, how many of them are armed, and who might take offence. It was a local version of a more general argument sometimes made against the excessive use of force by police officers: police services that use force more reluctantly appear themselves to be the targets of less violence in return.

Unfortunately, I hadn't read Wardop's research when I met Govender, or I could have told him that cops in Soweto might respond to him the way he'd responded to my story about Hannes. They might, in other words, decide that he is too risky to work with, but for the opposite reason to the one he'd offered for refusing to work with a man like Hannes. Nevertheless, Govender's response suggested something intriguing, that *hase* were not the only audience for an officer's acts of authority-assertion, and that there was another that was just as important: the officer's own colleagues.

Recall that Hannes had told me that his first shooting had been a rite of passage, a blooding instigated and encouraged by his colleagues and superior. It is a story about which we must be careful for, whatever may or may not have been the case in the 1960s when Hannes was in the force, the majority of police officers I asked told me that they had never shot anyone. To a man, they had all drawn their weapons at some point and most had either seen other cops shoot at suspects or had fired the odd warning shot themselves. But most I asked had never actually shot anyone, and of those who had, some had done so only when they had been ordinary victims of crime. That testimony accords with the facts as far as we know them, which are that in each of the past five years, somewhere between three hundred and six hundred suspects were shot to death by police officers. Even if woundings were ten times more common than killings, that would still leave a huge gap between the number of people shot and the 130 000-plus police officers on the streets.

Even so, even if tenderfoots aren't blooded in this way, it doesn't follow that police officers are indifferent about their colleagues' ability to obtain the acquiescence of the *hase* and suspects with whom they deal, and, therefore, about their proficiency with fist and baton, torch and firearm. Take the case of a patrol officer in Wynberg, Cape Town, whose unit had just acquired the services of an officer who had until then worked only in the station's back-office jobs. As soon as the unit's new member turned his back, the senior officer in the group nodded in his direction: 'When you penetrate a house, you need to know what you're doing. And you need to know that the other guys know what they are doing. He doesn't, and until he does, a whole crew can be at risk.' The same instinct, but this time spiced up by the organisation's deeply felt sexism, was reflected in the views of the officers who told me that they never worked with a woman without wondering whether she had the guts and the muscle to back them up.

All of which is to say that the aggressiveness that police officers must bring to their work is not determined solely by the nature of the work and the places in which it must be done. It is also affected by the need to demonstrate the flinty resolution of the police as a whole to the country's *hase*, and by the need for cops to signal their toughness to one another. And this last reason is related to another: like soldiers, it is in the heat of battle, so to speak, that the organisation's members bind themselves to one another. The violence they encounter and the violence they mete out in response are among the central pillars on which trust, solidarity and *esprit de corps* are built. This is a process that begins in basic training which – at least, until some of the more recent recruits were rushed through in three months flat – used to involve long days of intense physical training. Older officers regard these new recruits as impossibly undisciplined because they avoided these horrors, often personified in the semi-mythological figure of Patrollie Nel, who sounds like something of a caricature of a regimental sergeant-major, all curled moustache and parade-ground baton, and with a penchant for running raw recruits beyond the point of collapse. The shared suffering, however, was intended not only to get the student constables fit, but to build a sense of solidarity. This was an archetypal masculine solidarity, to be sure, and its forging was premised on a military psychology which recognises that in war, the only thing that keeps troops going forward is the belief that they are fighting with and for their brothers. Something of this sort works in policing too, where bonds are forged around moments of excitement and danger. And, as a result, part of the response to violence is a testosterone-charged exuberance, an excitement that is, for want of a better word, boyish. For all its adolescent pleasure, this is one of the essential elements of the police officer's experience, and it is this, as much as anything else, that explains why some men love this work.

But this is not costless work.

★

When I had asked Govender whether he would have any regrets about shooting a man stealing a car radio, he told me that he wouldn't, that such a man is a criminal and that it is a policeman's duty to deal with his sort. He implied that he couldn't allow himself the luxury of guilt or regrets, and he said he would distrust an officer who he thought might be plagued by this kind of doubt.

My sense at the time was that this was part bluff. I didn't think that Govender was stricken by guilt, but I felt that there was more texture to his feelings about the shootings than he had let on, and, on the last day I spent with him, I saw some evidence to back up my intuition.

We were driving into Johannesburg's southern suburbs on the way to Soweto because Govender wanted to introduce me to a former colleague of his who worked in the township. When I'd arrived that morning at Govender's baby-blue office with its battered safe and meshed

143

windows, he was on the phone, yelling into the poor instrument as if he doubted that it could carry his voice. I could only hear one side of the conversation.

'What's the name of that guy inside?' he asked.

There was a pause while the other man spoke.

'The laaitie who shot the cop,' Govender clarified.

A second pause was followed by: 'Ja. That one.' And then: 'Oh! Oscar. That's right. He's in big shit. He'll never get bail. Attempted murder! Of a police officer! You won't be seeing your friend for a long time.' Govender's chuckle seemed conspiratorial and I thought that Oscar's friend, whoever he was, wasn't all that bothered about his being behind bars. When it was over, I asked Govender about the conversation. 'Ag. It's just a druggie-bullshit thing,' he replied. 'The arsehole shot a cop and now he'll pay. That's the way it's supposed to be.'

The trip to Soweto was wasted, and by the time we got to the station Govender's buddy was on a murder scene and a call swiftly established that he would be there all day. We were late because a truck had lost its load on the highway, and traffic had been backed up for kilometres. As we sat in the monoxide fumes, Govender patiently tapping out an arrhythmic 'tune' on the steering wheel, we listened to the radio news, which carried an item about a police officer who had killed a wife or girlfriend before turning the gun on himself.

Listening to the news item, Govender grunted in derision.

Never missing an opportunity to pose the obvious question, I asked him why cops did that sort of thing.

'People talk about the stress, that stress makes these guys do this thing. That's bullshit. It's not stress.'

'What is it then?'

'When a member kills himself,' Govender said, 'you mustn't ask if he was stressed. You must ask if he was involved in a shooting before he died.'

Assuming he meant that the police officers who killed themselves after shooting someone else were guilt-stricken, I asked him why he didn't think that was a kind of stress.

'No, no, no,' he said. 'You don't understand.

144

'Africans have a saying,' he continued after a moment. 'They say that a mother never forgets her own child. It means that it doesn't matter how bad that child was, how much shit he got into, if you kill him, that mother will try to fight for him. She will go to get *muti*, and she will get a witch to curse you. She will fuck you up. That's why you must ask if the member who kills his family has been in a shooting incident. That's when you'll see what has really happened.'

I asked him if such a thing had ever been done to him after one of his cases, and how he knew what had happened. 'Once,' he said. 'After I shot someone, I wasn't myself. I was stubborn. Dangerously stubborn. I was fighting with everyone, and acting very badly. Then someone took me to a *sangoma*. And he helped. He gave me *muti* to cleanse myself. He helped me a lot. Now, if I kill someone, you won't find me at work the next day. I'll go straight to the *sangoma*. Before the body is in the ground.'

His view was unexpectedly eccentric. Nothing about our conversations had suggested a spiritual side to Inspector Govender, much less one that could support a cross-cultural belief in magic. I couldn't help thinking how attractive such an explanation would be to a man who consciously chose to regard killing as an act about which he ought to feel no guilt. I wondered if, instead of recognising his discomfort's origins in doubts about the morality of killing, he ascribed it to external forces, forces which, conveniently for him, could be driven out in a cleansing ritual. It wasn't the sort of thing I could ask about — how would I frame the question without sounding judgmental? 'Inspector, you're full of shit, you aren't bewitched, you're feeling guilty,' didn't sound like a smart thing to say to a man who shoots people — but I took it as a sign that the self-proclaimed hard-ass was paying a price for his hardness.

I had no doubt that the SAPS sometimes had need of its hard men. The only question I had, however, was whether it was a good thing or bad thing that Govender had temporarily hung up his spurs.

CHAPTER NINE

DRUG DEALERS, SIZZLERS AND THE RANDOM-FUCK-UP FACTOR: SEA POINT, SEPTEMBER 2003

'No-one who wasn't there can imagine what that place looked like,' Inspector Isaak Fourie was saying. 'It was an abattoir. All those bodies in a row. All of them covered in blood and piss. Mess, everywhere. You don't know how strong the heart is, how far blood flies. You couldn't breathe because of the smell. It made you feel like you were swallowing blood. Drowning in all that shit.'

We were talking about the Sizzlers massacre. Nine young men, peroxide-headed members of the sex industry in the prime of their lives, had been trussed like sheep before someone took a kitchen knife to their throats and then shot them in their heads. Miraculously, a tenth victim survived similar treatment. The crime scene must have been as grisly as any in South African history, comparable only to some of the more vicious deeds done in the name of apartheid or of liberation.

Fourie was quiet for a moment. A tightly-wound spring of a man with close-cropped hair, ears you could hang a trench coat on, and eyes that were just a little too intense, verging, perhaps, on the paranoid, he now made a tiny, unnecessary adjustment to a horizontal strap on his bullet-proof vest. Then he sighed the sigh of a man about to offer his last word on the subject, the sigh of a man about to seal it all up again: 'You knew that the guys who did it … Let's just say that they must have been seriously smoked up. No normal person could do what they did.'

We were sitting in a police car, its radio chirruping a flirtatious conversation between two cops – one man, one woman – who'd been at police college together. The house next to us, the house in which the horrors Fourie was talking about had been done, was small and whitewashed, with a *stoep* and a tiny front garden. It was an object lesson in quaintness, set though it was among the concrete beehives of the area's apartment blocks. Barely a block from five-star hotels and the local synagogue, it seemed a phenomenally unlikely spot for this kind of butchery.

It had all happened eight months earlier, in January 2003, and it had shocked even the most crime-jaded South Africans. It wasn't just that the crime had been committed so close to the heart of South Africa's tourism industry. Or that it was in a formerly white suburb. Or that the victims were white. Though all of these were part of the shock, at root, the horror the slaughter inspired was about the future. Where is our society going, South Africans asked themselves, if such a thing can happen? It was a question that was followed by another that was equally urgent, if somewhat less politically correct: where is our society going if such a thing can happen *here*? What forces – social, economic, criminal – had turned what should be one of the most valuable bits of real estate in the country first into an outlet for one of the more immoderate sectors of the local sex industry, and then into something that looked like the set of a teenage splatter film?

Almost immediately after the massacre became known, a conventional wisdom condensed, one that centred on two theses. The first was that Sea Point was going the way of Hillbrow, that it was becoming an urban ghetto in which only the poor and the vicious could survive. The second was that this transformation was being both exploited and encouraged by criminally inclined Nigerian migrants and predatory gangs spilling out of the slums of the Cape Flats in pursuit of new territories to rule and new markets to dominate. The result was that although the details of the Sizzlers massacre were not immediately clear, it was quickly concluded, by cops and pundits alike, that organised crime was involved. Perhaps this was a drug deal gone bad, or punishment for an unpaid drug debt. Perhaps the victims had failed to pay protection money to whichever gang ran the local racket, or had purchased drugs from the wrong supplier. Perhaps one gang was muscling into the territory of another, and this was a message to its rival's clients: your old protectors can't protect you from us, so pay up or move out.

Whatever the reason for the crime, it was quickly accepted that this

147

was not the work of 'common' criminals. There simply had to be more to it than that.

With all these possibilities, gang-watchers were uncertain about precisely why the crime had been committed, but insisted that there was some precedent for the apparently inexplicable and gratuitous violence in the ritualistic Nieuwoudtville killings in 1996, in which three people had died so that a Cape Town gangster could establish a reputation that would allow him to lead a prison gang. Indeed, they insisted that the violence was neither gratuitous nor inexplicable, and that gangsters, as well as their rivals, fellow-travellers and clients, would understand its message, written though it was in the language of blood. This was a crime, in other words, that had a logic. Terrible and incomprehensible as it might seem to others, in the codes of the underworld the meaning of the killing could be instantly understood.

To be sure, there were some contra-indications of gang involvement. It was, for instance, hard to understand why a rational gang intent on sending a message of this sort would have had to kill so many. More importantly, it seemed odd that any gang would consciously court the inevitable backlash, from a government inordinately sensitive to blows to its international image, that this kind of incident in the heart of glamorous Cape Town was guaranteed to generate. But, then again, perhaps the stakes were that high after all; perhaps the prospect of running Sea Point's sex and drugs industries justified these risks.

The suburb's residents, meanwhile, fearing the prospect of a full-blown gang war in the heart of the city, must have wondered whether this was the beginning of the end of the Mother City. How could they have done otherwise? If violence on this scale had come to the city once, what would stop it from coming again and again and again?

Given this background, I was more than a little surprised at the calm I encountered when I arrived at the Sea Point police station, a station that even hardened Johannesburg coppers had begun to speak of in hushed tones. I'd persuaded myself that I was coming to a precinct which had slipped over the edge of a precipice of violence, and that police officers would be at battle stations. Instead, I'd found a businesslike atmosphere of order and routine overseen by Superintendent Stander, its unflappable, ascetic commander.

When we'd first met, Stander had waved me into the library-like stillness of his office while trying to end an obviously irritating telephone conversation. I couldn't tell what the caller was complaining about, but Stander listened for five, then ten, then fifteen minutes, barely offering much more than the occasional tut-tut or solicitous, 'That's terrible.' But from the clenching and unclenching of his jaw, I knew that the level of sympathy he felt for the caller was falling precipitously. Eventually his irritation got the better of him, and, in a voice dripping with the most impeccable manners, he said, 'Madam, I'm not sure what you want me to do about this. You can't identify the man and, to be honest with you, I'm not sure that what you've described is a crime.' He listened a bit longer, then told her more forcefully that there was nothing he could do for her, but that if she wished to come in and open a docket for further investigation, she was welcome to do so.

After he hung up the phone, Stander looked down at his hands. He was either counting to ten or suppressing a laugh, so I took a chance on his sense of propriety and asked him what the call had been about.

'It's one of the older ladies in the community,' he said, making the word 'ladies' do a lot of work. 'She calls every once in a while with something new. This time, she says she was parked in the parking lot by Green Point when a man she didn't know walked up to her window and hypnotised her.'

Stander sighed to himself, and I thought he wanted me to ask a follow-up. Always happy to play the straight man, I asked what the alleged hypnotist was supposed to have done after casting his spell. 'Nothing,' Stander said without a hint of any emotion. 'That's all he did. He hypnotised her. And now she's calling me.' This time he didn't sigh. But he might as well have.

Whatever else one might say about the woman's story, one thing seemed obvious: if Stander had the time to spend fifteen minutes on the phone with this woman, neither he nor the caller thought that he was presiding over a suburb that had descended into open gang warfare.

★

Superintendent Stander was by reputation and self-assessment a member of the Police Service's old school, a commander, as the inexplicable saying goes, with hair on his teeth. He was not in Sea Point's hot seat at the time of the massacre, but was brought in, so the station's cynics say, so that the Police Service's senior management would be able to tell their political masters – and the public, of course – that something was being done to turn the suburb around. There was also talk at the time that the head of the station's crime prevention unit, having failed to prevent the bloodbath, would be moved sideways. But since the officer in question, Captain Pentz, was both the unit's commander and its sole member, it was thought, when the matter was reconsidered, that blaming him would be deemed a touch unfair by the rank and file in the province. So, instead of replacing him, management decided that they'd make his title more meaningful and actually allocate some members to his command. By the time I got there, Pentz had 18 men under him.

All of this seemed a little beside the point, however, because the official line from the station was that there was no dangerous build-up of gangland tensions, no risk that the suburb was going to become an urban wasteland, wrecked by criminal groups waging urban warfare in order to dominate its physical and economic turf.

'Crime is the lowest it's been in five years,' Stander told me before bemoaning the fact that the moratorium on the release of crime statistics meant that he couldn't prove that to me or to his community. It was a line I heard again and again from the station's senior officers. This was confirmed a year later, when station-level crime stats were released by the Police Service for the first time: every crime from murder to burglary, from rape to robbery was down on the year before, often by a very large percentage.

To his credit, Stander offered me no self-congratulatory explanation for the improvement in public safety. His crime prevention officers were working hard and making a difference, he said. But the truth was that he had no good reason to think that their work alone accounted for the fact that in the eight months since the Sizzlers massacre, there'd been only three more murders in the suburb. In a high-density urban area in which drugs and prostitution were part of the social fabric, and in which large quantities of alcohol were consumed every day, that wasn't half bad.

'We don't have a problem of gangs *per se,*' Stander told me. 'Drugs: yes. Prostitution: yes. Illegal immigrants: yes. Even the occasional high flier who lives in the buildings here. But *gangsterism* is not something you find here.'

It was a view reiterated by the head of the station's detectives, Captain Verster, a man with a wonderfully insightful turn of phrase to whom I had no trouble listening for hours at a stretch. 'You don't get gangs here for the same reason that you don't get lions in Namaqualand: the environment is wrong. They'd be like fish out of water.'

I'm not making that up. It's what he said: lions in Namaqualand would be fish out of water.

The Sea Point precinct, the environment he was talking about, is a long, narrow stretch of Atlantic seaboard, with ocean to the west and north, and the steeply-rising slopes of Signal Hill and Lion's Head to the east and south. The suburbs here are largely residential and expensive, and, despite the public wailing and gnashing of teeth, the processes of degradation and impoverishment visible ten years ago appear to have been arrested and reversed, the upturn propelled by the decade-long property boom that followed the emergence of Cape Town as a global tourist destination. Many of the high-rise apartment buildings are home to an elderly population, living out their retirements in genteel flats with heavy furnishings worn smooth with age and use. The rest are now holiday flats for sophisticates from Johannesburg, London and Berlin.

To residents who remember the current of decline ten years ago, much of the new glamour must seem artificial and transient, a brief remission in the long subsidence that preceded it. For them, what stands out when they look at the streets of Sea Point are not the obvious signs of improvement, but the equally obvious signs that, for all the slightly decrepit respectability of the older residents, and the glamour of its newer ones, there are also darker, more ominous threads running through the area's social fabric.

There are, of course, the *bergies* – homeless, alcoholic and sometimes threatening – who live in the suburb's parks and doorways. But they, the

Bible says, will always be with us, and their presence tells us nothing we didn't already know about South Africa. There are also, however, the streetwalkers and rent boys who patrol a stretch of Main Road, the escort agencies and strip clubs that proliferate at the end of Regent Street, and, above all, the groups of baleful-looking drug dealers who gather on a few street corners in the centre of the commercial area. These are the visible manifestations of an underground market that breaks through the local economy's veneer of respectability to offer the dangerous pleasures that can't be offered legally.

No-one knows exactly when and why these pleasures were first offered in Sea Point, but the cocktail of commercial sex and illicit drugs is often served up in areas in which the other needs of a rock-'n-roll lifestyle are met. Like other entertainment districts the world over, Sea Point's has developed an undercurrent of vice that both feeds off and stimulates the licit parts of its leisure economy. In fact, it may be that the illicit entertainment industry delivers as much knock-on business to legal establishments as the other way around. Both have boomed together.

And now it has become a 'reputation thing'.

'Addicts know that there are dealers here, dealers know that this is where addicts will look for them,' Captain Verster, the bluff, big-boned amateur artist who was also the head of the station's detective unit, told me. 'It's the same with the prostitutes. Because tourists and locals know that this is where you come to find a girl, girls keep coming here too.'

Verster was sitting in his office fielding the occasional question from a member of his staff. The office was quite big, and as most cops do, he'd pushed all the furniture back against the walls, making intimacy almost impossible to achieve. Above his head was a painting of his own. It showed a Spitfire attacking a German tank in what must have been the Algerian Desert. Something about the perspective was not completely successful, and the painting looked vaguely surreal. Later, when I asked about his painting, he told me that there was a market for African art and that he made good money. 'You have to get permission, of course,' he said. 'The bosses don't want you to paint anything that will hurt the reputation of the Police Service.'

'Anything sexy?' I asked.

'Sexy. Or political, I suppose.'

'So what about the theory that Sea Point has been carved up between the Firm and the Americans?' I asked, referring to two of the mega-gangs of the Cape Flats. 'What about the story that each gang dominates part of the drugs and prostitution and protection rackets in Sea Point, and that Sizzlers was a result of their conflict?' It was a theory that a senior police officer, the former head of the province's premier anti-gang operation and the current station commander at Elsies River, had propounded on national television shortly after the massacre.

'That's just a bullshit story,' Verster replied. 'Sizzlers was done by two lunatics. For money, not drugs. There is no gangsterism here.'

Perhaps I looked unconvinced by this, so he continued: 'There are some gangsters here, but they are runners. They come to town to bring drugs and to take out money. Maybe some of the bigger guys are into a few businesses or brothels, but the gangs don't control territory and they sure as shit don't fight it out. This isn't the Flats, it's a free market. Most of the drug dealers are Nigerians. They're not in the gangs. They do their own thing.' Verster gave a wicked smile before continuing: 'In any case, now that we have more uniformed members, we're fucking the dealers up. It's getting to the point where even the Nigerians can't afford good lawyers.'

★

It is important to record at this point that Verster wasn't engaged in idle speculation. As I spoke to him and avoided looking at his disconcerting painting, two men were being held awaiting trial at Pollsmoor Prison. They'd been arrested within a few weeks of the massacre and had made confessions to a magistrate. In them, they'd said that their motive had been simple robbery, that they were not members of any gang operating in the area, and that they had acted alone. We'll return to their story in due course, but for the moment I wish also to record that, at the time I visited the Sea Point police station, the emerging robbery-gone-wrong storyline struck me as somehow indecent; it offended against some innate conviction that terrible effects must have terrible causes, and the

153

misadventures of two petty thieves seemed altogether too slight a cause for this outrage. I was, in short, convinced that there was more to it.

I had a problem exploring this, however, because arrests had been made and a trial date had been set, and I knew from experience that a serious investigator would sooner pass through the eye of a needle than talk to me about a high-profile case before it went to trial. That route being closed to me, I decided instead to try to understand the local criminal economy by talking to detectives and tagging along on a series of patrols in the area, watching the cops work those who prospered or failed to prosper in Sea Point's underground. It was on one of those nights that I met the tightly wound Inspector Fourie, the man who described the scene at Sizzlers for me. His partner for the night was a young female constable, fresh out of college, and Fourie seemed to relish the prospect of showing off some of the street wisdom he'd accumulated.

The first question I'd asked as we'd set off from the station was about the gangs. Stander, Verster, and half-a-dozen other officers had already tried to convince me that gang activity in the area was extremely limited. But I thought I'd test the claim by feigning ignorance. 'I heard that the Americans and the Firm sometimes give you guys some trouble,' I offered a little vaguely.

'Not just them,' Fourie said. 'Here we've got Americans and the Firm, but we've also got some Triad activity.'

That was the first I'd heard of this, so I asked him to explain what they got up to. 'They're based at a restaurant in Sea Point,' he replied, telling me the name of its owner.

'What are they into?' I asked, hoping to find a route into the mystery of gangland activity and its relationship to the rest of the world. I was disappointed.

'Actually, they're quite quiet,' he conceded. 'They don't give us much shit.'

From that moment, I wasn't sure how seriously to take his insistent name-dropping and conspiracy-fiend tales about local bouncers who work as hit-men, security guards who run housebreaking syndicates by night, pornographers and paedophiles who work out of the local escort agencies, and body-builders who protect the top men in organised crime.

I wasn't sure if he was trying to impress me or his colleague with these stories, but some of them seemed too far-fetched by half, others too banal to record. None seemed particularly well founded on any evidence, and all seemed to break down after a little probing. But his conspiratorial convictions didn't make him bad at his primary job, which was to harry, hassle and harass the drug dealers and streetwalkers who were the more visible elements of the illicit economy.

★

Whatever else happens in Sea Point's criminal economy, the nights I spent with the local cops demonstrated that the street-work of drug peddlers is an unutterably unromantic business.

Sea Point's street-level drug-dealing problem is concentrated on a couple of corners in the middle of the commercial district near the notorious El Rio building – a formerly up-market apartment block now home to hundreds of immigrants and refugees from West Africa crammed into flats built for far fewer people. I wouldn't have seen its dingy interior, with its insistent bouquet of exotic cooking smells, and its tenants' rooms, each curtained off into separate sub-lets, if two women hadn't interrupted the cops working the drug bazaar to tell them that one of the building's occupants had obligingly stabbed another. This was not a place of luxury: the building was cramped and dirty, and the air seemed thick with the tensions and frustrations that come from poverty and overcrowding.

The dealers, many of whom live in El Rio, worked in groups of three: one to take the buyer's money from him, one to get the cash out of the area in case the notes were marked, and one to bring the drugs to the buyer. It's a hopelessly inefficient business model, but it took a lot of the risk of buy-bust stings out of the equation. The teams worked small stashes, hidden in cracks in the pavement or under loose bricks. But in the interminable gaps between attending to the needs of their clients, they could be found slouched against the street lights, huddled in the rain shadows of the buildings, or sitting in coffee shops. Everyone knew everyone else in these places, and all of them were in exactly the same boat.

The local cops didn't use the narcotics officer's traditional weapon, the buy-bust, preferring to leave it to specialised units. The arcana of the laws of evidence that govern these tactics were one reason for this, but the more important reason was practical: the dealers in Sea Point knew the local cops' faces and could not be relied on to make deals with them. But Fourie and his colleagues had other ways to disrupt the market. He delighted, for instance, in rummaging through bits of rubbish and the piles of urban detritus that accumulate around the buildings in the immediate vicinity of the drug bazaars. He did this under the gaze of a few dozen slingers whose impassivity was so studied they might have offered lessons to shop-window mannequins. Twice he sniffed out a handful of dagga cigarettes, but, since he could link no-one to them, he simply opened them up and let the dried leaves blow off on the breeze. He also enjoyed parking his marked vehicle in front of a pack of peddlers and sitting there just to scare off their customers. 'None of this makes much difference in the long run,' he conceded when I asked what he thought the effect was. Then, brightening, he added: 'The thing is that a lot of these guys live hand-to-mouth, so it pisses them off when I sit here or if I find the drugs they want to sell because then they may not eat anything tomorrow. And if they're hungry and pissed off, I'm smiling.'

At other times, Fourie would shift up from this passive aggressive approach to more forceful ways of asserting his authority, pushing men he didn't like the look of up against the wall to search them and inspect their refugee papers, looking for suspicious items – the serial number of a cellphone on one man matched that of a phone stolen in Kimberley a year earlier, for instance – and ordering those he couldn't find a reason to arrest to move on.

A general principle of South African law states that people have the right to stand wherever they damn well please, so I asked Fourie how he got around that. 'Ag, it's easy. It's true that they can stand where they want, but the by-laws say you can't obstruct pedestrians or traffic. We don't arrest people for that, but if they refuse to obey a police officer's instruction, well, we do arrest them for that. Otherwise, what's the point? That's when we get under their skin. And that's when we're smiling.'

This kind of drug dealer harassment is one of the pillars on which

156

urban policing strategies throughout the world are built. There is no doubt that it disrupts dealers' activities, puts large numbers of them behind bars, and eats into their profits. But there are serious doubts about its efficacy in shutting down drug markets, raising drug prices and reducing the quantities of drugs injected, inhaled and snorted into users' bodies because even if large numbers of vendors are sent to jail, drug dealers as a group are usually able to absorb the effects of aggressive police tactics. Arrested dealers are replaced, open-air bazaars move a few blocks down the road, dealers start making home deliveries. The market depends on no single arrested man. It accepts the loss and moves on.

The suppleness of the laws of supply and demand, it seems, exceeds the brute force of temporal legislation. This is true even in the seat of the global war on drugs, the United States, where three decades' worth of this kind of policing has filled prisons to bursting point even as the price of drugs has fallen lower and lower and the volume consumed has risen higher and higher. Even the best argument that can be made for this war – that it may have kept prices higher than they might otherwise have been – is of dubious value: since it is the high price of drugs that keeps dealers in the market, keeping the price up acts like a tax on drug users and a subsidy for drug pushers.

There are also other costs to this war. Station-house wisdom in Sea Point has it that too vigorous a crackdown on drug-dealing has the perverse effect of raising the number of robberies and burglaries. Even drug dealers have to eat, I was told, and if you take away their primary source of income, they will have to turn to others.

★

The discussion of the reasons why Nigerians have come to dominate open-air drug markets in the largest of South Africa's cities must be deferred to another place, but their dominance in the formerly white areas of Cape Town is, on the face of it, hardest to explain. These markets are, after all, practically in the backyard of the Cape Flats' gangs, gangs that are the biggest, oldest and most powerful criminal enterprises in the country. Why would they allow this market of middle-class

157

clubbers and adrenaline junkies to fall into the lap of a group of despised refugees and illegal immigrants? Of all people, surely these gangs, their teeth cut in ferociously fought turf wars, would be able to claim and defend ownership of this market. Why, then, aren't these streets daubed in their colours?

There are three possible answers to this question. The first is that the gangs, for reasons that passeth understanding, have no interest in this market. The second is that, notwithstanding appearances to the contrary, the gangs do control these streets. And the third, and most plausible, is that the gangs do work these streets, but that their strategy here is only a distant cousin of the approach they have taken in the ghettos of the Cape Flats.

The first idea – that the gangs have no interest in Sea Point – offends against everything we think we know about the insatiable greed of organised criminality. It is, therefore, very unlikely that there could ever be zero gang involvement in the local drug market. By contrast, the second answer to the question implausibly suggests that, whatever the nature and scale of the differences between the ghettos and Sea Point, they are, from a gangster's perspective, more alike than they are different, and that they can, therefore, be tackled using the identical business model. Roughly speaking, this account is the premise of the conventional wisdom about the Sizzlers massacre that formed so quickly after the event, and which I described earlier. It takes for granted the avarice of the gangs, so it meets that basic requirement for plausibility. But it also assumes that the gangs have the ability to project their power into an environment quite different to the ghettos of the Flats, and to develop both the business models and organisational culture necessary to flourish in so alien a habitat. This seems an heroic assumption: there are entrepreneurs in the gangs who are as nimble as they are ruthless, but their organisations were formed under the wholly different social conditions of the Flats and for wholly different reasons. They would have found it difficult to translate their dominance in one area of the underground economy into dominance in every other. Besides, their reputations for violence would have made them singularly ill-suited to selling drugs to middle-class users and the second-tier distributors from whom these users buy their drugs. Whatever their relationship with the law, middle-class drug users and their intermediary dealers would have been frightened off by the prospect of dealing directly with gangsters from the Cape Flats, and an overt presence in the market might have killed that market stone dead.

Hence the third answer to the question posed earlier: the gangs are not indifferent to the profits to be had in Sea Point's underground economy, but they cannot and do not dominate it the way they dominate the same market in their local fiefs. Instead they have had to adapt to the reality that the nation's drug market is heavily segmented, and that business models that are formidably profitable in one part of the market are ill-suited to its other segments. The territorial domination of gang turf is, for instance, utterly futile if your customers have cars. Trying to establish dominance is, in any case, an exceedingly dangerous enterprise unless conditions – economic, demographic and policing – are conducive to the project.

So, instead of trying to turn Main Road, Sea Point into some kind of local office, the gangs seem to have developed a more strategic, more commercial, relationship with this market. As a consequence, their touch here is far lighter than it is in their traditional stomping grounds. Instead of trying to dominate the streets and extract tribute from all who would do business here, they have sought to occupy some of the ecological niches to which their particular skills and resources are best suited. Perhaps they push drugs and sex through some of the kerbside prostitution. Perhaps they have a stake in some establishments operating in the twilight between the licit and illicit economies – the handful of cheap hotels and brothels, a liquor outlet or two. Perhaps they sell some of their merchandise to other retailers – the Nigerians, the second-tier distributors who sell to middle-class users, unaffiliated prostitutes and their pimps. Perhaps they offer themselves as musclemen to other members of Sea Point's criminal fraternity. What they have not done, however, is carve up the Atlantic seaboard into distinct turfs, the boundaries of which are staked and marked, and then defended against intrusion. Gangsterism of this sort is something that has not yet crossed into this part of town. Nor does it seem likely that it ever could.

But this assessment is only part of the answer, for it implies, as much of the talk about Cape Town's gangs often does, that the gangs are like well-oiled machines, flawlessly implementing a business strategy developed by their generals in a way that would make the CEOs of even the largest and most successful corporations envious. This seems doubtful. Gangs do have chains of command, and they do have the organisational machinery to discipline their members. But they have that machinery because their members are seldom entirely trustworthy (some, one imagines, verge on psychopathy). Nor are they meticulously competent branch-managers and bureaucrats. They are, as a result, at least as likely as anyone else to ignore, misunderstand or defy their instructions. That means, of course, that any explanation cast in too rational a set of terms risks missing the essential element of the capriciousness and unpredictability of people involved in long-term criminality.

And this, then, was how I thought Sizzlers may have played out. The idea that the gangs ran Sea Point in much the same way as they did the ghettos seemed patently false. Yes, they were in the market, but this didn't seem the kind of place they could divvy up between themselves and then dominate as they do the streets and the economies of the Flats. But perhaps not everyone in the gangs recognised that the realities of Sea Point made the approach they adopted in the townships inappropriate, and perhaps some among them had sought to impose themselves using tactics that had evolved in and for other ecological niches. The massacre at Sizzlers might not, in other words, have been a subtle, albeit vicious, message authored by a vampiric protection racket operating in the area for a local audience, but perhaps it was a sign that someone in one of the gangs was looking for new ways to wring cash from Sea Point's underground economy or, more prosaically, perhaps it was simply the aftershock of a drug deal gone bad.

The official line on all of this speculation is that it is, in the words of one of the case's investigators, Superintendent Mike Barkhuizen, 'a crock of shit'.

Superintendent Barkhuizen, a senior commander at the Serious and Violent Crimes Unit, was put in charge of the investigation into the killings almost immediately. I hadn't met him while I was in Sea Point because I knew that he wouldn't have spoken to me about the case before it went to court, but I phoned him a short while after two men – Adam Woerst and Trevor Theys – were convicted of the crime and given multiple life sentences. 'There's no debate about how it happened,' he said, before recounting the basic facts as established by his investigation.

Initially, it seems, the idea of a robbery was Woerst's, a young man who was, as they say, without prospects. A waiter, Woerst had come to hear about Sizzlers, and about the money that was kept in its safes, from an embittered former employee of the brothel who ate at the restaurant where he worked. Ironically, given the subsequent speculation, the reason the man had lost his job was that he'd been caught using drugs on the premises. His employer, it turned out, brothel-keeper though he was, either disapproved of narcotics or, as is more likely, disapproved of the idea of being bust with narcotics in his house. Hearing the man's story, Woerst started to 'think rands and cents' and approached Trevor Theys, another regular at the restaurant, with his scheme.

The idea was probably simple. They may not have planned to kill anyone, or they may have thought that only one or two people would be in the place in the early hours of that Monday morning. They would arrive, pose as potential clients to gain entry, and then hold the residents up. Perhaps they thought they wouldn't get caught. They might have doubted whether a troupe of rent-boys and their pimp would even report them to the police. Would they really want that kind of attention? Would they really want to involve the authorities? And, even if they did, what exactly would the cops do for these low-life moffies? The effort they would put into the investigation, the prospective robbers might have reasoned, may well be no more than half-hearted.

What plan could be simpler? they must have thought. What on earth could go wrong?

In the event, however, things did go wrong. And badly.

It started in the kitchen, probably with Theys, when one of the men being held at gunpoint fought back unexpectedly. Theys may have lowered his guard for a moment, or maybe the man simply fancied his chances. But whatever happened, he miscalculated and, in the ensuing struggle, he was shot dead.

That incident changed the odds. Now, instead of Woerst and Theys committing a robbery which might well have gone unreported or under-investigated, they'd killed someone. Murders, they would have known, get reported. They get investigated. And, in this case, there were two handfuls of witnesses who would be able to describe the killers and pick them out of a line-up.

Something would have to be done about that. That 'something' was mass murder. So, playing the odds as they must have imagined hardened gangsters rationally calculating the risks might do, the two petty thieves stalked the house slashing throats and then administering the *coups de grâce* with their guns.

No wonder Fourie thought that the smells and the fear must have been like something out of an abattoir.

But they didn't kill everyone: despite catastrophic injuries from two gunshots and the cutting of his throat, one man survived. And, just as Woerst and Theys must have feared, he was able to identify the attackers, picking Theys's face out of an ancient photo album of local criminals. 'It was a fucking old picture,' Barkhuizen told me, smiling at the implausibility. 'I think the damn thing was black-and-white.'

Without that photograph, it is quite conceivable that neither man would ever have been arrested, but the photo led to a name, and the name led to an address. Within hours, a small house in Mitchell's Plain was surrounded by heavily armed men, and Trevor Theys, a 42-year-old taxi driver whose only previous conviction, and the reason why he had a photo on file at all, was for using his employer's vehicle for his own personal gain, was under arrest. It didn't take long for Theys to give up Woerst's name, and he too was quickly arrested.

It was a straightforward case of a vicious crime, dumb criminals, and good policework. But it all seemed so petty. How could something so large be done for reasons so small? Was there nothing else to it? No gangs? No drugs? Nothing?

'People think, "Nine people died and you only arrested two men",' Barkhuizen told me on the phone. 'They think that that doesn't sound right. That's why you get all this speculation, but there was no evidence to back up those stories. Nothing. We looked for it. But there was nothing.'

I admitted to Barkhuizen that I was one of those people who instinctively thought that there must be more to this crime than meets the eye, and pointed out that even the judge, in passing sentence, had suggested that the men's confessions posed more questions than they provided answers about the motives for the crime. I told him that I could see the attraction of the official account of events for local police officers: it implied, after all, that the case had been solved, that there was nothing left undone, that they had fulfilled their sacred duty. As importantly, it suggested that whatever Sea Point's other problems, the officers manning the police station had not relinquished control of their territory to brutes and gangsters. But how can it be that these two men with no previous history of violence persuaded themselves so quickly to cut the necks of ten helplessly bound young men? The only previous conviction sported by either man was pretty ridiculous, and nothing about them suggested a history of violence. And yet these two men had decided to slaughter ten others. How, I wondered, could two such conscienceless beings have gotten this far without having done something similar before?

'It's a mistake a lot of people make,' Barkhuizen offered solicitously. 'But the most violent crimes are usually done by amateurs. They're much more dangerous than people who know what they are doing because when things go wrong, they panic. They don't have plans for emergencies. They don't know how to handle themselves. That's why amateurs are dangerous: when things go wrong, they go off like fireworks.'

OK, that's not unreasonable, I thought. But what about the initial claims, made repeatedly in the press in the wake of the butchery, that before attacking Sizzlers the killers had been looking for a former employee known as 'Maroewan' who was said to have stiffed some drug dealers in Johannesburg? And what about the sole survivor's evidence to the court that Woerst walked around Sizzlers on the phone asking someone to send a car to fetch him and Theys, and was getting increasingly agitated at the lack of response? Didn't that suggest that there was a wider conspiracy? How did that fit with the robbery-gone-wrong storyline?

These were ghosts and glimmers that hinted that there might, after all, be more to the crime, but Barkhuizen was adamant that they were, individually and severally, a crock of shit.

'It was a robbery and robbery was all that it was,' he insisted. 'We looked at all of the speculation, and it was all a bunch of red herrings. All they did was delay the investigation.' When I asked about the phone calls, he said no such calls had been traced. Maroewan, he said, was an ex-employee of Sizzlers and he probably did have problems with drug dealers in Jo'burg. But that was a coincidence, there was nothing to link the two stories. He was, in short, unmoved and immovable by this speculation. '*Hy wat beweer moet bewys*,' he said: he who alleges must prove. 'But, really, there's nothing there that we didn't find.'

★

I believe Barkhuizen and Stander and Verster and all the other officials who insisted that the Sizzlers case had been solved. I have no basis to doubt their word, and, in any event, a judge of the High Court gave two men nine life sentences on the basis of the evidence put to him. But I also know that good cops are good actors – the job demands it – and I can't help wondering whether we've all been suckered by an organisation which thinks the proclamation that the case has been solved refutes the idea that the gangs are heavily involved in Sea Point's criminal economy. Why might they try to do that? Because they think that it's more reassuring than the alternative.

But whenever these creeping doubts arise, I recall a warning given to me by an ex-cop who used to investigate organised crime in Gauteng. He told me that it's always best to leave a healthy amount of space in any explanation for any crime for what he called 'the random-fuck-up factor'.

'Organised crime exists,' he said. 'But people out there think that there are mafias pulling the strings in every hijacking and every bank robbery. That's rubbish. A lot of times, shit happens because shit happens. You won't find the masterminds behind it because there aren't any. All there is, is a bunch of misfits who think nothing of shooting their way to a fortune. They pick up a gun. They rob someone. And only then do they think about what they're going to do with the car they steal or whatever the fuck they end up with. Most of these little shits aren't acting on orders from customers. All they know is that there is someone in the township who'll buy a car from them. There's no big organised machine behind it. Just robbers and people willing to buy from them. That's all.'

Why, I asked, did so many cops and pundits think that there was more organisation than he allowed for?

'You know what people are like. Many think that every bad thing that happens must have a bad person behind it, someone who made it happen. They think that if there are lots of crimes that seem the same, then there must be one mastermind behind it all. But really, what is there to a hijacking? All it takes is a gun and some guts. Most of the time the people who write those reports about organised crime, in the press and in the police, watch way too much television.'

So Sizzlers was a robbery that went wrong. A random fuck-up, not a tightly scripted message from one world to the next or a by-play in a complex war for turf and status. Two men, neither of whom had apparently ever before committed a violent crime, simply slit the throats of ten men during their first criminal exploit.

Now, when I think about it, I wonder whether that is really much less worrying than the theory that gangs run Sea Point's drug scene.

CHAPTER TEN

LIKE AN ELEPHANT WITH A DART IN ITS ARSE: CAPTAIN LOUIS DE KOSTER, JOHANNESBURG

'Sometimes you think to yourself, "what the fuck do I do this for?"' Captain Louis de Koster was saying. 'The hours are *kak*. The work is dangerous. And I've got less chance of promotion than Eugene Terr'Blanche has of becoming president.'

'Is it as bad as that?' I asked.

'You better fucking believe it. There'll be no more white captains who get promoted. Not in the detectives. Not this year. And maybe not for the next ten years.' He stopped the car to let a pedestrian go by and, when he pressed the accelerator again, he sounded more resolute: 'No, my career is over. I must start looking for something else.' And then his voice changed again: 'The trouble is that I know a lot of guys who left. It isn't a piece of cake. They've got no job security, and most of them are worrying themselves into a coma.'

It was an unseasonably rainy Johannesburg evening and water had leaked under the bullet-proof vest that didn't quite fit me. The freezing touch of water between my shoulders made me twitch and shift about irritably. But De Koster had started his disquisition on the inequities of police promotion policies, and was as undistractable as a cobra in front of a lute.

'Half the detective units in this city are on the point of collapse,' he said matter-of-factly. 'Even where there are good commanders, most of the time he's up to his arse in paperwork and he can never get out to scenes. All they do is push paper and try to get their useless fucking members trained. They don't do any real work.'

De Koster himself didn't command a detective unit. 'There are three officers at the station,' he said. 'And I don't know exactly where I am in the pecking order.' Until a few months before this conversation, he'd been a senior officer in one of the area's specialised units. Then he'd been the reluctant victim of police redeployment instructions after the unit was restructured into oblivion, and had been sent to one of the northern sub- urbs' bigger police stations. I'd met him before the restructuring when he'd been deeply cynical about the move, and had followed him to his new post just to see how it was panning out. As it turned out, he was enjoying the work far more than he'd expected but, not having worked at a police station for more than a decade, he professed to being horrified at the workload and the lack of resources. It was nothing compared to some of the township stations he'd had contact with, though. 'They're the weak links in the chain,' he said. 'The *tsotsis* live there, and that's where they take the cars they steal. But the detective branches there are hopeless. There are whole stations that go weeks without making a decent arrest.'

'And you wouldn't want to work there? Just to make a difference?' I asked.

'No way. Not a chance. When whites go to those units, they get fuck-you files six inches thick chop-chop. It's just reverse racism and double standards: when whites are in command, everything has to be done by the letter, but black officers can get away with it if the cars are fucked or if dockets go missing or if their members get arrested. In any case, those units don't stand a chance. They've got no resources. The members are useless. No-one in the community wants to give evidence. It's one big fuck-up and they can fucking keep it.'

De Koster was driving us towards Hillbrow and was following three detectives and a witness in another vehicle. He'd arranged it this way so that he could sound off about the fate of middle-ranking white police- men without being overheard by his colleagues. He was new to the station, most of his members were black, and he didn't quite know whom he could speak openly in front of and whom he could not. He and the other detectives were looking for a home-invasion gang who had killed two people in one of their recent escapades, and the witness had come forward to lead them to a man he said might be one of the gangsters.

The crime had been committed ten days before, when an apartment that had been sub-divided and sub-let to three families had been stormed by four men. They'd tied up the residents and put them in a bedroom under the guard of one of the robbers while the other three had started to search the rooms. Somehow, one of the residents had managed to free himself and had attacked and disarmed the man guarding them. Prudently, he decided against taking the other men on, and had simply locked the door from within. When they realised what had happened, the rest of the gang had tried to force their way into the room and, in the process, had fired a stream of bullets through the thin wood of the door. Two people were killed. One was a resident of the flat, while the other was the now disarmed robber who'd been guarding them. The three remaining robbers had fled.

On the theory that robberies of these sub-lets are often inside jobs, the cops had initially pushed the surviving victims hard, looking for one who might have been involved in the planning of the crime. But ten days later they had nothing to show for their efforts. Then they caught a break: earlier that afternoon, the brother of the dead robber had called the cops. He said he had a name and address for one of the other robbers, one of the men he regarded as responsible for his brother's death, and he wanted to turn him in. One of De Koster's men had arranged for the caller to come in to the station that evening to lead the police to the suspect, and they were now driving through a damp landscape of asphalt and concrete in the hope and expectation that tonight a killer would be caught.

★

De Koster was a thin, reedy man with a bushy moustache that had no business on a face so tight and angular. His brown hair was flecked with grey and stood at all angles, as if a mild charge had been passed through his body. He was in his early forties, but the pack-and-a-half he smoked every day had left his skin pasty and washed out. Like his moustache, it seemed to have been recycled from another man. The car we were in, on the other hand, fitted the man perfectly. It was a dilapidated Mazda, the signature vehicle of the detective service. Aged and vaguely disreputable, the car looked like a recovering alcoholic who had resolved to turn his life around.

'I've been in this game a long, long time,' De Koster said, pursuing the course he'd set out on. 'But this affirmative action is going to be the death of the police. We can't survive like this, with all the old detectives getting negative and leaving.'

I asked De Koster whether the organisation hadn't in fact turned the corner, suggesting that the mid- and late 1990s, when thousands of senior white officers left under the generous terms of the 'voluntary severance packages', had been the low point. These were financial incentives offered by government in an effort to open up some gaps in the senior ranks of all public service institutions in order to facilitate the promotion of more junior, black employees and some party loyalists. Some who had left had done so because they couldn't stomach the idea of working for a black government. Others left because the terms of the offer were generous or because they felt they could do better in the private sector or because they felt that their careers had plateaued. The brain drain affected the paler detective service more profoundly than the rest of the organisation, and came at a time when detectives felt their vocation under threat with the ascendancy of *platkeppe* – the 'flat caps' from the uniform branch, resented and scorned by detectives – in the higher reaches of the organisation. Predictably, morale plummeted.

I'd first encountered all of this distress and disillusionment in 1998 when I researched a monograph on the state of the detective service. But that process had also taught me that complaining was part of the organisational culture of the detective service. Its members, I discovered, tended to develop a more individualist sensibility than those in other parts of the organisation, a sensibility that often manifested itself in a need to condemn as bureaucratic and excessively militarist the organisational culture of the rest of the police. Coming into conflict with or, at the very least, loudly expressing contempt for the Service seemed intrinsic to the detectives' make-up. Nevertheless, the unanimity among white detectives about the horrors of the practice of affirmative action, even amongst those who expressed understanding of its aims, suggested that something was going profoundly wrong with the policy, particularly since this was an organisation that could be only as effective as the experience, skill and morale of its members allowed. Now, five years later, the organisation seemed more stable, more at peace with itself. It was also a great deal blacker, a fact that still didn't rest well with many a white cop I encountered.

De Koster said he agreed that the late 1990s were worse. 'Those times were very bad. And some of those things are a bit better. But what you don't see is how many cops are getting stuck as inspectors or captains with nowhere to go. There are no posts above that, and even when a post does open, there's no way that a white detective will get it. No way at all. So those guys are getting very frustrated and we're going to lose a lot of them.'

'Would that be terrible for policing? Don't the police actually have to be more representative if they are going to be legitimate, if they are going to get the cooperation of the community?' I was being a little provocative, but he responded calmly enough: 'Policing will be OK if the commanders have skills. But most of them are useless: no experience, no training, no management skills. I heard that there was a commander appointed in SANAB who had no narcotics experience. Not even one single day. He doesn't know what crack is. He wouldn't know cocaine if he was standing in it. But he's the "commander" and his men are supposed to respect him, but they don't. He's supposed to be able to instruct them, which he can't. He knows sweet fuck all about the work. You tell me, does that make any sense to you? It can't go on like that.'

By now we were in high-rise, low-income Berea which was very like the neighbouring Hillbrow, but without the glamour. The rain had kept the streets emptier than usual but, even so, even after dark on a wintry night, the streets pulsed with a rhythm that was powered by entrepreneurialism, desperation and hope in equal parts. 'Fucking Nigies,' De Koster said, motioning towards a group of men on a corner. 'All of them. I bet half of them are called "Kingsley" and the rest are "Jude" and "Ike".' He pronounced it Ee-kay. The men stood about shiftlessly, alternately giving the passing traffic malevolent looks or gesturing that they were open for business. This was an open-air drug market, a crack corner served by scores of dealers who were the local face of a food chain that stretched back to the mountains of South America. Our business wasn't with these men, however, so, with officers and drug slingers pointedly ignoring each other, the cops emerged from their vehicles and focused their attention on a building that was brown with dust and acne-scarred where its paint had flecked. De Koster turned to his witness, who lived in the area, and told him to go home: 'It's better if no-one sees you with us.' Then he turned back to the heavily gated entrance of the building and called the man guarding it. He flashed his ID and his gun, said he was a policeman, and told the man to open up.

Never has any human being so begrudged a duty as greatly as the gate guard did this one, but eventually the gate was open and the detectives were following their shadows up the building's stairs.

They found the flat they were looking for on the third floor. De Koster's men took up defensive positions around the door and below the window next to it, trying to keep away from the likely trajectory of any bullets that might come through either. They had drawn their guns and the sharp, oily sound of metal on metal as they cocked the weapons sent a chill up my spine. It was a horrible sound, utterly alien and evil, but familiar, even comforting, too: a theme song for the SAPS.

One of the detectives, back against the wall, knocked on the door, and, in response to the inevitable question, said they were friends of John Sithole and would like to see him. Locks could be heard turning, and then the door opened to reveal a young woman whose hair, which she must have been washing and plaiting, was standing on end. It gave her a comically startled look, a look heightened by genuine surprise as three armed men rushed past her into the flat and out of my sight. Moments later, shouting could be heard from the flat's inner recesses. Then, in the silence that followed, De Koster and I followed the men into what turned out to be an over-stuffed TV room containing three gun-wielding detectives, two children and a man dressed for bed.

It was quickly established that this was not John Sithole. He told them that Sithole was a relative of his sister's husband, that he used to live in the flat, but that he'd left a few months before. He professed to having no idea where Sithole might have gone. De Koster, however, said he didn't believe him. 'Rubbish. You people always know where everyone is. You must know someone we can ask.'

'*Angazi*, boss,' he said. 'I don't know anyone. I don't know where he is.'

'Then you must come with us,' said De Koster, sighing theatrically. 'I've come here to arrest someone, and if he's not here then you must come with me instead. I'm not going back to the station with no-one.' Then he looked at me with a conspiratorial grin. 'This man is a researcher. What will he say about me if I come back empty-handed?'

I had come to hate these moments. Entering another human being's home, accosting him in his underwear in front of his children, bullying him with the authority of the law, and then taking him away. It was all horribly invasive. These are the bluntest edges of our law enforcement machinery, its sharpest elbows, and, necessary though they are, for those on the receiving end they must feel like violations.

The man was told to get his clothes and was then led, protesting, down the stairs where he was deposited in the car De Koster had followed to Berea. Once he was seated, De Koster leaned into the window and told him that he had better cooperate or this was going to be a very long night. If this frightened the man, he gave no sign of it. De Koster stepped back and the three detectives climbed into the car while he and I retreated to the second vehicle. 'You're not really going to arrest him, are you?' I asked as I ducked into the passenger seat.

'For what?' he sneered. 'I've got nothing on him. But maybe if he's frightened then he'll take us to where the real suspect is. We'll see what we can get out of him before we let him go.' The action in the flat had wound De Koster up tighter than he'd been earlier and, despite the rain, his hair seemed to bristle more proudly around his sharp face. Once he'd started the car, however, he seemed to put the whole business out of his mind, and picked up the thread of his sermon on the plight of the pale male in the new Police Service as if nothing had happened. 'I don't know if senior management knows what it's doing,' he complained.

'How do you mean?' I asked.

'Look what they did with the specialised units. Those units used to work. I mean really work. There was no space for passengers. If you couldn't carry your dockets, they got rid of you. Simple. Then they brought in affirmative action commanders. They didn't know the work.

172

They couldn't work scenes. They couldn't close cases. They could never testify in the High Court. But they were the new commanders. Talk about lunatics running the nuthouse.

'I don't know if you watch documentaries about animals. Have you ever seen one where they dart an elephant?

'There's this big fucking elephant, running along. He's afraid of nothing and nobody. And then bam! they hit it with a dart. At first, nothing happens. It just keeps running and running. But then you start to see changes. First it runs *skeef* and crashes into a few things. Then it stumbles. Then it stops and just stands there all confused, like it doesn't know where it is or what it's doing. Then it falls over. Now anyone can do what the fuck they like to him. He's helpless.

'That's what happened to the spec units. The changes didn't kill them at first. But they made a difference. Morale was low. On-the-job training stopped. People started doing funny things – getting into corruption, not doing their work ... Then they just stopped. Just like an elephant with a dart in its arse.

'Now all they can do is close them down.'

'Is that really fair?' I asked. 'I mean look at you. You say that the whole organisation is falling apart, but here you are. It's raining. It's cold. But instead of being in bed at home, you're in Hillbrow looking for a suspect.'

'Ja,' he replied. 'Here I am. I sometimes think I must be fucking mad. But, like you say, here I am. But you must understand that just because I *come* to work, doesn't mean that I *do* the work. Do it like I used to, I mean. In this game you have to be committed to do it properly, but the commitment isn't there any more. Not like it used to be. I've been in units where people could easily work two or three days without stopping when the big cases come in. But we don't do that any more.'

'And it's because you think that you have no future in the organisation?' I asked.

As if to give him a chance to consider his answer, De Koster allowed his attention to be drawn to a sparkling two-door BMW that had stopped in the lane next to me. Two affluent-looking white men were listening to pounding dance music. 'Fucking ravers,' De Koster said, glaring across me at them, challenging them with eyes they didn't seem willing to meet. 'Fucking scratch your noses. Just once. Please,' De Koster implored, hoping for an excuse to pull them over and search their pockets for the cocaine he sensed they had on them. Then the lights changed and we were off, and I asked about his feeling that he had no future in the organisation once again.

'That is a lot of the reason. But the way that you say it, you make it sound like it's just about the money and the career. It isn't. Take me. I joined the police in 1980. I was a laaitie, just out of school, and they put me in the riot unit for three or four years. I was in Soweto. I was 19, 20, 21 years old and I was fucking scared. But I also loved it because I thought I was doing something for my country. A lot of white cops won't tell you that any more. It's not politically correct to say we were fighting for our country. But we were young and dumb and that is what we thought. And it gave us a helluva lot of pride. We were proud of what we did. I was proud to tell people what I did.'

He paused to light the umpteenth cigarette.

'Today it's not the same. It's like I'm not welcome here, in the police. They don't want me and all my shit. They tell me I'm negative. I still want to help people, and I like being a policeman. But the pride about being in the police is gone. Today, if you tell your neighbours that you're a policeman, they start to wonder about you: are you corrupt? Are you too useless to get another job? And it's the same inside the organisation. Half the time you think that management thinks it would be better if you packed your bags and fucked off. It's like they don't want you around any more, and they'll make you as miserable as they can so that you'll just fucking leave.

'And you know what? If I had somewhere to go, that's exactly what I would do.'

While we'd been talking, the car De Koster was following had been gliding through the slippery streets of Yeoville. The buildings around us, frozen in the act of collapse, loomed above their car like object lessons in what happens when insufficient care is taken to keep things working.

'Where the fuck are you going?' De Koster muttered to himself before picking up his phone and calling one of the men. 'Where the fuck are you going?' he asked. He listened to the response, offered an eloquent grunt of self-congratulation, and hung up abruptly. 'He's taking us to Sithole's sister,' he said.

The car pulled up in front of a shabby building in the heart of the neighbourhood. In front of it, an oak tree had pushed itself through the asphalt pavement which had cracked into treacherously splayed plates. The three detectives got out of the car with the man they'd brought from Berea. 'Let's see what we see,' De Koster said to himself as he uncoiled from his seat into the night air, flicking his smouldering stompie against the low stone wall that surrounded the building. It died in a shower of sparks.

'What number did he say?' he asked one of his colleagues.

'He doesn't know the number, Captain.' He replied. 'He just knows the building.'

'Oh, for fuck's sake,' De Koster grumbled. 'How the fuck does that help us?'

'It's OK, Captain. He knows where the door is. He's been here before.'

Security consciousness among the building's tenants was not what it could have been, and although there was a gate someone had left it unlocked, so it wasn't long before the four cops were standing in front of a door pointed out by the man they'd brought along in a grimy corridor that was filled with kitchen smells. Once again the men took up positions around the door outside the likely fields of fire before one of the detectives knocked. Inside, a television set was blaring, so it was a moment before a response was heard.

'It's the police,' the knocker said. 'Open up, we want to talk to you.' This was the scary moment when those inside knew who was outside, and those outside had no idea who was inside. The men tensed, but soon the sounds of bolts being thrown could be heard. Then locks were turned and a chain clanked. Eventually the door opened to reveal a middle-aged woman with dark freckles across her broad features.

'We're looking for Sithole, John Sithole,' the detective who'd knocked said. 'Is he here?'

The woman looked confused and relieved. 'There's no Sithole here,' she said.

Next to me, De Koster kicked a wall: 'Fuck.'

'Do you know John? Do you know him?' the first detective asked. But the woman shook her head, pressing her lips together as if she had a bitter taste in her mouth.

'Is this the woman? Is this John's sister?' De Koster asked the man from Berea, hauling him into the room to look at her. He just wanted to be sure.

'No,' he replied. 'But it is the flat, boss. I'm definitely sure of that.'

'How long have you stayed here?' De Koster asked the woman.

'Three or four months,' she replied. The flat was a dead-end.

While this was going on, I was reflecting on what De Koster had told me about his disillusionment with policing as a career, and with the Police Service as his employer. His views were an echo of the wailing and teeth-gnashing that I'd encountered amongst detectives – especially white detectives – in 1998 and which I still encountered occasionally now. But his unhappiness had a slightly different flavour. He didn't talk darkly about a campaign waged from the highest levels of the organisation designed to leave South Africa defenceless against criminality, as some of his colleagues had done in 1998. Nor did he deny that apartheid had been cruel and ugly or that promotions policies in the old South African Police had been skewed horribly against black cops. But he was, nevertheless, despondent, and his despondency was more human and more sympathetic for being smaller and more personal. Cut to its core, his unhappiness came from feeling unwelcome and unwanted. It was, perhaps, a little childlike, but it was real and intense, and he was giving voice to an under-appreciated issue in the transformation of the police.

In some ways, policing is just an occupation like any other: people are paid for the work they do and that is that. But for many of the men and women concerned, it is as least as much a calling as it is a trade. That could mean that those who are called to this work would be less troubled by career-related difficulties because money wouldn't be everything to them. But it could also mean that the Police Service becomes more than just an employer. It is a community, a brotherhood, a semi-sacred community of the elect. And, being a community, the transformation of the rules of entry and exit, status and hierarchy that are inherent in the changes through which the organisation has gone, has been more traumatic than it might be if the Police Service was just another employer. In this organisation, more so than any other, these changes have been experienced almost like betrayals of trust, rather than a simple, technical matter of adjusting promotion policies and prospects. Of course the effect on expectations about careers and earnings is an important reason why many white cops of a certain age seem so pissed off. But so too is the soft-tissue damage that has been done and which expressed itself in De Koster's sense of being unwelcome in his community. I doubted whether much could have been done to avoid this problem, but I wondered whether anyone had even begun to think about its long-term effects.

Back on the street, De Koster took the man from Berea aside to give him the usual *shtick* about helping the police: how if he saw Sithole, he must call De Koster; how if he helped the police, he – De Koster – would personally put in a claim for informer fees or a reward; how they would be checking up on him, and if they found Sithole in his house, how he'd be arrested for harbouring a criminal. 'You must help us,' he concluded. 'No-one will know it was you, I promise. It will just be between you and me. So, if you see him or hear about him or anything that will help us, call me.'

The man didn't seem likely to declare his undying love for the police, but it was clear to him that he could go if he made a promise to help, so he did.

'OK,' De Koster said. 'My men will take you home now.'

Getting into the car I asked whether he thought the man would help if he found Sithole. 'We can only hope,' De Koster replied. 'Miracles do sometimes happen.'

CHAPTER ELEVEN

MAKING *MUKHU*:
THE DECLINE AND FALL OF YEOVILLE,
JULY 2003

I would dearly like to write that I grew up in Yeoville, to cast myself as a child of the inner city and to lay claim to the street-cachet that comes of such an upbringing. But, sadly, I had a privileged childhood far from Yeoville's streets and to claim otherwise would not be true. What is true, however, is that it was in Yeoville that I came of age.

I moved to Yeoville when I was a naïve twenty-year-old. My first flat had a spectacular view of the Hillbrow skyline, and I shared it with a friend who'd once been detained in solitary confinement for six months for her activities in the ANC underground. I didn't tell her that our neighbour was a warrant officer in the Riot Squad. He moved out within a couple of months, however, and was replaced by one of the last surviving spliff-toking, acid-dropping, heroin-using, long-haired hippies of the 1960s, a printer named Ty. Over the course of a life I can only barely imagine and which he, no doubt, could only vaguely remember, Ty had fried his brains so thoroughly that every time we bumped into each other on the stairs or in the corridor he'd feel obliged to introduce himself anew. 'Hi,' he'd say in a lilting, sing-song voice that suggested he was only half aware that he was talking to another human being. 'I'm Ty. I'm your neighbour.' I'd take his hand, say that I knew who he was already, and silently lament the fact that our relationship just didn't seem to be going anywhere.

This was the early 1990s, and Yeoville was undergoing a profound transformation. Always one of the greyest of Johannesburg's suburbs, the death of apartheid had seemed an affirmation of the free-wheeling bohemianism of the place. This is where the new South Africa is being born, residents – at least those of my generation – would tell themselves. It is in our streets, cafés and bars, our homes and flats that a new country is being shaped, one whose ethos might overturn the morbid fear and icy cynicism that had preceded it.

Perhaps every twenty-something thinks like this, but the world seemed ripe for remaking, and we all believed that the seeds planted in Yeoville would soon yield the timber needed to do the job.

We knew, of course, that Yeoville wasn't all sunshine and light. There was, for instance, the horror of the Yeoville rapist, a serial brute who terrified women in the area. When an arrest was eventually made, the suspect turned out to be a man I knew vaguely. That upset me. I was made only marginally happier when it turned out that the investigation had been horribly botched and that the arrested man was obviously innocent. His treatment by the community, cops and media left a vile taste in the mouth.

There were other indications of decline too. A popular jazz club closed and was replaced by a 'massage parlour'. It died quickly, but the change seemed to portend changes to the local economy. More visibly, drug-dealing, long a feature of community life, seemed to be becoming more brazen and, when the owner of a popular coffee-shop was murdered by a dealer, more frightening too.

I started noticing other indications that all was not well with the area's ambience. The flat in which I'd lived for four years was sold sectional title – 'What bank will give me a bond?' Ty asked me in a moment of clarity as he packed the litter that cluttered his floors – and my next building was owned and run by a former South African wrestling champion, then in his eighties, who walked around his property with a suped-up battery-powered phone on one hip and an enormous handgun on the other. Unrepentantly, he would tell me how he preferred to keep black people out of the building. But times were a-changing and sometimes he'd allow himself to make an exception, only to find some reason to kick the new tenant out soon after. Then he'd spend weeks bitterly regretting, to anyone who'd stand still long enough to listen, the original decision to lower his standards. When he died, an evaporated, hateful old woman named Joy took over the management of the place and set herself against anyone in the building who was younger, happier or darker-skinned than herself. That covered everyone but her emphysemic sister. Even she would not always be spared what I came to think of as 'the wrath of Joy'.

I still loved Yeoville, but by the late 1990s it was obvious that it had not fulfilled the utopian promise its residents had once seen in it. Now there were whole buildings that had gone bad. Windowless, lightless and peeling, these were home to a growing underclass of really poor people, among them prostitutes and pimps and drug dealers and thieves. One night, a man was beaten to within an inch of his life in my driveway by a gang of brick-wielding robbers. On the streets, the atmosphere had soured to the point that it became possible for a man with the sallow, open-pored skin of the meths drinker to spend his days sitting outside the local laundry making tsk-tsk-here-kitty sounds at the women who used it. I don't think anyone ever confronted him. Certainly, he never moved.

We residents consoled ourselves with jokes that celebrated the decay – how could you tell whether the bang you heard was a car backfiring or a gunshot? It's a car if you hear no return fire – but eventually I moved. After about a decade in the neighbourhood, the tipping point came when a man stopped on the road beneath my window late one night and emptied a full clip of ammunition into the air. I say 'into the air', but I might equally have said 'in my general direction'. Apparently he enjoyed the experience because he quickly reloaded and did it again. Sixteen shots seemed more like a potential massacre than a legitimate way to celebrate a long weekend, and I decided that it was time to get out.

I recount this bit of autobiography here because I offered it to cops at the Yeoville police station at least a dozen times when I visited with them. I wanted their account of the changes that the area had gone through, their explanation for why the bubbling bohemianism of the early 1990s had, by the end of the decade, been replaced by something more desperate, more angry and a good deal more violent. Their response could be summed up in precisely two words: illegal migrants. Some were 50 per cent more efficient even than that, condensing what social scientists and urban planners saw as a complex array of social, economic and political factors into just one word: Zimbabweans.

'In the past this place was all Jews,' one officer told me in my first hour at the station. 'If you came here on a Saturday morning, you could drive the wrong way up a one-way street with your eyes closed and you wouldn't hit anyone. Then, after 1994, the borders opened and the illegals, Zimbabweans especially, started coming in. Most of the Jews ran away, and the buildings were taken over by foreigners and criminals.'

His prognosis for the suburb? 'It's too late for fillings,' he said. 'All the teeth must be removed.'

★

'Why do they come here, all of these people?' Inspector Pule asked me. 'What do they want in our country? What do they want with our people?' He and his partner, the nuggety Sergeant Zintle, had just stopped a run-down car from the darkened interior of which a Coloured man who said he lived in Eldorado Park, a Congolese and a Nigerian were taking in the sights. Nothing suspicious had been found in the car or on their persons, and the two cops had studiously avoided seeing the blue hundred rand notes that poked out of the foreigners' papers. I wondered how circumspect they would have been if I was not present. But that is a story for another place.

As the three men drove off Pule gave me a meaningful look. 'That,' he said of the group, 'that's a match made in hell.'

'Why do *you* think they come to the country?' I asked, responding to Pule's semi-rhetorical question.

His look said don't-play-the-stupid-*umlungu*-with-me. 'They come to steal,' he said simply. 'They come here to steal and we South Africans, we are so soft that we let them come. We make it easy for them. Now we have all of these problems, all this crime.' He leaned forward, thumb hitched under a strap on his body armour, and spat in the street.

'But surely they don't all steal,' I said and then summarised some research work that had been done on the role of migrants in the local economy. 'Some have proper jobs. Others work as hawkers or barbers or builders in the informal sector. They are making a contribution.' I didn't add that their contribution usually didn't extend to paying taxes, so when they used public services, they did so without paying their fair share of the costs. That would have been handing Pule ammunition.

'Maybe some of them are working,' Pule shrugged, emphasising the qualifier. 'But our people are suffering without work. Those are jobs that South Africans should do, so they are stealing those jobs just like they steal everything else.'

Pule's resentful views about foreigners were far from unique among police officers. Everywhere I went, or so it seemed, illegal migrants were deemed the cause of the troubles of whatever area it happened to be. In Ivory Park, it was Mozambicans who clogged up the morgues. In Barberton, it was Mozambicans and Swazis who stole from homes and farms. Maluti had a stock theft problem that lay at the door of the Basutho. While in Sea Point (and pretty much everywhere else), it was the Nigerians who were turning the streets into drug bazaars and the buildings into no-go areas. In Yeoville, my old haunt, it was the Zimbabweans and, to a lesser extent, Nigerians and Congolese, who had turned the once-safe streets into the danger zones they'd become.

★

While never exactly catering to the moneyed classes, in the 1980s and early 1990s, before the property market collapsed and residential buildings throughout Yeoville went bad, bars and clubs and restaurants jostled each other on and around Rockey Street. Middle-aged drunks caught jazz bands in tiny Rumours. Students sipped beer on the roof of the Tandoor or drank dreadful cappuccinos in the comfortable darkness that was Coffee Society. Across the road, rock bands played at Dylans, while, a few doors further down, bikers raised their voices above the din at BaPita to threaten each other with mortal injury. The white-belt-and-stone-washed-jeans crowd hung out at Rockafellas. Afro-optimists passed joints around at the Poli-Poli, ignoring the pleas of long-suffering residents of the apartment block above them to keep it down. During the day there was tea and cake at Crackers in the Bizarre Centre, with its trees and damp brickwork, or the cooler-than-thou Times Square for something harder. The drums of dried fruit and 14 squillion varieties of soya at Fruits and Roots kept hippies from starvation, and the Army Surplus Store (where did all those Nato overcoats come from?) did sterling work keeping the same lot from freezing in the wintertime.

Perhaps Yeoville didn't have the middle-class respectability of a village in middle England, but this was a functioning community with real prospects and, whatever the level of disorder created by the alcohol- and dagga-fuelled nightlife in the 1990s, they were the picture of prim civility compared to the volatility that was to come.

'One of our big problems is a place called The Zone,' Captain Madiyiye told me. 'There's a lot of fighting there. Lots of knives and stabbing. Last June we had nine cases in one week from that place.'

'Why there?' I asked. 'What's special about it?'

'The people who go there. Lots of Coloureds from Cape Town and Durban.'

Madiyiye was a solid, quiet man whose thick glasses made him seem more librarian than cop, an administrator – 'bureaucrat' would be too pejorative a word – who would eat the proverbial elephant that was his job piece by carefully annotated and recorded piece. Stolid, stable and steady, he was precisely the sort of man I hoped would one day lead the Police Service. Poor man! It wasn't his fault that he'd been handed the most inappropriate, least officious-looking workplace in the entire Police Service. His office was the master bedroom of a mansion which once served as the embassy of one of apartheid's faux-independent bantustans. It had somehow wound up in the possession of the police after 1994, and Madiyiye's desk was surrounded by built-in cupboards, painted wood panels and a crescent-shaped bay window that looked out over a large estate that had long gone to seed. Fifteen office chairs were pushed back against the walls creating an empty, plushly carpeted space the size of a squash court in front of Madiyiye's desk. The ambience meant that when one or another of Madiyiye's men interrupted us to get a requisition signed or to have a docket inspected, he would seem like a naughty child compelled by early childhood memories to tread softly and disturb nothing in a space that might have reminded him of his parents' inner sanctum.

'So what do you do about places like The Zone?' I asked.

'It's difficult for us. Sometimes we get places closed because they violate their licences. There was one that was called The Blue Goose, where Crackers used to be. We closed that one, but then the people just go somewhere else. The problem just moves to another place.'

But it wasn't the clubs that gave Madiyiye and his colleagues their biggest headaches. That honour was reserved for the home invasions that plagued the area, sometimes at the rate of two a day.

'It's too easy for them,' Madiyiye told me. 'Usually they know someone who lives in the flat, so they knock on the door, ask to see that person and, when the door is opened, they produce a firearm.'

'Do they hurt people?'

'Sometimes. Usually they just tie people up and cover them with blankets. But sometimes the victims are aggressive. They want to prove a point, to prove that they are men. That is when they get hurt.

'The problem is the way people live,' he continued. 'There are many, many people who live in the flats in these buildings. Many foreigners. You find that people don't even know the names of the people they live with. Then someone moves out and a week later there is a robbery. It is that same person who was living there with you. The same person you were cooking with. The same person who shared the toilet with you. But you don't even know his proper name. There are just too many strangers.'

I'd spent the previous night with three of Madiyiye's men looking for complainants and suspects in cases they were working. They didn't like the night work, but it was much more efficient than looking for people during the day, when they could be sure that the flats they'd visit would be empty. Not that their success rate was much higher at night, for Yeoville's residents relocate more often than weaver birds in the spring, packing up and moving every time they miss their rent or get an opportunity for a cheaper room. But what Madiyiye had said was true: the flats and houses were filled to bursting point.

Even the buildings that had been dusted and mopped were seldom well-maintained. Nor was the lack of upkeep just a matter of whether the structures had electricity, working drains and running water, although many lacked these. It applied also to the details. Cupboards went door-less and doors went knobless. Locks were broken or jammed. Lights were bare. Thickets of electrical wires sprouted from wall sockets. In the bathrooms, tiles were coming off floors, baths were impossibly stained, and seatless toilets gaped stupidly at broken ceilings. In some areas, a row of unbroken windows was as rare as a full set of teeth in a Cape Town prison, and cracked panes were held together with glue and tape and odd scraps of paper.

All the residences were uncomfortable. Some were little better than rented death-traps.

'The magistrates should write down "no fixed abode" when suspects say they live in Yeoville,' one of the detectives had muttered to me after we left the umpteenth flat at which he'd been told that his suspect had moved. 'You'll never find someone at their address in Yeoville. The whole fucking place is like a hotel.'

Madiyiye's men, more so than Madiyiye himself, had talked about Yeoville's crime problem in the uncomplicatedly intolerant terms for which South African police officers are often berated, and they had taken special care to point out to me how many of the people they were looking for were known to be foreign or had foreign names. 'How much work must they make for us before someone closes the border?' one asked at some point. 'Maybe there are problems in Zimbabwe, but those are their problems. They mustn't come here and then make prob-lems for us. I don't go to my neighbour's house and then make trouble.'

★

Pule and Zintle had been driving around Yeoville's crowded streets all morning. 'This is where the Angolans live,' they'd say. Then, a little later: 'Here you find the Congolese' or 'This whole area is Little Harare.' At one point I took them to my old building where, just for the hell of it, they pulled over a car. It turned out to contain two Nigerian men. Both had official papers, having married South Africans. Oddly enough, nei-ther could give the cops a phone number at which his spouse might be reached. Neither remembered even the name of the company at which his beloved spouse toiled away. The officers took the reasonable view that the marriages were probably bogus, that the women concerned had no idea that they'd been married off to men they'd never met. But they drove off rather than pursue a suspicion that could easily consume an entire day.

At lunch time Pule stopped outside a fast-food outlet in Rockey Street. 'You shouldn't eat where you police,' Zintle had said when we'd pulled up to the curb. 'Maybe someone is going to poison you.'

'So why are we eating here?' I asked, conscious that he was making fun of me.

'The food's good,' he shrugged while Pule laughed. 'And we've got an *umlungu* with us today. No-one will dare to touch us.'

Pule was good health personified. His forearms rippled with muscle, his skin gleamed. His eyes shone with a Hollywood-confidence beneath a dome conscientiously shaved and then, apparently, buffed for good measure. He ought to be on a recruitment poster, I thought. If nothing else, thousands of women would apply.

The street scene beyond the cracked glass doors of the store wasn't anywhere nearly as well turned out as was Inspector Pule.

Outdoor traders, staking claims to a fragment of pavement like miners at a gold rush, were hawking DVDs and carrots, blue jeans and live chickens. I wondered whether they were caste-bound to a particular corner and a particular set of wares, or if they were fired by an impatient ambition to find new angles, to diversify their merchandise, to widen their margins and grow their incomes. The urban poor, unemployed and unemployable, were also out and about. Some looked bowed down and beaten. Others seemed brazenly predatory. There were women out shopping, their handbags held tightly against the depredations of the bag-snatchers, and young men in topless BMWs and expensive clothes who shouted greetings to men they knew and women they didn't. Nearby, taxi drivers and their touts yelled for custom. The smells were of rotting garbage and aromatic meat. Beneath those aromas, the occasional whiff of urine and worse bubbled through, hanging in the air like a hint of worse to come. Mercifully, the sharpness was blunted by the chemical smell of the traffic.

The energy generated by all the motion pumped and flowed through the streets. But it would have been a mistake to think the vibrancy a sign of life. It could also be seen as a symptom of disease or as a mania of some kind; it might just as well have been the death agonies of a community that was coming apart.

We were eating our lunch in the car, the doors open to let what breeze there was blow the smell of fried chicken out of the vehicle, when a robbery-in-progress call came through over the radio. Pule, answering the radio, asked for the location and was given a street address about two blocks from the police station. He moved quickly (but not so quickly as to forget to secure his lunch, a feat made possible by the cop-practice of only buying soft drinks in resealable bottles), started the car, put it in gear and sped off. In the passenger seat next to him, Zintle drew and cocked his firearm. 'Hold on,' Pule called to me over his shoulder, as he took a corner in front of on-coming traffic. He hadn't put on the siren – he hoped to surprise the robbers or muggers, or whatever they might be, in the act – and the wild turn across the traffic left motorists with alarmed looks on their faces.

Arriving at the address he'd been given, Pule looked at Zintle and shrugged: the street was quiet. There was no-one around apart from a small group of men sitting and chatting under a tree. This didn't look like the scene of a crime-in-progress. 'Did you call the police?' Zintle, leaning out of his window, asked a heavy-set man with a Lenin beard, dressed in jet-black pants, a matching turtleneck, tan boots and a checked yellow jacket. He looked nonplussed at the suggestion.

For no precisely definable reason, I had the impression that Zintle knew this man, and that his question and body language were intended to convey the subliminal message that he'd prefer, just for the moment, to be treated by this man as just another anonymous officer. 'There's a story here,' I thought to myself sadly. 'One to which I will gain no access.'

'No, sir,' the man replied with a softly lisping foreign accent. 'What would I want with the police?' At this some of his companions smiled. There seemed little reason to think that this tranquil scene had been the site of a robbery in the recent past.

Pule picked up the radio and was about to call in a 'negative' to radio control, when a car squealed to a halt next to us and a frantic-looking man jumped out waving a piece of paper. 'Those men robbed me,' he cried, pointing at the group Zintle had been talking to.

'I robbed you?' the man in black roared back incredulously, his lips curling in scorn. 'What are you talking about?' His friends quickly joined him in his outrage, a furious argument breaking out in a language I didn't recognise.

'I have a case against this man and this man and this man,' the man with the slip of paper said to Pule, gesturing towards the man with tan boots and two others. The document in his hand turned out to be a point-out note, an official police record which is given to complainants. Armed with it, a victim can approach any police officer and request that an arrest be made if he spots the perpetrator. It helps get round the pesky provisions of the Criminal Procedure Act, which provide that cops can't arrest people unless they have some basis other than the word of a potentially malicious passer-by, rules that have a sound basis even in societies less fractured by divisions than our own. Usually, point-out notes are handed out when investigations run dry, cases must be closed, and complainants must be fobbed off. More often than not, detectives expect that that will be the last they hear of the matter. This particular note, unlike some others I'd seen, made that plain enough: it said that unless there was significant progress in the case, the detective would not be in touch with the complainant again because 'it is more important to investigate than to engage in administrative tasks.'

'It looks like a case of robbery has been opened,' Pule said to both Zintle and the men. He seemed saddened by this.

The three suspects were still loudly arguing with their accuser who, in his own defence, was becoming louder and more hysterical by the second. Zintle was trying to get the men to quieten down so that he could make some headway in getting the matter off the streets. Failing with less direct approaches, he eventually punched one of the suspects in the chest and yelled at him to shut up. Then he took the arm of the man with tan boots and Leninist beard and, almost apologetically, told him that he'd have to take the three of them to the station to let the

188

detectives sort the problem out, before pushing them into the vehicle and telling the complainant to follow them in his own vehicle. A charge had been laid, a note had been issued: this was his duty.

We were only in the car for a minute or two, but it was time enough to establish that the two other men deferred to Mr Lenin and that one of the ways they could show their deference was by expressing their outrage at their, and especially his, arrest. 'He doesn't know what he has done, chief,' one of the men said to him. Then, addressing himself to the cops, added: 'I don't know this boy,' he said, referring to the complainant. 'I have never seen him, but he doesn't know what he has done!'

At the station the arrestees and their accuser were reunited in the prefab office which the uniformed crews use. Once again, their combined presence set the complainant off and he started yelling about how he'd been robbed. They in turn protested their innocence and made vaguely threatening noises. 'You don't know what you have done,' the one who had spoken in the car said to him. Then he turned to the cops and said: 'We have lived in this country for nine years. If we were behaving like this man is behaving, then we would all be sleeping under ground.'

Surprisingly, Pule and Zintle didn't react to any of the threatening sounds being made. Instead, they were concentrating on writing out their arrest statements and filling in the forms which record that an arrestee has been read his rights. 'We are going to have to take you to the cells,' Zintle said to the three men. 'There is a case against you. It is out of our hands.'

'But we don't know this boy,' one of them insisted. 'I have never seen him before.' At this the leader of the group interrupted. 'Leave it,' he instructed. 'The sergeant is only doing his work. We will sort this out later.' Then, contradicting the we-don't-know-this-boy claims of his associate, he asked the cops what they would say about a man who first threatens to have someone arrested, then opens a case against that person, and then decides a few weeks later to have him arrested. 'What do you say about that?' But neither Pule nor Zintle was playing this game, and their only response was to have the complainant, still shouting the odds, led out of their office so that they could finish their paperwork in relative silence.

The Yeoville police station has no holding cells of its own, so the three men were handcuffed together, put in the back of the car again, and were then taken to the grey-concrete cells of the Hillbrow police station. They arrived in time for the late-afternoon meal. Bread and gravy was being prepared in the courtyard under the watchful gaze of scores of pigeons. There the men were stripped of their phones and belts and shoelaces. Bizarrely, the leader of the three protested when his belt was wound into a loop with those of his fellows, feeling that this was somehow beneath his dignity. One of his lackeys seemed to agree, and fought a winning fight to have their leader's belt accorded the honour of being placed in the safe with a tag of its own.

After they were taken to the cells and we had left the station, I asked Pule what he thought that had all been about.

'They were making *mukhu*,' he sighed. 'All of them together. And now they are fighting about money.'

'Making *mukhu*?' I asked. 'What is that?'

'The Nigerian scam. You know. Stealing money.'

'So you think it was just a falling out among thieves?'

'You get it a lot,' he replied, and then told me about an incident that had happened when he'd been stationed in Hillbrow. A Nigerian – Pule was careful to insist on his nationality – had complained that two cellphones had been stolen from him by another man, also a Nigerian, who operated a bank of payphones on a street corner and doubled as a buyer and seller of cellphones. A day after the suspect was arrested and the cellphones recovered, however, the complainant withdrew the charges and the arrestee was released. It was clear to Pule that a deal had been struck between them, because the following week he found the complainant now running the payphone business that had belonged to the arrested man. 'The whole thing was a scam,' he concluded. 'That complainant set the man up and then got us to do his dirty work so that he could take over his business.'

'Do you think something similar is happening here?' I asked.

'Of course. Wait. You'll see tomorrow that the charge has been withdrawn. Someone will pay the complainant and he'll come and say that the matter is solved between them.'

'So this is standard procedure?' I asked. 'People use the police to get money out of each other?'

'You must understand something about the Nigerians,' he replied, instructing me as one might a naïve student constable. 'They are only interested in money. When they sleep, they dream about money. When they go to church, they pray about money. Even when they are with their girlfriends, all they are thinking about is money. So you must know that when they come to the police, that is also about money. When they have real problems, they sort them out by themselves and they don't come to the police. They will only come to the police to use us. We are not policemen to them. All we are is a weapon to use against each other.'

'And do they give you other problems? Do they cause a lot of crime?'

'The Nigerians?' Pule snorted. 'Of course they cause crime. That is natural to them. But there is one thing you must know about them: they are not violent. Nigerians are afraid of blood. Not like the Zimbabweans. Those are the violent ones. You must know if you must arrest a Zimbabwean that he will resist. So you must go there with back-up. But the Nigerians are like these three, they don't give you trouble.'

'But maybe that is because they know that the case will be withdrawn later?' I offered, but Pule just smiled the calm, self-satisfied smile of a teacher who was finally getting his point across.

★

Why is it that members of the South African Police Service distrust foreigners so much?

Ask a police officer this question, and I guarantee that after he has closed his mouth and rubbed the incredulity from his eyes, he'll tell you that cops don't like migrants because migrants are involved in crime. Duh!

It is important, at this point, to note that, whatever apologists, lobbyists and knee-jerk activists might have you believe, cops are not inventing the problems that are posed by migrants, and that there are,

191

in fact, a great many migrants who make their way by stealing or by dealing in illicit goods. In this, of course, they are no different from the rest of the urban underclass. It is also true that there are migrants who rob restaurants at gunpoint or con greedy businessmen out of cash, import narcotics or export stolen cars and cellphones. However they go about it, it is clear that more than a few migrants, refugees and 'refugees' survive, and occasionally prosper, through crime.

The crime problem posed by migrant populations, in other words, is not a figment of police imagination. Many really are up to no good.

Nor are all police stereotypes baseless. Take the example of Nigerians and the dominant role they are said to occupy in the supply chains for hard drugs. Here, the only daylight between reality and stereotype appears to be that markets are not dominated by Nigerians in general, but by Igbo-speaking Nigerians, a domination that has been traced back to 1967 and the brutally suppressed attempted secession of the mainly Igbo-speaking Biafran enclave in Nigeria.

Kurt Vonnegut, the American writer, was in Biafra in the final days of its resistance, and wrote that the hatred of Biafrans was natural enough – Biafrans were, after all, better educated, more entrepreneurial and more successful than their fellow countrymen. He described how that hatred found expression in military tactics remarkable for their indiscriminate savagery, and in a starvation-inducing blockade. In all, about a million people, something like a tenth of the Igbo-speaking population, were killed. Not surprisingly, in the 35 years since, this community has seen itself as an oppressed minority. This has been reinforced by the fact that they have felt excluded from the formal economy and the public service. Without prospects at home, thousands of people, many highly educated, left Nigeria to make their way in the global economy as academics, doctors and businessmen, and it wasn't long before the Igbo diaspora had outposts in Bangkok and Brazil. There, some among the community developed the contacts needed to make a substantial living in the narcotics trade. This is a trade in which the essential ingredient for success is having a wide network of trust, an asset the diaspora provided in spades: cultural and kinship networks of this kind bring industrial scale to the notion of a 'crime family', which explains why organised crime often takes the form of more-or-less culturally-discrete gangs. Nigerians had other advantages too. One of these is that Igbo is a difficult language peppered with dialects none of which is, for obvious reasons, much taught in police colleges outside of Nigeria. In a crime policed at its highest reaches largely through surveillance and intelligence-gathering, this is an efficient, low-tech shield against even the most sophisticated of eavesdropping operations.

Having found their niche in the criminal economy, Igbo-speaking drug rings began to lay out a web of contacts extending to street corners in cities in the American north-east, the United Kingdom, Europe and South Africa, fed along a supply chain that, in the case of cocaine, stretched from São Paulo but wound its way through any number of less suspicious destinations. Estimates of the size of the market share claimed by Nigerian smugglers and dealers are notoriously unreliable, so one should not take too seriously the claim made by America's Drug Enforcement Agency that 40 per cent of cocaine sold in America was at some point handled by Nigerian organised crime. It is known with more certainty, however, that some supply routes to the first world either run through Nigeria or are dominated by Nigerian operators, a fact illuminated by an experiment conducted by Dutch authorities in 2001. Aware that Nigerian cocaine smugglers often came through Schiphol Airport from Aruba and the Dutch Antilles, they decided to search every Nigerian passenger arriving from those locations over a two-week period instead of the random handful their profiling software would normally have kicked out. Sixty-three of the 83 people stopped were found to be carrying or to have swallowed cocaine.

What evidence exists about the development of the crack market in South Africa suggests that it too was the creation of Nigerian traders. They had come to this country in the mid-1990s to take advantage of its open borders, high volumes of international trade, and its vulnerable trade infrastructure, in order to transship narcotics from South America and the Far East to Europe. As a sideline, and as a way of exploiting the fact that young Nigerian men apparently wanted to come to South Africa to see streets paved with gold, they sought to grow a local market.

At the time, crack was an exotic drug, used by few addicts and sup-plied by fewer dealers. Some organised crime groups had tried to insin-uate rock cocaine into the market – cops talk of 'Yugoslav', 'Eastern European' and 'Israeli' syndicates. Each wanted to develop a market for crack because it is a retailers' ideal product: the drug is cheap but mar-gins are large; it is very addictive so it is relatively easy to recruit buy-ers; and, unlike other drugs, there is no biological satiation point to stop the user from pumping more and more into his lungs. It is, for this reason, only the very rare user who, once on a binge, is able to resist spending every last cent he can in pursuit of his blast. These psycho-chemical traits mean that returns on crack are enormous, the only challenge being the creation of a more-or-less permanent presence on the street to satisfy addicts' urges. This is a crucial variable for dealers since the same chemical properties that make the drug so profitable necessitate establishing a full-time street presence. Without that, you simply cannot dominate this market. The groups that had previously tried to create a market had failed for this reason, and South Africa's inner-city drug users, hooked primarily on depressants like Wellconnel, had not moved to crack in any great numbers.

The Nigerians solved this problem.

Taking a leaf out of their drug distribution practices in other coun-tries, they targeted street prostitutes in Hillbrow who took to crack like politicians take to freebie study-tours. Many quickly became the mod-ern equivalent of indentured labour, working off their crack-needs and crack-debt to their employers. This they did in part by selling sex. But they also began to deal crack to their clients, their colleagues, their friends. Anyone they could get to buy the stuff.

Soon crack use was spreading like the flu, with users infecting people around them, and, like a disease, the germ of addiction touched ever-greater numbers of people across an ever-wider spectrum of society. This was the first major cross-over drug in the market and soon rich adrenaline junkies, poor oblivion seekers, and dropouts of every stripe were flooding to a drug that could quickly create obsessive addiction.

This led to other crime problems.

A big problem for narcotics slingers the world over is that few of their clientele are upstanding members of society commanding full-time employment. Many are poor, and those who aren't quickly become so. The result is that dealers, if they want to maximise their profit, soon find that they must be willing to take payment in kind. Cellphones are nice. So are cars and computers. Users also want other drugs: depressants to come down with, hallucinogens for quiet Sunday afternoons. These too must be available.

Crack dealing must, in other words, become the basis of a wider criminal economy in which stolen goods and narcotics flow between buyers and sellers. Something like this happened in Johannesburg, and the Nigerian communities in the heart of the city became a hub for all sorts of criminal enterprise, from drug-dealing and pimping to dealing in stolen goods and developing sidelines in corrupting cops, customs agents and immigration officials. And that is leaving aside the extravagant frauds committed against the unwary.

They are, as Kurt Vonnegut himself might have said, busy, busy, busy.

★

That the figure of the illegal migrant – part criminal mastermind, part parasite, part vicious cur – features prominently in police officers' accounts of the causes of crime, often leads activists, Human Rights Commissioners and assorted lobbyists to accuse the police of xenophobia and racism. There is something to this, of course. But, despite its sounding like a psychological illness, a phobia like any other, xenophobia among police officers is not simply a baseless, irrational response to a neutral stimulus. The truth is that some important parts of the criminal economy really are dominated by foreigners, and, even if police officers were more sympathetic to the plight of political refugees and economic migrants, this is something none who work these streets could have failed to notice. For the average policeman, the fact that there are good reasons why ethnically and linguistically homogenous groups might dominate such markets – they're hard for law enforcement to penetrate, they have far-flung networks of trust, they have no bonds with the community affected by their activities and, therefore, nothing but the law to rein them in – is less significant than the brute fact of these groups' dominance. And that, in turn, has created a proto-Darwinian assessment of how different national groups fit into distinct niches in the criminal economy: Mozambicans are burglars; Zimbabweans steal at gunpoint, usually in gangs; ethnic Chinese deal in abalone and grey goods. And Nigerians? They fill all the gaps: running prostitutes, selling drugs, defrauding the unwary, and trading in every kind of stolen goods.

Bad boys, these 'Nigie motherfuckers', as a cop of my acquaintance insists on calling them.

Given all of this, it is hardly surprising that police officers think those who would deny the connection between migrants and criminality are barking mad. But, at the same time, that doesn't mean that the cops' attitudes reflect only the realities on the ground, and there are two important reasons to be suspicious about the strength of their convictions. The first is that blaming outsiders for criminality is always convenient and ought, therefore, to be handled with care. This is particularly so in South Africa.

Consider how the figure of the criminal outsider might have been fruitfully deployed in the parade rooms of police stations in the mid- and late 1990s, when morale was low and the organisation was riven along racial lines. In such circumstances, it might have been possible to heal divisions by devoting resources – emotional and financial, organisational and intellectual – to creating a sense of common purpose and a new camaraderie, to focus inwards and to look to new systems and structures and symbols with which to foster a new ethos and a new organisational loyalty. Such an approach might have worked, and a new fraternal 'us' might have been constructed on the basis of introspection and analysis. On the other hand, that same 'us' could be built in another way too: by focusing on a new 'them'.

In the 1990s, black cops and white cops, men and women with much to divide them, but trying to see themselves as the defenders of the new South Africa, the rainbow nation, would have wanted to find a hook on which to hang a new-found common purpose. There might have been any number of such hooks, but illegal migrants would have

fitted the bill particularly neatly. Today, the sheer handiness of the conviction that migrants are to blame ought to suggest that there is more
to it than that. It is, in other words, the glibness with which blame is
apportioned to foreigners that makes me suspicious. It reminds me of
Freud's definition of an illusion. This, he said, was a belief which, while
not necessarily factually false, is as much an expression of a deep-seated
wish as it is a reflection of empirical reality.

The second reason to doubt the claims about the foreign sources of
South African crime relates to a problem of prejudice-amplification
inherent in the way criminal justice systems work. Take, for example, the
case of African-Americans in the United States, who are massively over-
represented in prisons and parole programmes. Part of the reason for this
is that African-Americans are poorer than their compatriots, and often
come from communities beset by all manner of problems: more unemployment, more family breakdown, more street-level violence and more
drug addiction. They are, therefore, more likely to wind up being involved in crime. But, however much greater the odds that members of
this community are to commit crime than are members of other communities, the fact that police officers are driven by the need to make as
many arrests as possible in order to secure promotions means that they
concentrate their attentions on African-Americans. The result is that the
difference between black criminality and white criminality is made to
seem much greater than it really is. Cops, in the meantime, justify their
concentration on African-American communities by reference to all
the arrests that they make. 'These guys are bad news,' they'll say to one
another, as if in an echo-chamber. 'Just look at how many are behind
bars.'

The same pattern of prejudice-amplification occurs in South Africa.
Here too we have identifiable, geographically defined communities
which, because of their socio-economic profile, are sprinkled with their
fair share of criminals. Felicitously enough, those same areas are filled
with large numbers of people who are criminal in the technical sense
of being in the country illegally and who make a habit of concentrating in relatively small areas. Neighbourhoods such as this are an obvious
place to turn whenever the police wish to 'crack down on crime' and

bump up their arrest rates. The result is that those communities attract a disproportionate amount of police attention and create the same self-fulfilling justification as does the police attention devoted to African-Americans in the United States. 'These guys are bad news,' South Africa's police officers will say to one another. 'Just look at how many of them we arrest.'

There are consequences to these police tactics, consequences that will affect the quality of policework for years to come. A generation of cops is learning their trade by implementing tactics that place a huge premium on the volume of arrests made rather than on their quality. It is fish-in-a-barrel policing in which crime sweeps are used to mop up literally thousands of wretched migrants because, in doing so, a few hundred more dangerous characters are also, almost unwittingly, arrested. This is not wise or fair or precise. It is crude and heavy-handed. It is to use the machinery of law enforcement as a bludgeon rather than a rapier; it is a thousand-bomber raid rather than a surgical strike. Precisely what this will do to policing in the long term is hard to know. It seems unlikely that it will make those involved much smarter.

★

The day after Pule and Zwane had arrested the three Nigerian men, I was standing with them at the gates of the police station. The sun had already set, and the parking area in front of the station was a tight knot of vehicles each blocking the others' paths. A wind was choreographing a frantic dance of leaves and bits of paper. We were chatting about the night to come and whether it would rain or not, when the complainant from the day before walked out of the police station. Pule recognised him first and called him over.

The man was smaller than I'd thought him the day before, but perhaps it was just that he was now no longer hysterical and seemed to occupy less space. His calmness, however, was laced with a hint of sheepish self-satisfaction, and so, when I asked him how things were going with his case and whether he was happy with the way the police were handling it, I half expected him to say that his encounter with the police had restored his faith in the Rule of Law, that he felt a new man. I even wondered vaguely if he'd come to the station to compliment the cops. In spite of what Pule had predicted the day before, therefore, I was a little surprised when he said that he'd withdrawn charges that morning and had merely come to the station to finalise some paperwork in another matter.

Hearing this, Pule laughed, his scorn directed more at me than at the complainant. 'I'm going to arrest you,' he warned light-heartedly. 'What you are doing is defeating the ends of justice. You should be in the cells now.'

'It's not like that,' the man replied, a little plaintively.

'What is it like?' I demanded. 'Yesterday you were so upset and today you withdraw charges. How can that be?'

'Those men stole from me,' the man insisted. 'I came here, to South Africa, with $1 000. I wanted to find some work and I heard that those men could help me. They said I must give them $400 and that they will use it to buy me some phones so that I can make money. So when I went back, that man told me that the money I gave him was fake. He said that he couldn't buy phones with that money. When I said that he must give it back, he said it was gone.'

Preying on their fellow migrants, suddenly the three who had been arrested sounded like participants in a pyramid scheme, feasting off the funds new migrants brought with them. Would this diasporic economy collapse if the borders were closed, I wondered.

'So why did you withdraw charges?' I asked.

'Because last night his brother phoned me and said he will give me my money.'

After he'd left, I asked Pule if he believed the story. 'Never,' he replied. 'Those men were making *mukhu* together. The only thing that happened was that there was a conflict of interest between them. It's always like that. Now they have solved their problem and they will go to start making *mukhu* again.'

CHAPTER TWELVE

A NIGHT ON THE TOWN: INSPECTOR 'FATS' MAKAYE, IVORY PARK

Among South Africa's police officers there are many with the spirit of warriors, men and women who burn with a rage that might be quixotic. It is as unyielding as the flow of horrors they encounter. Not all are like this, however. There are some in the Service whose motivation is less noble. Some are drones, clock-punchers who handle the calls they get and carry the dockets they must, but whose detachment from all the ugliness around them is so complete, it suggests that they are interested only in securing their pensions. They never do more than they have to. Among these, the most expedient are the 'uniform carriers', the officers who actively avoid anything that smells of policework, doing less than is expected and then only when there is no other option, preferring to devote themselves to the cafés and taxis and carpentry businesses that are their sidelines. And even they are not the organisation's worst. That title must go to the law enforcement's entrepreneurs, the minority who wear the uniform for the 'perks'. They serve no-one, working the streets with something close to hatred, looking for opportunities for self-enrichment, shaking down immigrants and prostitutes and habitually pocketing what they find on the people they search.

Not all the shirkers and uniform carriers are corrupt, but they and the entrepreneurs both wear cloaks cut from the cloth of their shared disenchantment. In policing, world-weariness is an occupational hazard. Few of us could spend our days and nights swimming in society's sewers and emerge as fresh as a daisy, and there is good reason why one of the staples of Hollywood is the danger to the health and integrity of a man's soul that is posed by a career in uniform. Perhaps the most embittered officer I met was Inspector Solomon Makaye, a man whose conviction that the world conspires against him was so profound and unequivocal, it resembled a religious faith.

★

Inspector Makaye, an abundant man of pure physicality, frightened me when he first walked into the room.

I was sitting with a group of detectives at a late-afternoon roll-call for officers preparing for an all-night operation, inelegantly described to me by the unit's commander as 'an operation where the police do an operation'. In fact, it was simply a concentrated burst of activity by the station's detectives who, in the course of a night, would try to advance as many cases as possible. The fifty-odd dockets that had reached a point at which arrests could be made or warrants could be served were tossed into three piles on a childlike one-for-me-one-for-you basis, and three groups – the number defined by the number of vehicles available – were formed.

Makaye was the oldest man in the unit and, perhaps a privilege of age, he was also the last to arrive. He was strongly built, with a powerful chest, short arms and immense thighs that stretched his silvery pants to the point of rupture. His face was acne-scarred and cruel, and his eyes were small. Unexpectedly playful, they danced with the mischief-making glow of the bully. In spite of all the competition, however, the first thing I noticed about him were his exceedingly thick fingers. Something about them suggested violence.

The unit's commander, a small, studious man with thick glasses, was telling his men that he wanted them to make ten or twelve arrests that night, but he warned them that he didn't want to receive any complaints from suspects in the morning. 'I don't want to hear about the *unnecessary* use of force,' he said, laying on a set of spoken italics. 'You can fight fire with fire,' he went on, pausing to look pointedly at me. 'But only if you have to.' He paused again. 'Does everyone have his ID?' he asked. 'I don't want claims against the police for damages to doors.'

In the brief silence that followed, his baritone raised in self-mocking complaint, Makaye asked: 'Why is everyone looking at *me*?'

The unit commander asked me to work with Makaye and two younger detectives. Makaye, the senior man in his team, picked up the pile of dockets assigned to them, and led us to the cars. The fifteen cases represented a full night's work. Each required either the making of an arrest or the taking of a statement and, assuming that the people sought were found, there was every chance the men would be on the streets until dawn. The prospect made Makaye, known unimaginatively to his colleagues as 'Fats', hungry, and he asked the other two detectives to wait while he went to buy some food.

While he was away, his two colleagues stood in the parking lot and pumped themselves full of nicotine and I wrote banal notes about the tension in the policemen's shoulders and the sinister hint of a change in the weather that was in the air. A chain-link fence separated the parking lot from the bubbling street scene that throbbed with battered taxis polished to a shimmering glow, and equally battered, if somewhat less polished, pedestrians. Across the street, houses and rude shacks hunched next to each other in the dying light. A dense fog of smoke was rising as fires were lit across the township, and the breeze carried the acrid smell of the flames.

Fats was gone about twenty minutes. When he returned, he bore with him rather more than anyone had expected. He'd made two arrests already, and arrived with one man in handcuffs and another gripped tightly by the belt. 'Look at this,' he said, holding out a fifty-rand note. 'Look at the change they gave me.'

The note was dye-stained, suggesting that it had come from a cash-in-transit heist. Stained as it was, it was no longer legal tender, and passing it off was a crime. More exciting for Fats, however, was the possibility that the men might know something about where the note had come from. They were street traders, and since the members of heist gangs seldom fry meat to pay the bills, they were probably not involved in the heist itself. But perhaps, he reasoned, they would remember, or could be made to remember, who had handed the note to them.

This was a genuine clue and, in a crime that was often impossible to solve unless informers could be found, such things were usually thin on the ground. It made for a propitious start to the evening.

202

What followed, however, was shambolic.

Makaye went off to phone headquarters for instructions about the handing on of the arrested men to a specialised unit, leaving them with some of the station's uniformed officers. Trying to get a jump on their colleagues, the officers began to question the men in the parking lot. The questioning was intimidating, verging on violent. But the men – who may very well have had nothing useful to tell – were giving nothing away, denying all knowledge of the note, the dye stain and the law they had violated. Theirs was a defence based on mute ignorance.

After ten fruitless minutes, the officers gave up and walked away.

Makaye too had had no joy in trying to locate someone from the Serious Violent Crimes Unit. When he returned he was muttering about his having to work all night but there being no-one at headquarters to take his call. His muttering soon turned to yelling: the two men he'd arrested had been left unattended and were gone. Unguarded, they must have simply walked off into the gathering gloom.

No-one had seen them go and no-one would now meet Makaye's eye.

All were relieved, however, that the arrests had not yet been entered into any of the station's registers and that there would, therefore, be no need to explain the escapes.

★

One of the first things Makaye said to me as we started the dreary, frustrating business of looking for witnesses and suspects, none of whom appeared anxious to be found, was that my project was an utter waste of my time and his. 'You can never understand the police,' he told me. 'No outsider can understand us.'

'It's not easy,' I agreed. 'But most people love to talk about their work. Surely if I ask enough questions, if I listen well to the answers, I can get an idea of what the Service is all about?'

Makaye was unshakeable. 'You can never do it. It's impossible. You will never understand the organisation because you will never understand the suffering of the ordinary policeman. He is a small man. He has a small salary. But he has a whole world of problems. I myself have nearly thirty years of service. Thirty years! And they pay me R8 000 a month. We are suffering, and suffering men are angry men. You will never understand that unless you are one of us.'

We were in a road outside a local tavern, early evening drinkers trickling past us into a concrete room brightened only by the odd poster advertising a local beer. The cops had come there to find one of the owner's sons, a witness to a pistol-whipping some weeks earlier. The other two detectives were taking his statement while Makaye and I were standing on the pavement. I was dressed in my 'uniform': jeans and a t-shirt, my chest wrapped in a bullet-proof vest, with the legend 'POLICE' emblazoned in reflective yellow on the front. It was understandable, therefore, when one of the local booze-hounds assumed that I was a member of the Service. He was anxiously, but unsteadily, trying to draw me into conversation, to thank me for the fight against crime and for my efforts in making the perpetual binge that was his life a little safer. I was trying to ignore him, rudely refusing to shake his hand because I thought that Fats would take this gesture as a sign of irredeemable weakness. Eventually Makaye, who was in plain clothes and was therefore not getting any recognition for *his* efforts in the fight against crime, had had enough of this.

'You're interrupting,' he said to the man. 'Can't you see we're talking?'

The man stared at him blankly for a moment before turning back to me with a wounded look. He didn't go away, however.

'You should apologise,' Makaye continued. The man gave this request some consideration. It seemed to meet whatever specifications he set for it, and, after no more than two dozen heartbeats during which Makaye and I watched the gears turn behind his eyes, offered his apology: 'I'm sorry.'

'But why are you apologising? What are you sorry for?' Makaye demanded, sending the man into utter confusion.

'For interrupting?' the man offered, timidly turning his answer into a question.

'If you were really sorry,' Fats told him with the air of one solving a Socratic riddle, 'you'd have left us already.'

Having disposed of the annoying man, Makaye returned to his earlier theme. 'I don't mind that you are trying to understand us. It's good
that you are with the police. But no-one can understand us. No-one
can know us like we know ourselves. The small policeman will not be
honest with you. He won't tell you all his problems.'

What he said was indisputable, and I had seen plenty of evidence of
the difficulties he was describing. But then, I had never been naïve
enough to think that I'd get anything approaching the unvarnished
truth from men and women I seldom knew for more than a few days
and who worked for one of the most defensive institutions in the country. Nevertheless, his was a counsel of despair and I was far too arrogant
to accept it in its entirety. So I asked him to tell me about his own story.

'I've been a policeman my whole life,' he told me with practised
anger. 'Nearly thirty years of this shit. And still I am only an Inspector.
In my career I have been at six stations, the special branch, the fraud
unit, the murder and robbery unit, and anti-hijacking.' He counted
them off against his chorizo-fingers and then continued: 'I have been all
over the place. But when it comes time to fill senior posts, it's always the
same. They always overlook me.'

'Why is that?' I asked.

'The old excuse was the exams. You had to write exams to get a promotion. But it was a trick to hold the black policeman back. It didn't
matter how hard we worked or how good we were as policemen. All
that mattered was that fucking exam. You'll find that they were failing
us because we were black. None of us could pass. We weren't supposed
to. They kept us back.'

'Deliberately?'

'"Deliberately?"' He mimicked my question with unconcealed irritation. 'Of course "deliberately". For them, to fail a black man was a
matter of must. How could they allow a black man to pass and to get
his promotion? Then he would be senior to the young whites. That was
one thing that they couldn't stand.

'But their own people they treated like gold. George Fivaz, he became the National Commissioner of the whole police. But he had a
standard six. A standard six! And he became a general. Why?'

205

He paused, expecting me to fill in the blanks. I didn't.

'I'll tell you why. Because they don't know a fucking thing about policing.'

By now the other two detectives had taken the statement from the witness and it was time to move on to the next address, this time to look for a suspect accused of beating up his girlfriend. On the way, we roared through a labyrinth of alleys cutting through the shacks and shanties that were all about. At times, the road we were on was so narrow we seemed to be driving on the spot where a welcome mat might have sat if the shacks' owners had had a mind to set one out. Just before we arrived at the address, a dog stopped to squeeze a reluctant turd out of his malnourished body, blocking our path. Makaye's driver hooted at the creature. But, unwilling to leave his task half-done, the dog looked at us over his shoulder, concentration furrowing his shallow brow: pressing police business be damned.

In the car, I sat next to Makaye, in constant fear that his thighs, straining against the close confinement of his pants, would burst through the thinning fabric. The radio was tuned in to one of the local stations, and the song they were playing irritated Makaye. 'It's a song about President Mugabe,' he told me, when I asked him to translate the lyrics. 'It says that he has no heart, that he has sold his heart. Imagine what we would be saying if the Zimbabweans played a song like that about Mbeki on their radios.'

Moments later, Makaye's cellphone rang. He answered it in a voice with a much higher pitch than his own, imitating the sibilance of a Zimbabwean accent. 'Mugabe speaking. What farm do you want?'

The girlfriend-beater wasn't at the address the cops had been given. Neither was the girlfriend. It had taken nearly an hour to find the house because, more often than not, in Ivory Park, streets are unnamed and houses unnumbered. Add the lack of street lights, and you present the police with one of the greatest navigational challenges since Magellan. It was not surprising, then, that when the man who opened the door said the couple had moved away but he had no idea where they'd gone, the cops' annoyance bubbled over. 'You see what it's like,' Makaye said. 'The complainant moves. She will never think to tell the policeman that she is going. The only time you will hear from them again is when they complain to the station commissioner that you are not working on their case.'

After that the detectives looked for a man who had allegedly beaten his wife's sister because he thought she had bewitched him. When the cops read that he'd kicked her pregnant belly, they were angered enough to make a special effort to find him. It turned out that she wasn't in, but his wife assured the officers that all was now forgiven, and that her sister was planning to withdraw the charge. 'If she does that,' Makaye warned her angrily, 'I will personally come to arrest her for perjury. Tell her that she mustn't waste our time.'

Makaye's threat was almost certainly empty: withdrawals, particularly when suspects and complainants are related to each other, are enormously common. Hundreds of thousands of cases are opened and then withdrawn every year, a practice that breeds cynicism among the police, and raises the blood pressure of researchers and activists keen to see more punitive steps taken in cases of domestic violence.

Later that night, when we went back to the police station with some pap and chicken, I asked Makaye whether things had improved for police officers in the last few years. Once again he told his apocryphal tale about George Fivaz, who, in reality, has a degree in public administration. Then he said: 'When they came into power, we thought that the new government would do something for the poor black police officer with all his years of service. But we forgot something: we forgot that those politicians were harassed by the same police who now wanted their help. So instead of helping us, now they are taking revenge by harassing us.'

'What should government have done differently?' I asked. 'What would you have Minister Nqakula do now?'

'Nqakula? Who is he?' Makaye responded, disbelief at my naivety making him raise his voice. 'Shouldn't a man who owns a large herd at least go out to see the cows sometimes? But he is nowhere. He knows nothing. What does he know about the police officer and law enforcement? No-one must come into my house and tell me how to run my family.'

While he was talking, Makaye was rolling angry balls of pap in his fat fingers and thrusting them into the juices spreading out beneath the carcass. His speech was accompanied by an oily mist of maize meal and chicken fat. The other two detectives were working the phones. It was well after midnight, but between the three of them they had worked through about ten of the dockets and were yet to make an arrest. Apart from the man at the tavern, they had found only the woman whose sister was going to withdraw the case she'd opened. They were frustrated by the hours wasted driving about, and were now calling ahead to see if people were in. While they were busy at their folders, dog-eared from handling that was not exactly tender, I asked Makaye about the previous Minister for Safety and Security, 'Didn't Steve Tshwete spend a lot of time with his "herd"?'

'Who was this Tshwete? Did he really come out and see what was going on? Did *he* know anything about policing? Those fucking people have no fucking idea. They were in exile for years. Ever since they were little boys. Then they came back here and are driven around in big cars with lots of bodyguards. They don't go back to where they came from. They don't see how people live. They are here only for leisure.'

He paused as if struck by a new thought, but I suspected that this was a speech he'd given before, one with lines he expected to draw laughs but which weren't so much funny as just resentful. 'I don't understand this democracy,' he said, sneering at the word as if it bit him. 'People have all these rights ... But if you have the right to shit in your own toilet and to make love to your wife, what more do you need? They have all these rights, but they have no respect. That's the thing. They have no respect for anyone or anything. Without respect, all the other rights are crap. You can wipe your arse with them.

'Now these people with all these rights, some of them are like animals. They kill you for nothing. For less than nothing. Then we catch them and they go to jail. In jail they get three meals a day. They go to expensive hospitals when they are sick. They get a roof over their head. It means that they aren't afraid to go to prison. If prison was hard, if they were made to suffer, then they would be afraid to commit their crimes. But instead of making them suffer, this government treats them like its children. It protects them and makes them so comfortable. That's bull-shit: if they are going to respect the law, then they must learn to fear it. But no-one fears the police in South Africa because we have no power any more. The criminals get everything, but government has treated us, the police, with no respect. How can they tell the world that we are corrupt? We, the ones that the people must turn to for protection. And yet they tell the world that we are dogs!'

'So are they wrong?' I asked. 'Are there no corrupt police officers?'

'What do you mean by "corrupt"?' he demanded.

'What about officers who accept money not to do their work? Officers who take money and turn a blind eye, who don't make arrests or don't do the investigation, who sell the dockets or let people escape?'

Makaye was affronted. 'That would never happen around me. And if it does happen, the commander must be a very stupid man. But it never happens around me. People are afraid of me.'

'Why? Do you have a reputation?'

'No. It's that I'm negative. So I have no friends.'

★

Makaye was an extreme example of the embittered, ageing, black police officer. These were men for whom democracy came too late. Their careers, stunted by the racist recruitment and promotion policies of the past, were coming to an end, but they were still doing the grunt work on the organisation's frontlines: going to crime scenes, attending complaints, serving warrants. Despite the years of service, they had never been entrusted with a command; they were never promoted to a rank which they felt accorded with their age and experience. Neglected by the old police force, they felt forgotten by the new. These men had gone through some really rough times in the 1980s when communities targeted the police, whom they regarded as sell-outs and traitors. Now, with a crime wave on their hands and the same communities baying for more policing, many seemed to think that their life choices had been vindicated by history, and few seemed even to comprehend my question when I asked them whether they had regrets about participating in apartheid's police force. It was just a job, they said in the face of my doubts: they were only serving their communities. They just couldn't understand why they got so little reward for having sacrificed so much.

Late that night, just before the shift knocked off, Makaye turned to me and spoke in quieter, calmer tones. 'It's not that I am a hard man,' he said.

'I know,' I said. 'It's that you don't think very much of me.'

'No. It's not that. Like I said before, I don't think strangers should go into a man's house to tell him how to run his family. But, if you want to talk to us, then you are welcome. The thing is that we are very negative because of the way we are treated. That is why you do get some young policemen who are doing wrong things, committing crimes and other rubbish. But I don't say they are "corrupt", because if you say that then you are blaming them. To say they are corrupt means that there is something wrong with them. I think many, many people would also commit crimes if they were as negative.'

'But is it an excuse? A man has a job and a responsibility, but because he is angry with the police, because he is negative, he can commit a crime? Is that right?'

'No. It is not right. But you can't expect angels if you treat people like dogs. You mustn't only blame them. Other people must also take the blame.'

With that, Makaye left. I tried over the next few days to make an appointment to see him again. But he never returned my calls. After he left, however, I turned to one of the other detectives I was with. He was a young man, a constable recruited in 1999, who was also studying for a law degree. I asked him whether he agreed with the things Makaye had been telling me, whether he was taken in by Makaye's bitterness and cynicism.

'Not at all,' he said. 'You must understand the difference between Fats and me. He was recruited into a police *force*. I applied to join a police *service*. I won't be here forever, but in this job, you must make sure you enjoy the work. And to enjoy it, you must love it. You can't do these things just to survive.'

CHAPTER THIRTEEN

EATING THE CORPSES:
INSPECTOR TEBOGO MORAKE,
THOKOZA

Thokoza is a small, knife-shaped township on the south-eastern edge of greater Johannesburg, an area that is home to some of the city's heaviest industries, many working round the clock single-mindedly pursuing the goal of turning the air into a noxious soup. In this, their results are spectacular and, when the wind is too light or comes from the wrong direction, eyes run and sinuses burn. Upwards of a half-a-million people living in Thokoza, Khatlehong and Vosloorus breathe this air all day, every day.

It is, as they say, better than the alternative.

Thokoza's claim to fame is Khumalo Street, a couple of kilometres of spear-straight tar which, in the first half of the 1990s, was one of South Africa's most fecund killing fields. Hundreds of people died on and around this road. For long periods, drivers couldn't use it for fear of snipers firing from the windows of the Inkatha-dominated men's hostels that blight one side of the road. On the other side of the road, parts of the location became a veritable ghost town. No-one but fighters aligned to the African National Congress (ANC) was prepared to sleep there for fear of the massed *izimpi*, armed with spears and sticks and iron bars, that would periodically emerge to wreak havoc.

The war took much of the country by surprise. Described with Pilate-like disingenuousness and a staggeringly unhelpful literalism in contemporary government statements as 'black-on-black violence', the East Rand War, erupting barely half a year into the process of negotiating a transition from apartheid, sent a wave of blood washing through the streets.

211

All the explanations for the dramatic upsurge in violence within the black community are at least partly unsatisfactory. Some are racist and contemptible. Others, by focusing too greatly on the presumed political calculations of one or other of the contending factions, assume a rationality and guiding intelligence – be it of the ANC or the Inkatha Freedom Party (IFP) or the 'third force' – that stretches credulity too far and obscures the questions of how and why ordinary people got swept up by mass hysteria and bloodlust. Perhaps violence on this scale, of this nature, is always inexplicable; to our credit, such violence defies human reason, and attempts to explain it founder when confronted by those elements that are altogether psychotic.

There are, however, some things about the violence that we do know and can explain. We know that there were historical tensions between the ANC and IFP. We know that the Security Branch in the police systematically stoked those tensions in the early 1990s. We know that they also assisted the IFP, providing weapons and training, and forewarning hostel-dwellers of police raids so that those weapons could be hidden. We know that the ANC encouraged its members to form self-defence units, and provided them with some of their weaponry. We know that many SDUs were little more than ragtag gangs with the most threadbare discipline. And we know that, however the violence began, an ever-accelerating cycle of vengeance took hold and that for long stretches of time all reason was lost: the targeting of victims became ferociously indiscriminate as the long-delayed revolution noisily began to consume its children.

At the heart of this mayhem were the South African Police. Some, it is clear, actively participated in the fighting. Many others, probably the majority, the members of less overtly politicised branches of the police, played a role that would be hard to characterise as openly partial: all they did was pick up bodies.

Perhaps that was why Inspector Tebogo Morake, a detective at the Thokoza police station then and now, told me that the township is quiet these days. 'There are only one or two murders a week now,' he explained, without apparent irony.

It was spring, and Morake and I were coming back from a Monday morning murder. We had just passed the mortuary van on its way to collect the corpse. 'I'm not going to go back with the van,' he said, his long, bloodhound face looking wearier than usual. 'It's very traumatising.'

'Does a scene like that stay with you?' I asked.

'Yes,' he replied, staring into the morning street scene. 'But not like it used to. In the time of the violence I would sometimes pick up six bodies in a day. Most were shot and weren't so bad. But some were hacked and burned. Sometimes the bodies were old and rotting. Eaten by dogs.

'I couldn't eat meat for six months. I could swallow nothing but milk and vegetables. I kept thinking that I was eating those corpses.'

★

The crime scene we were returning from had been harrowing.

The woman who had first reported it had told Morake that there was a body in a room rented by her son, Andile. She'd been called to the house because an almighty quarrel had taken place the night before. The owner of the house and his neighbours didn't know the victim, but, since they couldn't locate Andile, their tenant, they had called his mother. At first she'd been afraid to enter the room. She didn't know who or what she would find. When she braved her way in eventually, she recognised the deceased as Busi, a friend of Andile's. Inspector Morake assumed that Andile must have been the killer, but the woman insisted that Andile and his girlfriend were not in Thokoza that weekend. They'd left the room in the care of another man and had gone to visit with family in Tembisa. She was terrified that the police would blame her son. But it wasn't Andile who had done the deed, she insisted, it was the man in whose care the room had been left.

'What is the man's name?' Morake asked.

The woman thought for a moment before replying. Perhaps she was contemplating whether to tell the police at all. But having already walked all the way to the station, and seeking to deflect suspicion from her son, this was a decision that she had already made, even if it still left the faint taste of betrayal in her mouth. Eventually, speaking softly, as one who knows she is venturing into a strange and dangerous land, she gave the name: Sello Radebe.

Morake smiled. He recognised this as the name of one of the township's more troublesome customers, a man previously convicted of housebreaking and robbery, a man who had only recently been released from prison. The result was that even before he left to attend the scene, Morake had a picture of the man's gaunt, vicious face copied from the album of the area's known criminals and had pasted it to a wall in the reception area with the hand-written legend, 'Sought in connection with murder.'

The house in which the murder had been committed was a dark, dull grey with even darker, duller trimmings. Morbid though it looked, it had about it a prosperous air, an impression created by the four solidly constructed rental rooms built off the main house. These additional rooms had created an odd structure almost bursting out of the plot. There was little space that was still unroofed; just a parking place and a narrow path to the back of the house.

A billboard, unrealistically proclaiming that the Pepsi generation says no to drugs, hung on the front gate. I couldn't help noticing that members of that generation were blasting kwaito sounds from a neighbour's house. In the charnel atmosphere of the murder scene, the booming bass was tasteless and tactless.

Evidence of the nature of the assault that had killed Busi came in the form of shattered glass and bloodstains. It was scattered along the walkway around the building. It was clear that she had been beaten to death with beer bottles. Bloodstains on the seats, on the ground and on shards of glass suggested that the assault started behind the building where some old car seats in faux-leather were grouped together under an overhanging tree. After the initial attack, the killer must have pulled his victim down the path and through the door of one of the rented rooms. The dust looked as if something soft and heavy had been dragged through it, and there was more broken glass and blood. At about knee height, the walls on either side were stained by a gruesome constellation of blood spots the size of tennis balls. Either Busi had had blood on her hands and had tried to brace herself against the wall, or the killer had paused every now and then to slam her head into the bricks.

Compared to the fury of the tiny backyard and path, the room in which Busi's body had been found was eerily composed. It was a neat arrangement of bed, stove, television and sickly purple pot plants squeezed into a tiny space. On the bed, looking to be in a deep sleep, was a woman in her twenties. She'd been laid out, her arms crossed over her chest. A blanket covered her legs. Her face was bruised and swollen, and there were a great number of other wounds. To my untrained eye, they all seemed minor, little more than bruises, scratches and gravel-burns.

A Bible lay open next to her head. Five verses from Psalm 51 were circled individually in ballpoint by a hand that had hesitated initially, but, perhaps on rereading the message, had retraced its path with more confidence. The verses spoke of sin and redemption: 'Have mercy on me, O God, according to thy steadfast love; according to thy abundant mercy blot out my transgressions. Wash me thoroughly of my iniquity, and cleanse me of my sin! ... Create in me a clean heart, O God, and put a new and right spirit within me. Cast me not away from thy presence, and take not thy holy spirit from me. Restore to me the joy of thy salvation, and uphold me with a willing spirit.' I imagined a tearful murderer, belatedly distraught at his own brutality, fearful of the implications for himself in this world and the next, sitting next to Busi's body wishing that the past could be undone.

The police photographer arrived shortly after Morake and me. He had already taken a few pictures to establish the scene when he asked Morake to pull down the blanket so that he could take some pictures of any wounds it concealed. Then he wanted the body turned over. Morake got onto the bed, and, straddling her, he started to lift the body. It was only then that I fully grasped just how dead she was. Rigor mortis had set in, and her folded arms shuddered unnaturally as Morake lifted and turned the body. No living being would be that stiff, so dead a weight. Without the spark of life, she'd become nothing more than an unwieldy slab of meat, as awkward and uncooperative as a rolled-up carpet.

When her body had been raised from the bed, more wounds became visible on her arms, legs and torso. Her panties were bunched up beneath badly scratched buttocks, further evidence that she'd been pulled along the ground by her arms. There was surprisingly little blood on her. It was as if, having battered her to death, her killer had taken the time to wash her wounds just as he prayed that the Lord would wash him of his sins.

Even with her back exposed, none of the wounds she'd suffered looked fatal, so I asked Morake what he thought had killed her. 'It was a grievous assault,' he said, not quite answering my question and using a strangely archaic, strangely appropriate expression. 'A grievous, grievous assault.'

That it was, and it must have taken place over an extended period of time. Indeed, Morake later learned from a neighbour that the fight could be heard for hours, and that even before the fight Sello had been getting increasingly angry because Busi, his girlfriend, was not around. He learned that Sello had been drinking heavily most of the day, and when Busi eventually turned up early in the evening he exploded at her.

It began as a drunken shouting match like any other, but it must have gotten steadily worse: in the end, Busi died from the accumulation of over two dozen individual wounds.

I kept thinking that all the time she was being attacked – with a series of beer bottles which would have been close to hand – she must have been screaming. She would not have gone softly. Her screams would have been shrill and incoherent, but they would have communicated nothing but terror. No-one who heard them could have mistaken them for anything but mortal fear. Yet no-one had come to her aid.

No-one had come into the house to separate Sello and Busi physically. No-one had come up the driveway and told Sello to stop beating the victim. No-one had poked a head around a corner or coughed loudly to let him know that he'd been seen. No-one had so much as lifted a phone to call the police. No-one, it seemed, had consciously acknowledged the tragedy. Her neighbours must have sat, shamefaced, not meeting one another's eyes while Busi's life was ending. They had chosen ignorance, denying to themselves the horror happening next door.

And make no mistake, there would have been people close to the action. A township's stands are not large, and houses are little more than arms-length from each other. Not only are they close to each other, but homes are jam-packed with residents. Families, extended families, tenants, visitors. It simply isn't conceivable that all of the neighbouring houses were empty that Sunday night.

I have always had doubts about the plausibility of the case that is usually made for allowing the public to own firearms for self-defence: since criminals choose the time and place of attack, their targets, I reasoned, must have little chance of fighting back. Here, I couldn't help thinking that if an armed neighbour had intervened in this most serious of something-that-ought-not-to-be-happening-and-about-which-something-ought-to-be-done-now situations, Busi would be alive. But guns are reasonably common in the area, and, besides, they probably wouldn't have been needed to end the attack. Perhaps all that would have been needed was for someone, anyone, to have shown some interest. And yet no-one lifted a finger for Busi.

What despair must she have felt at the world's indifference?

'Why would no-one have come to her assistance?' I asked Morake.

'People are frightened to get involved,' he replied in a voice that evinced no astonishment. 'When people are drunk and violent, you only get involved if it is a loved one. It's not safe to do it, so people don't.' His views were echoed by a priest I met in Ivory Park: 'When you hear shouting in the street after dark, you don't go out. You want to help – of course you do – but you think about what you will achieve and what you will risk. In the end, you do nothing. You can't negotiate with Charles Glass.'

Even so, there is something altogether horrific about the idea that everyone who heard Busi's last shouts must have quickly returned to what they were doing after she was at last silenced. Were they relieved that it was over? That their consciences would no longer be pricked by the need to intervene? Had they been irritated by her pleas, deciding right from the start that they could not be bothered to waste time over something as banal as a murder?

★

The Thokoza police station stands today where it stood when the *izimpi* marched in the 1990s. It is a depressing sight, a run-down structure squatting next to Khumalo Street, a few hundred metres from the hostels that still dominate that side of the road. Much of the township, wrecked a decade ago, has now been rebuilt, and houses have been raised in what was once the unbroken shack-land of Phola Park. But the wave of reconstructive energy somehow missed the police station. It is dingy and dark, its structures scarred by the thousands of people who troop through it every year, its atmosphere poisoned by the desperation and misery that brought them to the station in the first place.

The violence that tore the township apart during the East Rand War was stupefying.

Pictures taken at the time tell stories of impossible brutality. There is one taken by Joao Silva in Khumalo Street in December 1990. It is of seven women. They are dressed conservatively in aprons and head-scarves. One has a blanket wrapped around her waist. From beneath the skirts they wear, petticoats appear. They are not young women – one may be in her twenties but the others are in their thirties and forties and have the busts and hips to show it. But age, it seems, has not mellowed them, and the camera catches them using heavy wooden clubs to pound the body of another woman, lying prone, helpless and apparently dead at their feet. One, the oldest and largest in the group, the proud possessor of a baseball bat, is in the middle of her follow-through. The blow had been aimed at the victim's head, and she has been pulled off balance by the force of her swing. Another two have their sticks high above their heads. They too are about to let rip. Disconcertingly, magnifying the horror, in the foreground of the picture a man in a white t-shirt and neatly pressed office-wear trousers ambles across the road, beaming a winning smile of greeting: 'Oh! what a beautiful morning.'

There is another picture which I remember sent chills down my spine when I first saw it on the front page of *The Star* in August 1990. It is a wide shot of an *impi* moving down Khumalo Street from one of the hostels. There must be a couple of hundred men marching in tight formation. Sprouting above their heads like wild flowers in the spring are clubs and sharpened steel rods, pangas and axes. You can all but hear the chanting of war cries and feel their adrenaline-pumping menace. The road they are walking on is wet, and seems muddy and grim. The sense of threat is reinforced by two figures caught in silhouette – a young girl holding the hand of her baby sister – sprinting across the road between the photographer and the advancing host. Their presence emphasises how empty the rest of the street is. It is an emptiness that speaks of a world frozen in terror.

Violence on this scale is impossible for police forces to contain. But it is studied self-delusion to believe, as many cops maintain that they do, that the security forces were applying the law impartially while the people on the East Rand were going at one another's throats. There is simply too much evidence against this. Testimony at the Truth and Reconciliation Commission, evidence led at criminal trials and eyewitness statements by journalists, priests and victims are too abundant to resist the conclusion that security forces sometimes failed to intervene impartially, and often actively encouraged, even sponsored, the violence. At the same time, it is just as mistaken to think that all police officers were equally up to their necks in these conspiracies. The organisation simply didn't work like that. What conspiracies existed would have been hatched among networks of trusted agents behind opaque organisational walls; most police officers would have known little about their mechanics. Some, trying to do their jobs in impossible circumstances, would have been obstacles around which conspirators would have had to work, avoiding or diverting their attention. In a few cases, police officers were murdered by their own colleagues in order to protect these plots.

The cops most likely to be out of the conspirators' loop were those at police stations. The overtly political dirty work was done elsewhere in the organisation. Certainly, there would have been a few trusted individuals who would work with the heavies from the security police and the military willingly, and there would also have been a larger number who might have helped one side or the other out of misplaced loyalty to a particular faction or political party. But, for the most part, station-level cops wouldn't have been directly involved. As far as they were concerned, they were non-combatants and their job was to do their best to prevent and investigate the crimes committed.

In reality, this was usually impossible: when blood is flowing in the gutters, when communities are utterly polarised, suspicious of outsiders and angry at the police, when armed men are marauding through the streets, ordinary policing, like everything else, breaks down. How do you conduct patrols in these circumstances? How are investigations to be run when crime scenes are too numerous and too vulnerable to attack to work properly, when they are, in any event, contaminated by the frenzy in which they were formed? Witness evidence is also hopelessly unreliable. Even the Truth Commission, with its confession-and-amnesty process, struggled, finding itself unable to hand out amnesties because, as it reports, 'applicants were usually barely able to recall the year of the incident.'

In the end, however, none of these considerations was as important as the fact that cycles of violence have their own logic. Why bother going to the police when it is far easier, and infinitely more satisfying, to exact revenge yourself? Or, as Morake told me, 'We didn't make convictions in those cases. People didn't trust us because of the government. They preferred to deal with those cases without us.'

This was not an environment for which any criminal justice system is designed. Here the whole world had turned into a something-which-ought-not-to-be-happening-about-which-something-ought-to-be-done-now situation, yet there was no way to intervene effectively using ordinary police powers. The rules of evidence and due process were also worthless. They come from a world that is more rational and less blood-soaked. Instead of becoming an instrument used in the rational pursuit of the truth after a crime had taken place, in battlefields like Thokoza's, policing boiled down to little more than the picking up of bodies.

The result was that station-level cops had the worst of all possible worlds: a community in flames about which they could do nothing with their standard strategies and tactics, and a growing reputation for, at best, incompetence and, at worst, anything from subliminal partiality to active involvement. Little wonder then that police officers were also targets for the community's collective rage, becoming subject to attack at any and all times, at any and all places, or that police officers' memories of those times revolve around the oppressive danger they felt. There were drive-by shootings and ambushes by gangs using petrol bombs.

There were police-initiated operations into hostile territory during which resistance could flare up at any time. There were dangers associated with getting between warring factions: standing between an *impi* and its target, trying to protect dignitaries going on tours of inspection, facing down marches by angry residents. These were fears an officer might have for his own skin, but layers of supplementary terror would be added when they thought about what might happen to their spouses and children, their siblings and even their parents.

Police officers, especially those who lived in the townships, lived with constant fear. For the most part this was little more than the background radiation of their lives, but it would sometimes flare up and become debilitating. Stress-related illnesses were endemic. So too was suicide, often accompanied by family murders.

★

If it was members of the police who had contemplated suicide in the 1980s, now there was someone else who was also thinking about killing himself: Sello, the suspect in Busi's murder. He had called his mother and had talked about ending it all. Morake asked her to come in. I was on a patrol when she arrived and missed the interview with her, but Morake told me she was very distraught. 'What was she to tell her boy?' she'd pleaded. He didn't want to go back to jail, and he was feeling very sorry for what he'd done. His mother thought that he was serious when he spoke of killing himself.

'I asked her for her help,' Morake told me. 'I told her that it would be better for her boy if he didn't run, and I told her she should assist the police by getting him to hand himself in. Or, if he wasn't prepared to do that, to help the police set a trap for him when he visits her. If he stays outside alone, he will definitely kill himself. It would be better if he is in the cells.'

Sello's turning himself in and confessing would be better for Morake too, because he might need the confession to make the case. 'The Captain shat me out,' he told me a little shamefacedly. 'I forgot to gather the bottles from the crime scene, and now we don't have the evidence.'

This was a setback for the case. Morake hadn't found an eyewitness. He had the neighbour's testimony that Sello had been looking for Busi for two days, that he had been very angry with her when she did eventually show up, and that he had been drunk and belligerent. The neighbour also said that after the shouting stopped, Sello had come to ask for a broom, and that he had seen blood on Sello's hands, blood that Sello didn't explain, but which he proceeded to wash off.

This was all compelling evidence and would probably be enough to secure a conviction. It was also strengthened by the fact that Sello had phoned his mother in distress and had confessed the whole dirty business. But you never know with mothers: when the time came to testify in a court of law against her own flesh and blood, anything could happen. Perhaps she would lie under oath or, more likely, retreat to her family homestead in some rural backwater and be lost to Morake forever.

Morake and his Captain would sleep easier, therefore, if they had some physical evidence linking Sello to the scene, ideally a fingerprint on a bloodstained beer bottle. But Morake hadn't gathered any bottles when he'd first gone to the scene and, when he returned a day later, everything had been cleared away.

'Are you worried?' I asked. 'Will you get a confession?'

'I think so. Usually it's not so hard. The only thing is you mustn't force it from him. It's much better to be soft. If you show you have sympathy with him, let him think you are his friend, that's when he'll talk.'

The art of the police interrogation summed up in three words: befriend and betray.

★

Busi's death, and the shoddy investigation of it, bothered me.

It wasn't merely the senselessness of the murder – a horrible platitude: are some murders more sensible than others? – or the ferocity of the assault. It was the stubborn passivity of the people who must have heard the attack but who did nothing.

The failure of a people to intervene when a violent crime is being committed in eye- or earshot is a popular theme in criminology, and is usually identified as a symptom of the anonymity and isolation that mark mass society. That was why no-one had intervened when Kitty Genovese was raped and murdered outside an apartment building in New York in 1964. Thirty-eight witnesses reported either hearing or seeing the attack, yet none had done anything to stop it. It was a crime that had spawned a veritable cottage industry of urban pessimism.

The irony of Busi's death is that the idea of community, and the valorisation of all the good things that are said to flow from belonging to one, figure so large in South Africans' thinking about themselves. One of the most potent beliefs we have of ourselves is that our communities are strong, bound together by bonds forged by cultural traditions favouring communal solidarity. These, we tell ourselves, have been hardened by years of struggle against a system premised on a logic of division and segregation, a logic that was the polar opposite of the thick web of bonds communities proclaimed themselves to have. All of this is, in some ways, true. But in other ways, the belief in the existence of community solidarity is a myth, a lie we tell ourselves because we want it to be so, but which is really just a nostalgic backward glance at the intimacies of village life.

Busi, we must remember, didn't live where she died. She was killed by her boyfriend while he was house-sitting a rented room in someone else's yard. The landlord knew her only by sight. The neighbours didn't know her at all. For all the sympathy her death struggle elicited from those living around her, Busi might as well have been dying in a foreign country.

Bear in mind that this wasn't in an informal settlement, exploding with new residents arriving every day. It wasn't a society of strangers into which new strangers continue to pour. This was one of the older sections of Thokoza, supposedly a place of established families and long-term friendships. Yet, even here, the churning of the population was rapid as owners and, in greater numbers, tenants moved in and out. Perhaps this wasn't exactly a society of strangers, but there were enough unfamiliar people to undermine the idea that this was a society shaped by people whose bonds were in any way intimate.

But the churning of the neighbourhood's residents would not, by itself, explain why no-one helped Busi. After all, when they heard the screams, neighbours wouldn't have known who was being attacked. No doubt they would have made sure that all their own loved ones were accounted for, but they wouldn't have known precisely who was on the receiving end of what must have sounded like a fearful thrashing. There must, therefore, be other reasons for their passivity.

One of those is that, as much as weaknesses in the social fabric cause crime, each crime doubles back and tugs on those same fraying threads, making the fabric that much more ragged. Every time someone is mugged, people retreat a little further into their homes. Every time a drunk fires his weapon into the night air, those in earshot hunker down a little closer to the ground. Every time a neighbour assaults his wife, the good people around them tuck their children in a little closer and whisper a little more fervently their thanks that such things don't happen in their houses, swearing to each other that they will do their best to live to watch their children grow. Crime makes people retreat from public spaces. They become more suspicious of others, and some of the precious fund of trust that oils social interaction leaks away.

Sello killed Busi and he alone is to blame for it. But every crime that preceded this one, every crime that frightened the good people of Thokoza, made Busi's death a fraction more likely. She died at Sello's hands, but there were nameless, countless others whose crimes had kept the people in nearby houses from intervening.

And some of this blame must fall also on the heads of the *izimpi* and self-defence units that fought their bloody battles in the 1990s.

One of the main effects of high levels of crime is the shredding of social bonds. But a conflict of the kind that swept through the East Rand in the early and mid-1990s doesn't have to have quite the same effect. Then, because the threat confronted by the community was identifiable and originated beyond its imagined boundary with the rest of the world, bonds of solidarity could be built. The shared threat, the shared horror and the shared mourning helped the community cohere. Its members were, after all, fighting a common enemy, and the habits of civility, solidarity and mutual assistance might have been expected to emerge. Something like this happened in London during the Blitz, and laid the cultural and political basis for the building of a welfare state in class-riven England after the war.

But conflict-fostered solidarity is only one effect of violence on this scale. The other is its brutalising of those affected by it.

Generally, the word 'brutalise' is taken to mean the cruel use of violence by the strong against the weak. The farmer, we might read, brutalised his labourers, the rapist brutalised his victim. But the word has a subtler meaning, and refers to the desensitising and deadening effects that violence has on those who use it. The victims suffer brutality; but it is those who wield the instruments of violence who are brutalised, becoming somehow less human, certainly less humane.

The people of Thokoza were neither wholly victim nor wholly perpetrator. They were abused as victims of violence, but, as perpetrators, they must have been brutalised too. Attacked by Inkatha and the police, ordinary people, like the women wielding baseball bats caught in Joao Silva's photo, dished out punishment in their turn. The coarsening effect of this on their psyches is, I think, as much an explanation of the disturbing passivity of the people within earshot of Busi as is everyday crime's continuing fraying of the social fabric. It has left in its wake a high tolerance for violence and a well-developed ability to ignore it.

Busi's death was not an act of war, certainly not of a war waged a decade before, but it was an act which that war had made easier.

But if the brutalisation of the East Rand War had done that to the people who'd heard Busi's screams, I wondered if it might have done something similar to Inspector Morake. What explained his failure to pick up the physical evidence that might secure Sello's conviction? It was a strange lapse, and could not be accounted for either by his being under-trained or by his being inexperienced. I wondered if he too, traumatised and brutalised by his own experiences as a police officer during the war and the crime wave that followed, was left unmoved by Busi's death and indifferent to the fate of her killer. Was that, perhaps, one of the reasons why some investigators did little more than the blindingly obvious to close their cases? Did they also no longer care enough to waste their time over something as banal as a murder?

CHAPTER FOURTEEN

EATING *TSHO-TSHO*: ARGUING ABOUT POLICE CORRUPTION, JULY 2003

It is extraordinarily difficult to write sensitively, persuasively and accurately about men and women who are members of a brotherhood to which you do not belong. Theirs is a different reality. Their language, the only vehicle through which you can access their world, is imbued with meanings you cannot grasp. Their motives are baffling; their intentions, obscure. This is bad enough if the people to whom you speak actually want to help you to understand, but you learn soon enough that in an organisation as politically charged as a police service, answers to your questions will never be completely frank or sincere. They are, instead, wrapped in layers of self-idealisation, half-truth and, sometimes, outright fabrication. That is just the way it is.

So, even if you don't know before you begin your quest that it will be hard to penetrate the fog of incomprehension that surrounds every living being, you quickly learn that this is true of police officers. You learn that any understanding you have will be tentative, that it will have been shaped as much from the clay of your own preconceptions as from the marble of the real world.

You learn, in other words, that you will fail.

Nevertheless, armed with a conviction that despite the inevitability of failure you will still have something useful to say, you press on. You spend weeks in vans driven by men who believe themselves to be the other brother of Michael Schumacher. You talk to scores of cops in rooms singularly ill-designed to build the intimacy you need. (Why are all the chairs pushed right up against the wall, as far from the officer's desk as possible?) You do your best to sympathise and, as importantly, to appear to sympathise with the policeman's lot, even when his truncheon has just bounced off the shoulder of a man who isn't going to be arrested because he isn't even suspected of committing a crime. You do all of this to build credibility, to encourage cops to open up and to provide the materials you need to shape your thinking. True, your knowledge of policing is partial and at one remove. True, you have had to negotiate the gulf between the meaning-intended and the meaning-conveyed that comes of your inability to speak the vernacular. Despite all of that, you think you know enough about policing to risk putting pen to paper.

And then you do something really stupid. Knowing that by adopting the course you are embarking on you will piss off 130 000-plus men and women, each of whom has been issued a taxpayer-financed handgun, you decide to write about corruption, a subject about which police officers are most reticent and around which they have erected an almost impenetrable scaffold of denial, wilful ignorance and repression. Despite that, you clutch firmly to the sides of your computer and you set sail.

But what exactly are you going to say, and how the hell are you to justify it?

★

That cops would rather not talk about wrongdoing in the ranks is neither surprising nor shameful. This is, after all, an organisation which, for perfectly reasonable, perfectly understandable reasons, seeks to persuade itself and its members that they form a fellowship, a tight band of like-minded men and women standing fast against forces which would sweep through their lines at the first hint of weakening resolve. Comradeship, loyalty to the badge are hardwired into the organisation, and as a result ranks have closed.

In such circumstances, an officer's merely talking about corruption can be an act of aggression against his brothers, a kind of betrayal, and even when it isn't this, that is often how it is interpreted. For many police officers, therefore, corruption is a taboo, a subject with which they consciously refuse to engage. It is a mistake, however, to see this as a sign of stupidity or blindness or naivety. It is, on the contrary, a demonstration of loyalty: it is part of the price of membership of the group, a sign of fidelity to one's brothers, and of loyalty to the cause.

Cops also prefer to hold their peace about any dubious activity in the ranks because anyone who consciously admits to knowledge of corruption faces an impossible dilemma. Either he must act on his suspicions and face being cast out, or he must be prepared, when he looks himself in the mirror, to confront a man who has failed to do his duty. In such circumstances, even the most honest cop would perhaps prefer ignorance over knowledge.

Loyalty to the group and the need to feel that one is living up to one's own self-image as law enforcer: each reinforces the instinct to resist thinking about corruption, much less talking about it to notebook-wielding outsiders.

Given all of this, an honest researcher must be suspicious not only of the silence his questions generate, but also of any allegations he hears. What, he must wonder, is he to make of those who break the vow of silence, who defy the rule of *omerta*? Is the officer telling the truth when he whispers that his station commissioner runs an armed-guard business out of the station, providing two colluding officers to act as security for clients (far outside the precinct, as it happens) when they cash up at the end of the day? Or is he taking this opportunity to stick it to a man who, for all the researcher knows, does his job well, and who may just have chewed out his source? 'Revenge cases' for theft and rape and assault, opened by disgruntled arrestees against the officers who have arrested them, are an occupational hazard. There is no reason to think that the practice is confined to drug dealers and prostitutes; police officers talking to journalists and researchers could be playing that game too.

The result is that we must regard most accounts of police officers about corruption in the ranks as unreliable. Some will understate the problem of corruption out of loyalty. Some, embittered and malign, will overstate the problem, declaring it a symptom of all that is wrong with the transformation of policing and the process of democratisation that underpins it. Others will seek to impugn colleagues for reasons of their own, never forgetting, of course, to cast themselves as the patron saint of clean cops. Since few will address themselves to the subject objectively, relying on any of their accounts is problematic.

Even so, many of the stories I heard, conveyed by people who seemed honest, in circumstances which mitigate doubts, had a ring of truth to them.

Some of the officers I became closest to told such stories. One, with whom I spent the best part of a week, and whose loyalty to the badge seemed unshakeable, told me that one of his colleagues whose dockets had a habit of disappearing had been photographed in the company of known hijackers. Another, equally reliable-seeming, muttered about officers who, he said, were knee-deep in the drug trade, bringing dagga across the Lesotho border and Mandrax in from Mozambique, for instance. Detectives often laughed about the ease with which the reward and informer systems were abused, or despaired at the blatant partiality shown by officers with relatives who operated taxis in highly contested markets.

In all these cases, I thought carefully about the stories and the storytellers, before deciding that they were probably true. In other cases, when I thought my sources were trying to make trouble for their colleagues and bosses, I kept my reservations to myself.

But if the word of police officers would have been an unreliable way to go about trying to understand police corruption, observation was, if anything, even worse. Corrupt cops are, after all, not fools. They don't solicit bribes from suspects, hawk dockets to defence attorneys or demand free sex from prostitutes when witnesses are hanging about. Graft is not a spectator sport. It is something that is done only among friends and preferably in the dark. For this reason, I had no expectation that I'd see any corruption in the flesh and no illusion that my failure to see any would imply that the officers I was with must, therefore, be clean. Besides, as I quickly learned, cops are great actors – they have to be to do their jobs – and it would be laughably easy for even the most crooked to present himself as a model of rectitude to an interviewer armed with nothing more compelling than a sharpened pencil.

All of which makes it somewhat surprising just how often there were incidents which raised suspicions and which created opportunities to talk.

What was I to make, for instance, of the Yeoville cop who stopped his van next to three men spangled in gold jewellery, and began the conversation with a part-assertive, part-unctuous '*Ngilambile*'? The three he was speaking to were lounging in a convertible BMW and dressed in expensive clothes, clothes that fitted in a manner quite different to the hand-me-down, patch-and-mend couture that dominated the suburb. I don't profess any great knowledge of either urban or traditional culture, but I did wonder why a policeman would open a conversation with an anomalously prosperous-looking civilian by telling him that he was hungry. Especially when the area is also renowned for being home to drug dealers. Nor can I say that I was reassured when, after we'd driven off and I'd asked who the man had been, the officer told me that the three men were police reservists, but professed not to remember their names when I said I might want to interview them.

Pull the other one, I thought. It's got bells on it.

Then there was the moment outside the holding cells at the Hillbrow police station when the three *muhku*-making Nigerians, arrested for the robbery that had never happened, were being processed. While the cops I was with debated whether one could have his belt stored separately from the others', two uniformed cops from Hillbrow brought another migrant into the room. One pushed him into a corner, went through the man's wallet and, having found what he was looking for – a copy of the man's refugee papers, I think – told him, 'You can buy this back from me when you get out of here.'

I also had to wonder why it was that when officers stopped foreign-looking people and asked to inspect their papers, the passports that were handed over would often have a hundred rand note poking out of the top. Were these valuable documents serving double duty as wallets, or was this a practice that had evolved in response to the numerous encounters with men in uniform? I couldn't tell, but I had my suspicions.

Another odd moment was when a senior officer at Rosebank told the two men to whom I was being assigned for the day not to 'eat *tsho-tsho*' while I was with them. Not, in other words, to accept any bribes. This was meant, I suppose, as something of a joke. But it was the sort of joke that only works if it is also partly sincere. Precisely why the officer was concerned about the *tsho-tsho*-eating habits of the two I would work with became apparent 14 months later when an award-winning current affairs programme caught cops from this station accepting 'spot fines' from journalists posing as prostitutes and johns. Senior police officers felt they had to pronounce themselves shocked! shocked! about this, with a dewy-eyed Deputy Provincial Commissioner saying that it was an embarrassment to the rest of the men and women who wear the uniform. But the truth is that cops in every jurisdiction in all the world know that prostitutes and drug dealers and illegal migrants are ripe for the shaking down. In South Africa, they call these people 'ATMs'.

Then there were all the arrests connected to police wrongdoing that happened around me, with seemingly every station abuzz with the latest incident. A detective who shared an office with Alida van Zyl, the detective who closed the restaurant robbery cases in Rosebank, was arrested for trying to sell a docket to a suspect. The case, as it happened, had already been withdrawn, but the man must have wanted to get something out of it before his boss had the file archived. Two other officers at the station had recently been arrested for their involvement in a taxi conflict. In Galeshewe, it was the suspension of the station commissioner who had taken the unusual step of replacing a detective assigned to a case seemingly because it took him out of town for a couple of weeks and allowed him to loot the travel and subsistence budget. That he'd taken a fresh, young, female constable with him, was, according to my informants, the giddy limit. In Maluti, an officer was arrested while I was there because the petrol card of a vehicle for which he was responsible had run up a R10 000 bill at a local service station, despite its not having moved in more than a month.

All these arrests and suspensions were disturbing. They were also encouraging, of course, because they suggested that some of the poison was being drawn, some portion of the swamp was being drained. Nevertheless, when I read that a majority of 200 detectives interviewed by an academic agreed with the statement that 'many police officers are corrupt', I couldn't help but feel that they knew what they were talking about.

★

The infrastructure laid on by the state at the Yeoville police station is far from ideal, and because the community's is usually worse, when nature calls, some of the station's cops find a visit to the hygienic loos at the Killarney shopping centre irresistible. The mall is typical of the genre: brightly lit shops, polished floors, elegantly dressed shoppers and an overfull parking lot, the chaos of which can be short-circuited if you have a police emblem on the side of your van. I was always delighted to visit the mall in the company of policemen. This was largely because I was convinced that I cut a dashing figure in my bullet-proof vest and had managed to persuade myself that I was turning heads. During one such stop, however, I was less concerned about how I looked, than with a quite heated debate I was having with one of the men I was trailing.

Our conversation revolved around the fate of two of the man's colleagues. They'd been caught red-handed the week before while committing a robbery at a house in a neighbouring precinct. As I understood it, there was absolutely no question of their guilt: they were caught on the scene, and the witnesses had had no trouble identifying them. Given that our sentencing regime prescribes a minimum sentence of fifteen years for aggravated robbery, these two had every chance of spending a large proportion of their lives in Diepkloof prison. Indeed, such is the punitiveness of our law in relation to offending by law enforcement officers, that the two would have been liable to the same minimum sentence if all they'd done was sell some dagga. Theirs was not an enviable fate. I was, nevertheless, surprised at the vehemence with which Sergeant Mulaudzi argued that the young constables didn't deserve this. Nor, he maintained, did they deserve to be held awaiting trial or, indeed, even to be suspended from duty. In his ideal world, the two probable-robbers would be patrolling Yeoville's streets even now.

The intensity of Mulaudzi's views made them eccentric. Even so, they were not a million miles from those of the many other cops to whom I spoke of corruption and criminality in the ranks. All of them would condemn wrongdoing forcefully in the abstract. But often, when a specific case was mentioned, particularly when someone they knew had been involved, their views would become more tolerant. They became more willing to understand, less prone to condemn. And, like

232

many people outside of the Service, they would seek to explain – not justify, of course! – the actions of the men by the supposed deficiency of their salaries.

'This government is very cruel to its policemen,' Mulaudzi told me as we sipped coffee from cardboard cups and looked at cut-price CDs. I'd bought the coffees in order to prove that the chicory blend favoured in police stations around the country tasted like diluted sewage compared to the real stuff. But the act had backfired. Mulaudzi and his partner now thought I was, at best, morally suspect, at worst, completely insane: who could spend more than R10 on a single cup of coffee?

'What do you mean "cruel"?' I asked. 'The men were arrested committing a crime. Shouldn't they be treated like other criminals?'

Mulaudzi was not yet ready to make any concessions to fact or to police experience, which dictates that people caught on the scene are guilty. 'How do you know that they were involved?' he demanded. Then he proceeded to offer a fanciful account of how the two off-duty cops might have been walking past the house while it was being robbed and, having intervened to try to save the victims, were now mistakenly thought by the people they'd saved to have been part of the original gang.

'Lesley,' I said, calling him over-familiarly by his first name. 'You don't really believe that, do you?'

Mulaudzi was a big man, his belly swelling up against the blue of his uniform. His arms, thick and heavy, hung at an angle from his shoulders and seemed to flap when he puffed his way up or down stairs. His speech was usually slow, wheezy and plodding, his movement oceanic in its languidness. 'I'm not saying they are innocent,' he replied, pedantically. 'But it is too easy for people to say that the police are guilty. If criminals can have rights, if *they* are innocent until proven guilty, isn't it the same for the police? But now those two men are locked up. What is happening to their families while they are inside?'

One of the things that was odd about this conversation was that for much of the morning Mulaudzi, his partner and I had debated the merits of reinstating the death penalty. Like most cops, the two were in favour. Predictably enough, I was more sceptical. Now I found myself defending the punitiveness of our criminal justice system, if only on grounds of consistency, while Mulaudzi had become an advocate of the virtues of restorative justice. 'It is too hard,' he told me. 'They want to suspend those men without pay. Without pay! How must they afford lawyers? Must they use those lawyers from the Legal Aid Board?' He seemed to think that that prospect was so horrifying that it alone decided the argument in his favour.

I asked him what he thought should happen to the two while the wheels of justice ground their way forward.

'They should be free,' he replied emphatically. 'They must come out of Sun City and they must come back to work. They are innocent until found guilty in a court of law. That is how the law is. A policeman is a human like other people. He must also have his human rights.'

Mulaudzi was wrong about the law. The legal regime governing the right to bail in South Africa was tightened considerably in the late 1990s and now, when people are accused of participation in serious crimes – murder, rape, aggravated robbery and the like – the onus falls on them to show that exceptional circumstances exist which would allow the court to release them. I pointed this out and then told Mulaudzi why I thought his views unreasonable: 'How can you expect special treatment for policemen? If the criminal justice system did that, then people would lose a lot of respect for it. How would the community respond knowing that police officers who were accused of serious crimes were on the street?'

By way of response, Mulaudzi shrugged. 'When you send a policeman to jail, it is a very serious thing. He is in danger from the minute he walks in the door. Maybe there are people there who he arrested. So if you must send them to jail, it is like you want to kill them.'

This was, I suppose, possible. I know of no cases in which a police officer has been murdered behind bars, but it was not inconceivable that cops might be in more danger than other inmates. I had only met one officer who talked of having spent time in jail on a corruption charge, but his experience was quite different. He was a detective in the narcotics branch who'd spent six months in Diepkloof prison – the Sun City of which Mulaudzi spoke – after he was arrested by the anti-corruption unit. I could make no sense of the convoluted story he constructed to explain this away. It was filled with uncertainties, and the connections, which must have been clear to him, were not so for me. He was constantly adding to and changing what he had said before. The narrative, when it emerged, involved a drug lord who bore a grudge who had set a corrupt member of the anti-corruption unit on him, and a false charge of possessing a stolen car was laid. 'There were always suspicions about me,' he told me another time, however: 'My wife is successful. She has money. They think it comes from me.'

Whether that narc was corrupt or not, he found himself in jail, and his version of an officer's life behind bars suggested that Mulaudzi might be exaggerating the danger the two Yeoville cops were in. 'Once the warders knew I was a policeman,' he told me, 'it was OK. There was a kind of respect because they knew what it is like to work with criminals. They made me do life skills training with prisoners.'

'But, Lesley,' I said to Mulaudzi over our coffees, 'what did they think was going to happen if they got caught? They knew the risks. They knew what might happen to them. They knew the criminal justice system, probably better than other criminals. How can they complain now?'

Mulaudzi thought about this for a moment, but then dismissed it and raised an argument that rears its head in pretty much every discussion of police corruption in South Africa: what did I expect to happen if police were paid so badly that they couldn't raise a family, couldn't buy a car, couldn't live a decent life? Of course policemen would steal if they were not paid enough for taking the risks they must take and for providing the services they do. Corruption was the inevitable result of poor pay.

The sheer frequency with which this argument is made shouldn't blind us to its obvious deficiencies, the most important of which is that it is quite perverse to allow this argument to apply to cops, but to draw back from making similar excuses for other criminals who are usually even poorer than the police. It is true, of course, that police officers are poor despite their doing policework and their having to take risks on behalf of the community when doing so, while other criminals have no grounds to believe themselves exploited. But the unemployed criminal is locked out of society more firmly than are police officers, so they too have their grounds for resentment. Besides, pleading poverty as an explanation for corruption amounts to little more than a thinly veiled extortion threat dressed up as sympathetic understanding: if you fail to pay us adequately to keep you safe, so the logic of the argument goes, then we will make you even less safe.

To buy into this argument means buying into mixed-up ideas about the world, ideas in which policing can be little different from a protection racket.

Another objection to this line of reasoning goes to what it implies about cops as self-directed moral agents. These are reasoning adults, after all, who, knowing the conditions of employment in the police as well as whatever options they may have elsewhere, have chosen a life in uniform. Having done so, they cannot beg for understanding when some among them supplement their incomes illegally. If the rewards don't match the efforts and the risks, members are free to leave. What they should not be able to do is have their cake and eat it: if the conditions of employment are voluntarily accepted, they cannot then be used as an excuse for subsequent criminality.

I made these points to Sergeant Mulaudzi with more vigour than I might usually have done in my earnest-if-slightly-dim-researcher mode. Perhaps it was because we were in the mall, and the familiarity of the territory had made me feel more confrontational. Perhaps I was just a bit bored. Perhaps it was the real coffee. Whatever the reason, the effect on Mulaudzi was electrifying.

'Do you know what it is to be poor?' he demanded, speaking faster than I thought him capable, and brandishing the coffee I had bought him. It had become a silent indictment of the frivolous wealth he thought I must have. 'Do you know what it is to work all day but when you go home there is nothing in your wallet? It is easy to say a member must be clean. But it is hard in practice. In practice, people make mistakes.'

'But surely the same is true about ordinary criminals?' I asked. 'Why should the police get special treatment?'

For a moment, Mulaudzi seemed to be boiling with anger, and for the first time he locked eyes with me. I had overstepped the mark. Cops, whatever they do, are never 'ordinary criminals'. On behalf of his colleagues, Mulaudzi was insulted. Our conversation, mutually uncomprehending as it was, was now at an end. Indeed, all conversation was, and we drove back to the station in an uncomfortable silence, broken only by the squawking chatter of the police radio. The silence gave me a chance to think through the implications of what he had said.

★

The idea that police officers are underpaid and that this explains, even if it doesn't justify, why some are corrupt, was one I heard often. In the past I'd expressed understanding, but silently rejected it on the grounds that I'd given Mulaudzi. Now I found it quite unsettling. It made me wonder about the psychology of the organisation. This, after all, was an institution committed to the enforcement of the law, one which proclaimed itself to have 'zero tolerance' for all manner of criminal wrongdoing, and which was, rhetorically at least, intent on stamping out all forms of criminality. And yet there were all too many members whose self-professed steely resolve seemed to go a little soft around the edges when it came to police corruption. Few would have gone as far as Mulaudzi had in seeking to defend colleagues who had apparently committed a crime of violence, and, in the abstract at least, all insisted that corruption was wrong and should be punished. At the same time, they insisted that it had to be understood, that it could be explained, and that, with the appropriate steps taken to fatten pay cheques, it could be eliminated.

All of which is true, as it is true of everyone. But in policing, there is much more to be said.

Every police service in the world has its problems of corruption. Everywhere you go, there will be officers shaking down drug dealers, copping freebies from prostitutes, holding up banks, and looting evidence lockers. Some will issue false documents to migrants, others will sell dockets to suspects, steal furniture from the office, or conspire to skim a percentage off the fees they are supposed to pay their informers.

Corruption, whether petty or grand, is a problem wherever laws are enforced and, after 5 000 years of recorded history, no-one has come up with a sure-fire strategy for eliminating it. The problem is as inherent a part of law enforcement as are the uniforms and badges, and arises from the fact that those against whom a society wants its police to act would generally prefer to be left alone. Some will be willing to pay up rather than submit, and that opens lots of space for entrepreneurial law enforcement.

Serious as this basic problem is, it is still only part of the problem, and to it must be added three other factors that combine to create the most challenging oversight problems in all of government.

The first of these factors is that police officers, unlike the officials of any other branch of government, do their work on the street. Officers, working as individuals or in small groups, attend to the complaints they receive, process summonses, and go after bad guys of all kinds. In all of this, they act in an oversight shadow, a managerial blind spot that extends from their commanding officer's desk all the way into the homes and alleys to which their work takes them. No-one can watch what officers do or do not do, because the nature of their work puts them in places where meaningful oversight is simply impossible.

A second factor makes the first even more knotty. This is that in the police, unlike any other hierarchical organisation in the public or private sectors, and despite its pretensions to being a disciplined, quasi-military force, discretion in decision-making actually expands the lower down the organisation one goes. Police officers know in their bones that the laws they enforce, and the powers they are assigned with which to do so, provide only a framework for action rather than a strict set of dos and don'ts. Your task as a street cop is often to deal with situations which don't admit of straightforward solution, and so you deploy your legal powers and your native ingenuity to cobble solutions together. How you do so depends not so much on what any given law says, but on which laws you wish to use and how. Police managers, on the other hand, cooped up in offices filling in forms and complying with procedure manuals heavy enough to sink a tugboat, actually enjoy less discretion in the course of their day-to-day activities. They never have to decide whether, when, where or how to engage with unpredictable people like civilians, suspects and wit-nesses. In making these choices, street-cops, young men and women with only limited experience of life, are guided by the law, their training and the established practices of their units. But, in the end, the choice of pre-cisely how to respond to any given set of circumstances usually rests on the shoulders of relatively junior officers.

So we have an organisation in which decision-making power lies at the bottom of the hierarchy and in which the reality of the craft means that those assigned that power must exercise their discretion in places in which their actions cannot be observed nor their decisions reviewed. This is already a recipe for problems. A final factor completes the mix. That ingredient derives from the nature of the laws officers are asked to enforce, some of which couldn't be better designed if their aim and object was to test the corruptibility of saints.

Corruption can, of course, arise when any law is broken, whenever a policeman is called upon to act. Cops could say to wife-beaters, bank robbers and even dog-kickers that they will 'lose' their dockets in return for some consideration. Here the wide discretion of, and limited over-sight over, junior officers is a problem.

But the corruption generated by these sorts of crimes pales into insignificance against the problems that arise when the law seeks to reg-ulate voluntary human conduct, when it seeks, in the interests of a wider public good or in the maintenance of social mores or in order to regulate otherwise legitimate commerce, to get people to desist from doing something they would like to do or would pay good money to do. The economic and political forces that drive voluntary migration, for instance, are often so powerful that the efforts of law enforcement agencies to police it seem Canute-like in their futility. Officers know this to be true, they know that no matter how hard they work, they can-not turn back the tide. The trouble with this is that if they know that there is little that their individual efforts will achieve, they will become more susceptible to turning a blind eye. The same is true of crimes like prostitution, drug-dealing and dealing in liquor. In these cases, the laws, in all their wisdom, have been designed to stop people doing something they plainly want to do. This sort of activity simply cannot be stopped, not with all the cops and laws and moral regeneration campaigns in the world. It can't be stopped by angry communities or vigilante gangs. It can't be stopped by overcrowded, gang-infested jails. These are crimes that arise from human needs, human desire. States, no matter how self-righteous, no matter how powerful, can do little to dam or direct or disrupt the flow of desire. All they can do is make it a little harder, a little more costly, to fulfil.

Cops, tasked with raising the costs of meeting these illicit but nonetheless undeniable needs, know from experience that there is little they can do, that their collective efforts are puny beside the force of human desire. They cannot stop men going to prostitutes, or drug users finding their fixes. They can't stop the majority of migrants. These things are bigger than they are.

This is a dangerous sort of knowledge for a law enforcement official, because once a cop doubts he can fix a problem, he may quickly decide that he might as well benefit from it. Besides, although cops are not liberals about drugs and prostitution and they don't believe these things should be decriminalised and regulated, they do know that there are worse things in the world than allowing a junkie to get his fix or a lonely man to visit a brothel. Sometimes cops look away not because they are paid to (even if they are) but because they know that no good can come of doing what the law tells them is their duty. That is why asking fallible men and women to police other people's morality is always and everywhere a fertile ground for corruption.

There are two ways a police service can seek to inoculate itself against this disease. The first involves traps, investigations, disciplinary hearings, prosecutions and jail time. It is enormously important. But, given how extraordinarily easy it is to hide corrupt activity, especially when it is reasonably widespread so that collusion between corruptible officers spreads, this is a strategy that is unlikely to immunise the system. The other approach is to foster an organisational culture that treats corruption both as a crime and, as importantly, as an act of betrayal, a violation which so offends the mores of the place that its members are shocked into casting out those who commit it.

This was why I worried about Mulaudzi and his colleagues' willingness to explain corruption, to speak of it as something with identifiable roots that extend from the act back to the disenchantments of the pay slip. When they did this, they were saying, in effect, that the true betrayal, the original betrayal, is the one committed by the organisation. It is as if they are saying that the primary treason belongs to the Police Service, not the corrupt policeman, and it leads to an odd, impossibly paradoxical notion: that a betrayal is justified.

I couldn't help thinking that a police service in which this kind of reasoning was accepted was one that had not completely bought into its idealised self-presentation as centurions defending the invisible boundary between order and disorder. The mere fact that this was how cops talked about corruption – as a way officers supplemented their modest pay, rather than as an inexcusable violation of a code they were supposedly committed to – was deeply troubling. It didn't suggest that corruption was condoned, accepted as part of the package of services offered by the police. But nor did it suggest outright, unequivocal, line-in-the-sand rejection. Even if few cops expressed as much sympathy as did Mulaudzi, many suggested at least the willingness to show understanding, to make gestures of sympathy.

Thought of in this way, corruption became as much a problem of organisational culture as it was of money, and a problem in which many more people were implicated than those who actually benefited from acts of corruption. It seemed as if something was missing from the way the organisation's members thought of themselves and their work, that there was a hole in the framework of norms and traditions needed to produce honest cops, that the intricate ethical scaffolding needed to keep the organisation's members clean was somehow warped and now could not bear the twin strains of temptation and opportunity.

It was a chilling thought. But, in retrospect, I wonder whether I should have been as surprised.

Institutions, after all, the police more so than any other, carry the weight of their history, dragging it behind them like a shadow, and it is hard to conceive of a police service with a history less conducive to creating the appropriate moral infrastructure to condemn corruption as betrayal, than the SAPS.

Think about the cynicism of law enforcement under apartheid. That, after all, was a system the closest analogues of which are the slave states that dot the history of the ancient and modern worlds. As in those social systems, society was neatly divided between victor and vanquished, the enfranchised and the disenfranchised, the master and the slave. And, as in those social systems, the law, though constructed on a foundation of high-sounding principles, was divided against itself. Its best values applied only to a privileged few of its subjects. For the rest, it was a mean, vicious thing, the chief aim and object of which was forcibly to exclude them from its protection. Great things were sometimes achieved in these divided societies. But securing the structures of inclusion and exclusion was a dirty, brutal and brutalising business. It could not but have left the apparatus of its enforcement drawn in the colours of its own cynicism.

No organisational culture, not even that of a police service, is static, of course, and the past ten years have introduced new tints and textures into the canvas. But after my talk with Mulaudzi, it occurred to me how few encounters I had had with policemen who demonstrated any deep-seated conviction that the formative years of their careers might have left them ill-equipped for the challenges of policing the new South Africa or of living up to the standards demanded by the new order. They seemed untouched by the idea that they might bear invisible scars from those times. But that this is so is incontestable. Certainly it is true of the practical, craft skills of policing. Why should it not also be true of the organisational culture which gives shape to its officers' work? Of all the world's policing systems, it is hard to imagine one less capable of building an organisational culture which respected the law and treated wrongdoing in the ranks as repugnant, than was apartheid's. And that system, with much of its organisational grammar left untouched by the transition, is what was bequeathed to the Police Service that would do democracy's dirty work.

Much has been done since the mid-1990s to prise open the question of corruption. Researchers have scurried about the organisation's entrails surveying officers about the extent of corruption in the ranks. Investigative journalists have lifted the lid and poked bright lights into the depths. The organisation itself has adopted an ever-growing pile of anti-corruption principles, policies and strategies. It has opened anti-corruption squads and then merged them into organised crime units. It has sought to recruit older, better-educated, less impressionable staff. It has raised average salaries by more than ten per cent a year for ten years. It has issued condemnation after condemnation, and has prosecuted literally thousands of members for wrongdoing. And yet, at the same time, and working against all of this, the organisation has also fostered a self-righteous sense of injury: the idea that cops are not paid well enough to expect compliance with the law is almost an official government position, and is certainly the view of every politician and newspaper in the country. 'Yes,' we keep saying to our cops. 'We *do* treat you badly.' That hardly seems the ideal message to send to men and women who have ample opportunities to extract a little more from the society of which they are a crucial part.

★

The last station I visited in my research was in Barberton, a lushly beautiful Mpumalanga town tucked into the folds of the second-oldest crater on the planet. Its commander was Superintendent Vusi Mdakane, an officer who treated corruption more forthrightly than any other I spoke to.

An example: a corridor pin-board next to Mdakane's office displayed dozens of articles clipped from local newspapers, each laminated and pasted on brightly coloured cardboard and pinned to the wall at odd angles. This is an effect, you might think, more appropriate for a nursery school than a police station, yet it is used in pretty much every station I've ever been to. Look at the articles on display here, however, and you discover that, unlike similar boards in other police stations too timid to show anything but the most complimentary letters to the editor, here neatly clipped stories of police corruption, of unsolved cases, and of communities marching to condemn police inefficiency, were also on display. One of these was a strongly worded article about Mdakane's boss, the local Area Commissioner, in which unionists were quoted accusing the man of being unable to communicate, unwilling to consult, and, most damningly, of running his office as another man might run his kitchen. That story was granted as much prominence as was one about a local police officer who had rescued a granny kidnapped during a farm attack. Others dealt with allegations of police corruption.

It was an unusually frank display.

Superintendent Mdakane had a face like a bust from the Solomon Islands: a large mouth, a broad nose, and a forehead in imminent danger of disappearing under the upward pressure exerted by his features. The artlessness of his face was exaggerated, one suspects intentionally, by a self-imposed baldness. But the ingenuousness of these features was a little deceptive. In an organisation of bureaucrats as nervous of outsiders as civilians in a war zone, this was a man subtle enough to see opportunity rather than threat in a writer's request to visit his station. And, where the relentless self-promotion of many in his organisation is nothing but a tremendous bore, when he showed me the awards he'd won in station-of-the-year competitions, it was done with disarming charm and seductive flair.

Pointing to the article about his boss, I told Mdakane that I thought he played a clever game, using the critical articles as a marker of his openness, building his credibility by acknowledging weakness. 'It's always like that,' he replied. 'If you are defensive, you will always lose.' This was the same view that he took about a case of corruption in the local government while I was there.

Mdakane's officers had received reports that a local councilor had been defrauding people living in one of the local informal settlements, 'selling' them their plots for a couple of hundred rand apiece. An arrest warrant had been issued and was to be served on the day I left the area. 'The guy definitely did it,' Mdakane said in response to my question. 'We don't make these arrests lightly. Last time we had to make this kind of arrest, the politicians tried to intervene.'

'What happened?'

'The mayor called me to have the man released. But sometimes I can be a thunderhead. I told him that there were many irregularities and that if he sticks his nose in, maybe we will end up tracing some of those irregularities back to him. It was the last I heard from him.

'He would have been much cleverer if he never phoned me and instead told his people that this councilor was a rotten apple and that he was not going to tolerate rotten apples in his organisation. That's what I will always say about our members when they get in trouble. You won't catch me on the wrong side of a statement about that.'

These were, it should be said, statements he'd become quite familiar with making in the recent past: two of his members had recently been arrested. One had been charged with robbery and kidnapping after he 'arrested' a fraud suspect who had duped a member of the officer's family out of money in a 'black dollars' scheme. But the officer had kept the money and failed to open a docket and have the case processed. The second, the head of the station's detectives, had been charged with corruption and fraud after allegedly forging the signature of the local prosecutor in order to close cases. 'It was a pill problem,' Mdakane offered by way of an explanation. 'He was a good officer, a clever detective, but his life was a fucking mess.'

In addition to these cases, his officers had also stung three cops from a neighbouring station involved in a case of corruption straight out of a Tarantino script. A police officer steals a car, alters its engine number and sells it to a trusting buyer for R50 000 cash. Days later, he sends two colleagues to visit the buyer, a Barberton man. They inspect the engine, note the altered number, and arrest the man for being in possession of stolen goods. Instead of processing him, though, they offer to dump the case in return for R3 000 and the vehicle. That R3 000 was a mistake. If they had not demanded it and had simply driven off with the car immediately, it might have been impossible to make arrests or to prove any charges. The cash demand, however, meant that the man had time to call Mdakane, whose men quickly arranged a sting, allowing the deal to go through but setting up a roadblock on the road out of town. The money, photocopied before being handed over, was still in their possession. Their careers were effectively over; Mdakane, you would think, was on the way up.

I asked Mdakane, whom I met right at the end of my research, about the origins of corruption. Could they be traced to the sense of frustration and anger that so many officers – I was thinking of Mulaudzi, but also of the Molefes, Makayes and De Kosters I had met – had about their work. Mdakane, with whom I spoke only in the presence of other officers from the station (he wanted them to contribute, but also, I think, to hear him speak), leaned back a moment in his chair. 'Everyone here,' he said, gesturing at the five or six men and women in his office, 'has their own problems with the police. It is a funny place to work and a lot of things go wrong. But you can't let people use that as an excuse. There is no excuse for corruption. The police have also given us many opportunities. Without the police, where would I be? I would be nothing.

'Corruption is only because of greed. And when a policeman does it, the other members all suffer. Everyone in the community looks at that man and says, "You see. The police are corrupt." It is very bad for us when that happens. So the only thing to do is that the police must get rid of these rotten apples. Maybe they are few. Maybe they are many. But we must treat them like rotten apples. They must be taken out of the barrel. That is the only way.'

CHAPTER FIFTEEN

CONCLUSION:
MORE COPS, LESS CRIME?

In 1994 I was teaching economics at Wits University and had almost no interest in policing. Shortly after the inauguration of the new government, however, I was approached by people working for the new minister for safety and security to help develop a view on the implications of the RDP for the police budget. (In the interests of historical accuracy, I should say that they approached someone else first, but he was unavailable: I was the second choice.) My job was to assess the advice the minister had received from police management, then still under the command of the decidedly untrusted General Johan van der Merwe, on the planned R400 million budget cut. Simply stated, this was that any cut would be an unmitigated disaster, the impact of which on law and order would be comparable only with Lenin's return to Moscow in 1917. The precise language, as I recall, was taken from the police submission on the 1993/94 budget which had stated, after every line item and in hysterical capital letters, that any cuts would mean that the requirements of the law would not be fulfilled. It then went on to say, 'This will have catastrophic implications for the police, as well as for the Republic of South Africa and it might/will lead to complete anarchy.'

It was, I think, that 'might/will' that put doubts in the minister's mind. Just how rigorous an analysis was this, anyway? How seriously should he take its conclusions?

My project took three weeks and, in the end, reached the only politically viable conclusion: although the police would hurt, the fact that the funds could be reclaimed for RDP-aligned projects, as well as the fact that increased root-causes spending might actually help reduce

247

crime, meant that the department could give at least tentative support to the budget cut.

In the meantime, I was hooked.

The minister, who received a great deal of unfair public criticism, was charismatic, smart, self-deprecating and hard-working. I liked him immediately and, over the next four years, came to admire him thoroughly. His advisory team, which consisted of a dynamic group of lawyers, criminologists and intelligence-types, was also a fascinating bunch. But it was the cops themselves whom I found most intriguing. I signed up the instant I was offered full-time work.

With only a few exceptions, the police officers with whom we civilians worked in those early days hated us. Part of that was their displaced anxiety about the transition to democracy. The rest bubbled up from a cop-culture that regards civilians as know-nothing *hase* whose every instinct is dubious and whose knowledge – if one can use the word – comes exclusively from books. We civilians, on the other hand, were more than a little sceptical of police management's politics, its competence and, indeed, its honesty. And, although we thought there was plenty of evidence to support those doubts, it is also fair to say that beneath our efforts to engage with the cops in developing a vision of a new Police Service, we were sometimes motivated by a *schadenfreude* that was both infantile and dangerous. This led to the perverse result that the more unpopular some decisions were among the generals, the more delight we had in pushing them through. If police management hated the new uniforms and rank structures, it was too bad. If they resented an open-doors policy to the TRC and the demilitarisation of the organisation's culture, so much the better. If they doubted the wisdom of some of the station-level restructuring that went on, or were concerned that some changes to the law would make policing more difficult, well, all we needed to do to win the argument was to point out that their knowledge and experience of policing had been terribly distorted by their enthusiastic enforcement of apartheid. Besides, some in the organisation's senior ranks, for all their pretensions to being professional cops, had last set foot in a police station in the Triassic period that ended in 1990. Their knowledge of practical policing in the new South Africa, and their street-smarts, were far from fresh.

Police-civilian relations, as you might imagine, were not always loving. For me, the turning point came some time in 1996. By that point cops were starting to adjust to the new realities, and I had come to the less-than-profound realisation that, warts and all, a reasonably effective police service was something the country actually needed. More important was another less-than-profound realisation: that police officers knew at least as much as anyone else about what it would take to get the organisation to function better. I cannot claim that this epiphany came as a result of any excess of humility or openness to argument on my part. Instead, I lived out the old New York adage that holds that a liberal is really just a conservative, law-and-order voter who hasn't yet been mugged. My turn had come at a Johannesburg fast-food emporium on a winter's night, and from that moment on I embraced a model of law enforcement that I dubbed 'boots-and-all policing'.

But even this felt suspect. How did I know what the police should do, what strategies they should adopt, how heavily their boots should tread? I'd read a bunch of books and talked to more head office cops than you could shake a nightstick at, but my knowledge felt brittle and unreliable, undermined by an ignorance of the real business of policing so profound I couldn't even chart its contours. I didn't know enough to know what I didn't know. All I knew was that the material to which I had had access, and even the officers to whom I had spoken, could engage only at the most abstract of levels about policing. Neither approach allowed me to get a feel for how ordinary policemen do ordinary policework.

That is perhaps the main reason why I wrote this book. It is also why it focuses on the day-to-day experience of grassroots, street-level polic-ing: it was here that my ignorance was most profound. I felt that even if I couldn't get real knowledge of how things worked, I could at least hope better to define the limits of my knowledge. If I could do that, I thought, it would be something. If, in the process, I could help other people understand a little more about the dirty work of democracy, that too would not be nothing.

What, then, have I learned?

★

Perhaps the most important thing I learned was also the most banal. It is that police officers are human beings.

This is hardly the stuff of intellectual revolution, but this simple fact has important implications. It means, for instance, that the Police Service is not like a vast production line, mechanised and run by computers, the outputs of which change predictably when structures, policies or resource levels change. If it was a car, we'd say of it that the gears slip and that the wheels are not properly aligned because what happens on the street often bears only the slightest resemblance to what policy-makers intend. Why does this happen? Because internal memos setting out new policies and procedures are poorly drafted and are then left unread. Because mutually contradictory instructions are issued and then wilfully misunderstood. Because individual officers interpret and re-interpret their instructions a half-dozen times before going ahead and doing what they have always done anyway.

It is not just poor communications systems, though.

On average, cops are probably as set in their ways as anyone else and, like most people, they don't particularly like change. Nor are they infinitely malleable. There are limits, in other words, to how much we can expect to change what cops do. So, when grand-sounding plans are developed to use the police to reweave the social fabric and help nurture new modes of social life, we should remember that few cops have the interest, skills or inclination to make this sort of thing happen. They are not social engineers or, indeed, social workers. Their jobs and their identities are forged around using the law to end the unpleasant situations that arise inevitably in mass society and, as a crucial complementary function, for finding criminals and evidence. These are reactive skills and require a reactive mindset. Yet cops are not fools. They may not believe themselves to be a mechanism through which all of society's problems can be solved, but they understand the value of approaches to reducing crime that focus on root causes (whatever they may be). It's just that that is not who they are nor what they wish to do. Nor should their reluctance to become the instruments of this kind of do-goodery be taken as some kind of appalling resistance to change or as a mark of any alleged moral deficiencies. It is simply the natural, human inclination to muddle through life without taking on more than one's fair share of burdens.

A concrete example will help explain what I mean, especially since it involves the issue that demands the most time and attention from patrol officers at most of the police stations I visited: domestic violence.

★

One of the most widely held views about the policing of domestic violence in South Africa is that police officers don't implement the Domestic Violence Act because, like most other men, they have imbibed the patriarchy and chauvinism of our culture. This, it is said, means that they side with abusers in abusive relationships. This analysis, in my experience, is wrong. It is true that the letter and the spirit of the provisions of the Act often go unimplemented. But the problem, I think, has less to do with police officers' attitudes than it has to do with the misconception of the role cops can play in dealing with these problems and, therefore, about the reasons they are unwilling to do more.

One of these is that the vast, vast majority of domestic violence cases which cops attend are quite petty. They involve shouting and swearing, threats and even some physical violence. But in most cases, none of the violence rises above the level of the most minor of assaults. Often the underlying act is no more serious than *crimen injuria*. Traumatic as this may be for the victim, the pettiness of the violence involved means that officers are often looking to get past these incidents if only because something more serious might be happening down the road.

A second reason for the lack of officer sympathy is that domestic disputes, more so than any other kind of incident to which cops are called, take them into the heart of the callers' private lives. At these scenes, they are asked to peer behind screens that shield a family's private world from others and, when they do so, they see the most unhappy of homes. This is unpleasant enough, and I would hazard that none but a saint could enjoy the work for long. But the problem is worsened by the fact that whatever it is that is the source of the family's present troubles – whether it is money or drink or any one of the many

251

other pathologies from which South African families suffer – there is seldom much that police officers, armed only with the power of arrest, can do to help. Cops can't make people richer or give them more room in which to live. They can't get mean drunks to stop drinking. They can't make difficult people easier to live with. They have the tools to do none of this.

Nor, it must be said, do they want them.

Odd as it may seem, given the amount of time taken by these incidents on an average shift, a deep desire to immerse oneself in other people's family problems is not, in my experience, the principal reason why people become police officers. Few have any desire to mend the torn tapestries of these families' lives. Besides, because these cases are usually withdrawn soon after they're opened, and certainly before they go to court, cops, perhaps unjustifiably, often see any effort to make an arrest as wasted.

Given all of this, officers are prone to thinking that they're better off conserving their energies than making an arrest, something that would be followed by hours of processing papers and arrestees. Instead, when they get to these scenes, they do little more than establish their authority and ask what happened. They insist that people talk consecutively and that they refrain from interrupting each other. They listen to all points of view and, after they learn that the fight revolved around money, the poor behaviour of one or another member of the family, or some combination of both, they ask a simple, if disingenuous, question: 'And what do you think we (meaning the police) can do about that?'

This is not an honest question posed in the hope of an answer. It is, rather, an assertion, framed as a question, that policing and police powers are too blunt an instrument for dealing with life's micro-dramas. It is a statement that the police can do nothing for the parties that they cannot do for themselves.

It is also, of course, a form of copping out. And this is why it is sometimes taken as a sign that the police are not interested in the problem of domestic violence. But before dismissing it in this way, we should note an oft-neglected subtlety of this approach: it may be a strategy that avoids paperwork and does not result in the visceral satisfaction that might come of the arrest of rude or abusive menfolk, but it also allows both parties to a dispute to withdraw from the argument and to go to bed without any loss of face. It offers them a way out of the trenches into which they have dug themselves. This, police officers tell me, is all they are reasonably able to do in these cases. The people involved are usually hardened by the privations of their lives and are, as a result, too proud to take a backward step because any compromise is seen by them as weakness, and they have learned that weakness is seldom rewarded. That may well be the reason why these arguments have escalated to the point at which police must be called in the first place. If that is the case, it may also be that the parties actually need a cop in their living-room to tell them to shut up and go to bed before they can do it. That, these officers argue, is all the couple really wants, and it would do no-one much good for the police to insert themselves more forcefully into the dispute.

For the most part, the failure of the police to implement the letter and spirit of the Domestic Violence Act is not because cops despise women. It is because the Act, by seeking to create a pro-arrest orientation towards cases of domestic violence, while also expanding the definition of domestic violence to include everything from withholding grocery money and screaming matches to physical and sexual violence, is actually less complex and human than the parties themselves or, indeed, the officers who must deal with them. Cops, it is true, hate these incidents and often think those involved are losers. All they want to do is manage down the temperature and then get on with other business. The results of their efforts are partial, temporary and unsatisfactory. But that, unfortunately, is inevitable in these cases, which are messy in the way that life is always messy, and which admit of no easy solutions.

It is hard to believe that any legislation will change that.

★

Another way in which cops' humanity affects the way they do their job is more troubling, even if it is also entirely predictable. This is that, given perverse incentives, police officers will respond perversely.

An example will help explain what I mean.

A night shift at one of the police stations I visited was dominated by a series of pursuits of a group of young boys. They'd been pointed out as suspects by a pedestrian we passed who said they'd mugged him seconds before the cops turned the corner. Three times that night the cops spotted the group on the street, but each time the young thugs sped off into the darkness of the township night, slipping between houses and shacks, and leaving in their wake widening circles of barking dogs, sonic ripples across the township night. The fourth and final chase was around dawn, and at last one of the boys was nabbed. When he was taken back to the station, however, it was found that the victim, who was asleep in the charge office, had not yet been able to open a case. Perhaps this was because his loss, the grand total of R6, was deemed too trivial by the counter-cops to justify police attention. Perhaps it was because he was too young and powerless to force the officers to take his statement. Whatever the reason, the unblushing response of one senior officer to this dereliction of duty was revealing: 'It is a pity that we made this arrest,' she told me. 'Robbery is a serious crime. Now we will have to open a docket and our crime stats are going to look bad.'

It is tempting to say at this point that the officer's reaction reflects a profound dishonesty in the heart of the police, one which renders suspect the use of any and all crime stats as a measure of police performance. If they massage the numbers, so this argument would go, then we can feel justified in concluding that the cops are failing to keep crime in check. Why else would they cook the books?

But the primary dishonesty here doesn't lie with the police. It lies with a society that knows, or ought to know, that policing can only do so much about crime, and that to use crime levels as a measure of the effectiveness of the police alone, does them a serious disservice. Obviously all crimes that are reported to the police should be recorded by them. But when a society disingenuously, and in the face of its own better instincts, places so much emphasis on crime levels as the key measure of how well the police do their work, it has only itself to blame when its officers try to find ways to make their performance appear more impressive.

254

So why, then, do we do it? Why do we hold only the police account-able for crime?

One reason is that the police themselves tell us that they can man-age crime levels. This they do in the way they talk about their work, in the way they designate some among their number as 'crime prevention officers', and in the tone of self-congratulation with which the Service greets any evidence of a decrease in recorded crime. This attitude is also evident in the Service's plans which have set the 'stabilisation' and sub-sequent 'normalisation' of crime levels as strategic objectives. If this is the police's self-imposed aim and object, then surely, we are justified in holding them to it? Finally, this idea is written into organisational processes that require individual station commissioners to account for every increase in reported crime. Depending on the temperament of the officer to whom reports are made, these meetings can be a gruelling assault on both the person and competence of the station commissioner concerned, who is told, in effect, that it is he who is responsible for crime levels, and that, if they have gone up, he must not be any good at his job.

The trouble is that although good policing can help to reduce crime and bad policing can lead to increases, a vast array of factors are at least as important in determining how safe a society is. These factors – social, economic, cultural and political – are seldom much influenced by polic-ing. It is possible, even probable, therefore, that changes to crime levels often, even usually, have nothing to do with changes in the quality of policing.

Why, then, do the police themselves say they are responsible for crime? Why don't they reject the burden and say that they can do noth-ing about the fact that people are unemployed, that they drink, that they have experienced early childhood traumas, and that, as a result, they have poor anger management skills and unhealthy responses to tempta-tion? Why embrace responsibility for something as important as crime while having only partial control over it?

One reason, of course, is self-deception. This is a useful, often enjoy-able, and very human capability, and cops, like researchers and farmers and artists and businessmen and anyone else, tend to overestimate their own importance. Another is naked bureaucratic calculation. There is much for the organisation to gain from punting the view that policing is the primary vehicle through which crime levels might be brought down. If this is so, if policing really is the last, best hope for reducing crime, it would be insanity itself for government to turn down the Service's requests for more money, men and machines.

But that raises another question: why would a left-of-centre government, one which believes that most of our problems come from the social and economic debris left by apartheid, buy into a more-cops-less-crime argument? Why would it pump resources into the police instead of into any of crime's root causes? Why would it allow the police to imply, as they do when they say their objective is merely to 'stabilise crime levels', that trends in our society are such that, without special efforts on their part, crime must forever get worse?

One answer is that government honestly thinks that the police are the sole factor governing the level of crime. Certainly there is much evidence in everything from ANC election material to the president's state-of-the-nation address that can be proffered in support of the idea that government sincerely believes that policing is the answer to crime and violence. But sincerity, as political sociologists will tell you, is usually disguised calculation, and political language is always layered with strategy. But to say this means we must ask another question: why would government say something it doesn't truly believe? What would it have to gain?

The real question, though, is this: what is its alternative?

Despite the fact that most members of the ruling party would argue that crime is caused by adverse social conditions and can best be combated by dealing with those conditions, they also know that to adopt such a view as official policy is fraught with danger, because to do so risks spreading responsibility for crime and violence more widely across government. The result would be that instead of any rise in the level of crime being used as a rod to beat the Police Service's back, the whole of government might suffer. From government's point of view, then, the danger associated with seeing crime as deriving from social conditions is that there is no way to contain the twin cancers of external criticism and internal self-doubt. If crime has many causes, blame for it might stick to every state institution; if crime control is the responsibility of the police, on the other hand, they alone carry the can.

All of which leads to perhaps the biggest question of all: notwithstanding lay and official views on where blame for our crime problems really lies, just how much responsibility should the police shoulder? How much responsibility should they bear for any increases, and how much credit should they get for any declines?

These are extraordinarily difficult questions to answer. And the problem is not just that there is a lack of firm empirical evidence one way or the other. It is worse than that: what evidence does exist is usually ambiguous, and is frequently flat-out contradicted by other bits of evidence. Indeed, in some areas, the data are so hopelessly confused and confusing that no more than the most tentative answers can be given. So tentative, in fact, that, despite public consensus to the contrary, it is impossible to be sure of so seemingly obvious an assertion as the claim that South Africa is the world's crime capital. This is because the international data are unbelievably poor. The result is that we can be sure that our crime levels, particularly for violent crime, compare very unfavourably against levels of crime in the developed world. But there are so few reliable data for the developing world, that it is literally impossible to say whether South Africa is a more violent country than other poor countries, or whether we simply have better data-gathering infrastructure. Only one example is needed to prove the point: the only available data on murder rates in Nigeria – home to about a quarter of all people on the African continent – are more than twenty years old, and imply that per capita murder rates in that country are a good deal lower than those of the European Union. One need not be a rabid Afro-pessimist to think that is bunkum.

A more pertinent problem relates to how one interprets changes in the recorded level of crime in South Africa over the past ten years. To begin with, we have no country-wide data for any time before 1994/5 against which to compare current crime rates. We also know that reporting rates for most crimes will have been affected significantly by the roll-out of police infrastructure into previously under-serviced areas, and by the growing legitimacy of the police after the end of apartheid. It is possible, in other words, that increased reporting alone accounts for the increase in crimes like assault and robbery. This claim is often made, and is apparently supported by the fact that levels of murder, which is by far the best-reported and -recorded crime, have fallen from nearly twenty-seven thousand in 1995/6 to less than twenty thousand in 2003/4. If that is so, the argument goes, we can conclude that other crime must also have fallen, and that the apparent rise is no more than increased reporting and recording.

The trouble with this argument is that the rise in some kinds of criminality seems to be both too steep and too prolonged to be no more than a reporting phenomenon. Besides, there is at least some evidence, coming from a 2003 victimisation survey, that, by the first years of the new millennium, victims were reporting to the police a smaller proportion of robberies than they had done in the late 1990s. That this happened even as the number of robberies recorded by the police rose quickly, suggests horrible underlying trends.

The data are puzzling, then, and, even before we start apportioning blame and credit for our crime levels, we have to acknowledge that, with the exception of murder rates which we unquestionably know are considerably lower than they were a decade ago, we actually don't know a great deal about what has really happened to crime rates. Let us, then, stick with what we do unequivocally know, and focus on murder rates. What role might the police have played in their decline? In answering this question, we should note immediately that there are grounds for thinking that policing has improved and that it might have had something to do with the decline in murder rates. This is so because police numbers have increased dramatically since 2000, as has spending on essential equipment, especially vehicles. The police, then, are much better resourced than they were. The organisation, which is now over the most traumatic phase of its transformation, is also much more stable than it was and has also, under the unimaginative operational name 'Crackdown', adopted a far more aggressive, boots-and-all approach to dealing with high crime areas. It is, in other words, not beyond the realm of possibility that changes in policing really did lead to changes in murder levels.

If this is the case, however, one thing seems fairly clear: police did not reduce murder rates by reducing aggravated robbery rates, the recorded levels of which have basically doubled at more or less the same time as the number of murders fell by 25 per cent. Despite failing to reduce the number of robberies, however, it might be that policing has reduced the average lethality of these crimes. This is possible because the Police Service has devoted vast energies to recovering illegal firearms. Fewer firearm crimes, even if they are replaced by knife attacks, could well lead to fewer murders because knives are less lethal than guns. It is also possible that the reduced lethality of the average robbery has something to do with changing *modi operandi* since the spread of cellphones has led to a dramatic increase in the kinds of robberies – muggings, bag-snatchings and smash-and-grabs – that tend to result in fewer fatalities. Thus the increase in robberies may not have led to a commensurate rise in murder, even if the police had not focused on guns. It is impossible, however, to be sure which effect was more pronounced.

So, it is possible that the police may have had something to do with robbery becoming a less lethal crime of violence, but, given the rise in the number of aggravated robberies, it would be very surprising if this accounted for the drop in the number of murders committed every year. Besides, we have other evidence that robbery is not the principal driver of murder rates, a fact that is evinced by a police docket analysis which found that the motive for most murders was something other than robbery. In fact, a very large proportion of all killings result from something as banal as an argument between people who know each other. Since a fall in robbery-murders probably doesn't account for the large fall in all murders, then, a steep fall in these other kinds of murder must have played a role. If this is so, how much credit do the police deserve for this?

Once again, this is a difficult question to answer.

It is possible that improved policing has discouraged these crimes. It is also possible that the focus on firearms has paid off here as well. In addition, it seems that murders have fallen fastest in those places into which new resources have been pumped – notably the Cape Flats and central Johannesburg. All of which tends to suggest that policing has made a difference to murder rates. But there are other factors that might also account for the decline.

One of these is the enormous increase in funds that government has allocated to the paying of social grants, the value of which has grown at more than twice the rate of inflation from R14,4 billion in 1995/6 to R41,4 billion in 2004/5. It is clear that this has not been enough to lift the majority of the poor out of poverty, and it is almost certainly insufficient to have made any significant difference in predatory crimes like robbery – much of which is not, in any event, committed out of genuine, rob-or-starve need. But it is possible that a cash injection of this magnitude has helped ameliorate some of the worst privations suffered by the poorest households. This, in turn, may well have reduced the levels of frustration and desperation which might otherwise have resulted in more interpersonal violence. Growing welfare rolls, in other words, may account for some of the decline in murder rates.

Another factor that has gotten altogether too little attention and which, I think, has probably played an important role, is the political stability that has settled on this country. This should not be taken to mean that I think that there were seven thousand-odd more political murders in 1995/6 than there were in 2003/4. Obviously that is not the case: even at the height of the violence during the transition, it is unlikely that as many as seven thousand people were killed for political reasons in any one year. However, the fact that people entering adulthood today are less likely to have direct experience of political violence than were their predecessors, means that trauma levels are lower now than they were then. Since we know that the experience of violence in childhood is a predictor of later violence, it is plausible that the reduction in trauma levels is being felt in the dampening of cycles of violence. It is also possible that the habits of moderation, self-regulation, compromise and self-control – the habits that come of living in a less volatile society – have begun to take hold. If these hypotheses are correct, the decline in murder could be as much a 'peace dividend' as it is a marker of improved policework.

These arguments might suggest that I think that the police are not especially effective. But again, we must return to my central premise:

policing can only do so much about crime because much of what drives criminality is not significantly affected by how well or how poorly a country is policed. Our police may not be perfect, but then our crime problems have their origins in places policing cannot get to. Still, that doesn't mean that policing is irrelevant or that crime levels depend wholly on factors other than policing. It is, therefore, worth asking a final question: how well are the police performing? To answer this question, however, we need some context.

★

Collectively, the police forces inherited by South Africa's first post-apartheid government were in a shambles. Poorly led, poorly trained and thoroughly bewildered by the transition to democracy, grassroots police officers entered the new era with little real sense of where the institution would be going. That was unsurprising since their leaders – uniformed and political – were equally uncertain about the place of the police in the post-apartheid scheme of things. In such an environment, misplaced hopes and fears thrived.

White cops, fearful for their career prospects and, in some cases, simply unwilling to work for a black-led Service, either nursed new grievances or left the organisation. Black cops, having spent decades being despised both by their communities and by their white colleagues, dreamed of the opportunities for social acceptance and for promotion that would soon be theirs. In retrospect, both white cops' pessimism and black cops' optimism were overblown, but both flowed out of a not-unrealistic sense that much would have to change in the police if the institution was going to flourish: there was simply no way that policing or the police organisation could continue to function as they had done. Not after the world had been turned on its head.

The changes, when they began, were thoroughly disorientating. Suddenly, in an organisation dedicated to preserving the *status quo*, too much was going on. Old rank structures were swept away and replaced, new curricula were introduced, out-dated rules of criminal procedure were junked, a fresh management team was appointed, and organisational structures were torn down, redesigned, re-erected and then razed again, all at a head-spinning pace.

Given the ferment, it was inevitable that management systems would begin to soften, that discipline would slacken, that command and control would become less fluent. It is hard, after all, to concentrate on the job at hand when the institution's bush-telegraph is humming with rumours and when, from a career cop's point of view, all that was solid is melting into air. Naturally, morale slipped badly.

Police management of the day was in an awful position. They knew that change had to happen, and they also knew something that was related to this but which was also slightly different: not only did the organisation have to change, it had to be seen to be changing willingly. The trouble was that they knew that ordinary police officers were experiencing these changes as little short of cataclysmic, but there was little space for them to acknowledge this either to their troops or to the general public. To do so would have seemed an implicit indictment of change itself, and, besides, would have reflected badly on their assessment of their own managerial skills. In the end, they did what anyone would do in similar circumstances: they tried to buy enough support from the rank-and-file to help ease the Service into the new South Africa by allowing grade inflation and salary improvements to lift police salaries. This sounds like a good thing, and it was. But it was also irresponsible in its own way because, by the mid- and late 1990s, salary growth so far outstripped the growth of the police budget as a whole that a moratorium had to be put on new enlistments, existing staff had to be encouraged to leave, and the budgets for new vehicles, vehicle repairs and even petrol had to be looted. It was something of a scorched earth approach to organisational development. The result was that by the turn of the century there were 20 per cent fewer cops than there had been in 1994, and each was worse equipped. Given the increase in most crimes between 1994 and 2000, that meant that workloads had exploded. Despite the increased salaries, no-one was especially pleased with the outcome.

Since the nadir, however, police management, assisted by a rapidly growing budget, has executed a remarkable, but largely unacknowledged, turnaround.

Between 2000 and 2005, police numbers grew by nearly a third, and had rebounded to their 1995 level and are projected to grow still further. This massive growth in numbers was not, however, effected at the expense of investment in the complementary goods and services needed by police officers. In fact, expenditure on these items grew far faster than did spending on personnel. Nor were these the only improvements. Money has been spent on hi-tech solutions to age-old problems. A state-of-the-art computerised fingerprint identification system, for instance, has helped dramatically speed up investigations and, by cutting to a fraction the time taken to produce criminal records for sentencing procedures, it has helped reduce the awaiting-trial prisoner population. Policing is also much smarter now than it was: patrol work is directed by more careful analysis of crime patterns and the use of more sophisticated patrol and problem-solving strategies; high-density operations have been used to crack down in areas with specific problems; guns and repeat offenders have been targeted as never before; and asset forfeiture legislation has hit organised criminals in the pocket.

Some of the softer aspects of management also seem better than they once were. Police head office, for instance, appears to be exerting far more pressure for delivery on its underlings than was the case ten or even five years ago. In an institution in which managers 'with hair on their teeth' command respect, the newly felt pressure (combined with the swelling numbers of officers and all the new goodies) seems to have improved morale. For the ordinary police officer, the brief experiment of a more decentralised, less militarised form of command and control was experienced largely as a period of organisational drift. Many actually prefer the kick-arse-and-take-names approach of the new national commissioner.

The police, then, have effected a hugely impressive turnaround at strategic, organisational and operational levels. They have gotten more resources, and they are deploying them wisely. More, I think, could not really be asked of its management.

★

This is a book about grassroots policing, not police management, and I want to end by paying final homage to South Africa's men and women in blue. This time I will do so by reference to a policeman to whom I said not a single word. His name was Inspector Mbambe and he was on the first shift I worked. It was 31 January 2003 and, as it turned out, it was his very last day at work because that month he had reached the Service's mandatory retirement age. The final shift to which he'd been assigned started at seven in the evening and was to finish at seven the following morning. Anyone I know would have taken the night off. Not Mbambe. He arrived at work in a pressed uniform, was allotted one of the vans, and drove his crew around the township for five hours. At midnight, he drove the vehicle back to the station where the shift commander offered a short speech of thanks. Then he said goodnight and goodbye, and went home.

It was a remarkable, remarkably sad, spectacle. What, I wondered, had kept him going all these years?

When I started researching this book, I wasn't coming at the subject entirely ignorant. I had spent years in government working on issues of policing either for the minister of safety and security or for the National Treasury. I had taught on station management courses offered by a consortium of universities. I had done docket analyses and ride-along research projects. I may have known too little about real policing, but I was not entirely ignorant.

One thing I suspected was that good policing would turn out to be maddeningly difficult, that it would result in partial, lesser-of-two-evils kind of solutions to society's problems, and that, as a consequence, police officers would have to have the skills of Chinese jugglers if they were to balance all the competing values our society holds dear. In this, I was not disappointed: good policing really does need to be as nimble and quick-witted as that. What was surprising was how many officers grasped that, how many understood how complex and changeable the problems they confronted were and how limited were the means at their disposal to effect solutions. I expected, I suppose, to be confronted more often with a naive, boy-scout-ish enthusiasm that would also be something of a sham: cops, I thought, would talk themselves up. Instead,

264

most turned out to be hard-bitten realists with a fine-grained under-standing of the nuances of the job. They didn't look like philosophers, but many acted with more wit than university-trained researchers, aca-demics and journalists would have given them credit for, or would them-selves have been capable of.

They were, nonetheless, often depressed by their job and the frustra-tions that come of it. Most seemed to have found some way to live with the difficulties of the work itself, but seemed angry at the way their institution has treated them, at the way their ambitions have been thwarted. It is easy to see how this could lead to cynicism, slackness and even dishonesty. But often the depression was mixed with determina-tion and, paradoxically, flowed from a conviction that, however hard the job, however frustrating, this was work that counted. They didn't do it for the pleasures, but because it mattered.

No-one, I think, could do this job without an edge of bitterness, but that it must be done is incontrovertible. Police officers do our society's dirty work, and we owe men like Inspector Mbambe more gratitude than we can say.

AUTHOR'S NOTE

One of the challenges of writing a book of this sort is how best to collect one's primary data. In an ideal world, every interviewee would consent to being interviewed, have no fears about speaking openly, and would speak nothing but the truth throughout. It would also be a world in which every interviewee could be interviewed in his or her first language, and interviewers would be able to recall verbatim every word spoken. Better still, every conversation would be recorded, especially if there was any possibility that doubts about the accuracy of recollections and interpretations would be raised.

Unfortunately, the real world is not like that.

In the real world, people don't like to be quoted being rude to the boss. In the real world, even the most honest among us cloaks himself in the most flattering garb. In the real world, people make mistakes, they struggle to tell stories chronologically, and they choose to hide what they would prefer you didn't know. Nor does it help that an interviewer's understanding is seldom linear, that it often comes to him in waves and layers, and that, as a result, there are always questions he wishes he'd asked. In the real world, conversations that take place over 12-hour shifts in rattly old cars can't be recorded, and contemporaneous note-taking in the dead of night is impossible.

All of which means that readers of any material based on the kind of work I did to complete this book, need to take on faith that I tried to capture as accurately and honestly as possible the sentiments and words of the officers with whom I spent so many hours. It is, however, impossible to demonstrate that what I have written reflects what I saw and

266

what I heard. All I can do is acknowledge frankly that the book I have written is not rigorously scientific. I used no standardised questionnaires. I drew no representative samples. There was no quantification of opinion. The argument, where it refers to people and events, relies on the quality of my note-taking skills and on the depth of my recollection and interpretation of events and words. Those who wish to, are free to dismiss it for that reason alone.

In response to those who would dismiss the work on these grounds, however, I would say that the approach taken was an attempt, amateurish and flawed no doubt, to understand policing ethnographically, to attempt, in other words, to describe the nature of the organisation, its culture and its attitudes by immersing myself in its day-to-day operations. This is an approach which is fraught with dangers. There is, for instance, an enormous risk that the researcher who adopts so freewheeling a method as this will emerge from his endeavours with little more than confirmation of the prejudices with which he began. The equal and opposite risk is that, in raising all methodological anchors, the researcher risks losing all critical and intellectual objectivity and becoming little more than the organisation's publicist.

These dangers, real as they might be, are also unavoidable. There is, quite literally, no way in which questions about the organisational practice of institutions as large and as sedimented as is a police force can even be framed, much less answered, unless and until researchers are willing to set aside preconceptions and to seek to understand the organisation from the inside out. If that means running the methodological risks already referred to, so be it. And if the results are, for these reasons, harder to defend by reference to the rigour of the methodology which underpins them, that too is a price that must be paid.

Whatever reputational risks the researcher is prepared to run, however, he cannot ask the same of his subjects. For this reason, I have gone to great length to disguise the identities of many of the people described in these pages, both by changing their names and, in many cases, altering their physical descriptions. This does not apply to everyone. Some people, those whose positions made them easily identifiable and who did not request anonymity, are named. All the station commissioners mentioned, for instance, are properly identified, though some have now moved on to bigger things. So too are heads of units like Captains Verster and Pentz at Sea Point. I have, however, sought to avoid naming anyone doing anything about which they might be embarrassed. Inspectors Kirsten and Van Zyl from Parkview, bless their cotton socks, are both real and are completely undisguised. In other cases, however, dramatic changes have been made.

I have said already that Inspector Makaye, the subject of chapter twelve, does not now work, nor has he ever worked, in Ivory park. The real Captain de Koster described in chapter ten does not live and work in Johannesburg. In both cases I shifted the geographic backdrops, drawing on time spent with other cops in the places into which I have inserted these men, so that their identities could be hidden. In other places, notably chapters seven, eleven and fourteen, composite characters have been created out of more than one individual. In each case, this was partly for ease of exposition and partly to disguise individuals through synthesis. In the case of Ronnie Govender, the rough, tough, no-shit-taking cop described in chapter eight, I have inserted one or two pieces of biographical disinformation so misleading that the real Govender will doubt that he is reading about himself, while in chapters six and thirteen I have subtly changed some facts of the cases the men I called Inspectors Mokhosi and Morake were investigating so that these cannot be identified with any certainty because I would hate for anything I have written to affect any trial that might ensue. None of these changes, however, affect the substance of the chapters: Morake really did leave crucial evidence behind; Mokhosi really did delay taking statements, and really did get incompatible accounts of events.

I am pleased about none of these changes. But they were unavoidable. It simply would not have been fair to expose individual officers to criticism simply because they'd been unlucky enough to be on duty when I arrived at their station. For all I know, given the fact that their commanders knew what I was doing when they assigned me to these men, these cops were the very best the station had to offer.

Finally, I need to acknowledge my sources. This is not a comprehensive bibliography. Instead, it covers only works to which I have referred, usually without explicitly identifying their authors, in the course of the text. Many, many other writings have affected my thinking.

★

The form of this book – studies of individual police officers going about their work – was inspired by two quite different sources. The first is the work of journalist-turned-author-turned-scriptwriter, David Simon, whose books *Homicide: A Year on the Killing Streets* (1991: Ivy Books) and (with Edward Burns) *The Corner: A Year in the Life of an Inner-City Neighbourhood* (1997: Broadway Books), demonstrated the power of close, individual studies in throwing light on more general problems. He is also the inventor of the wonderful word 'eyefuck'. The second is the extraordinary travel writing of VS Naipaul, a man quite capable of putting an entire civilisation on the couch by describing a casual conversation with a single person met fortuitously in the foyer of a hotel. The writing is sublime. The insight is better still.

George Orwell's semi-autobiographical, experiential essays were also the source of much inspiration for the form of the book. His much-anthologised essay 'Shooting an elephant' provided the book's title, and *Homage to Catalonia* (2003: Penguin Classics) provided the title of chapter seven.

The theoretical framework from which I have approached policing has been most rigorously developed by Egon Bittner and Carl Klockers. Bittner's collection, *Aspects of Police Work* (1990: Northeastern University Press), especially the delightfully titled essay, 'Florence Nightingale in pursuit of Willie Sutton: A theory of police', which is the source of the notion of a something-is-happening-about-which-something-ought-to-be-done-now situation, and Klockers's *The Idea of Police* (1985: Sage Publications), were the most valuable.

In chapter two, the account given of Chief Galeshewe's rebellion on pages 16 and 17 comes from Shillington's *The Colonisation of the Southern Tswana* (1985: Ravan Press) and the idea of the police as 'street-corner politicians' on page 24 comes from Rob Reiner's *The Politics of the Police* (1992: Harvester/Wheatsheaf).

Chapter three's title mirrors that of Joseph Conrad's short story which is also quoted at some length. My copy is in a 1999 collection edited by J Lawton, *Joseph Conrad: The Secret Sharer and other stories*, and is published by Phoenix. For the account of the resolution of the cattle war, I relied in part on two presentations made at a 2001 conference on rural safety organised by the SAPS at which I was the report-writer. One was made by Captain Batha Mlata (who was still the head of the Stock Theft Unit in Maluti when I visited, and was one of the nicest cops I met) and the other by Captain Erasmus. A 2001 Idasa-published, Southern African Migration Project monograph, *Cross-border Raiding and Community Conflict in the Lesotho-South African Border Zone* by G Kynoch, T Ulicki and various collaborators, provided important background material. The statistics about the state of police infrastructure and training offered on page 33 come from a 1994 study by Antoinette Louw and Mark Shaw called *Stolen Opportunities: The Impact of Crime on South Africa's Poor* which was published by the Institute for Security Studies. The data on the visibility of policing in the Eastern Cape on page 37 comes from an article written by Eric Pelser for the *South African Crime Quarterly* in 2000.

In chapter four, the statistic that over sixty per cent of police officers who are murdered are killed while off duty comes from the national commissioner himself, who gave this figure to a summit on police killings in 2003. It was reported by Ted Leggett in the fourth *SA Crime Quarterly* of 2003. Accounts of the studies showing the relative futility of rapid response referred to on page 46 can be found in a number of places: two of the most useful were Larry Sherman's 1995 article 'The Police' in Wilson and Peterselia's collection, *Crime*, published by ICS Press, and 'Response time and citizen evaluation of the police' by Stephen Percy that was published in a collection edited by David Bayley and published by Oxford University Press in 1998. It was called *What Works in Policing*. The account of the difficulties of and limitations on police investigations offered on page 62 relies on a Wesley Skogan and George Antunes article called 'Information, apprehension and deterrence: exploring the limits of police productivity' in the same Bayley collection, and on a 1975 Rand Corporation study of police investigations of which I have read two summaries – one by Peter Greenwood and Joan Peterselia, and another by Jan Chaiken, Peter Greenwood and Joan Peterselia – without ever seeing the original, which seems to be out of print. The first was published in the Bayley collection already referred to, and the second was printed in *Policy Analysis* in 1977.

Much of the thinking about gangs and gangsterism in chapter five is derived from two extraordinary master's dissertations completed at UCT in the early 1980s. The first was Don Pinnock's *State Control and Street Gangs in Cape Town: Towards an understanding of special and social development* completed in 1982. This dissertation is also the source of the account of how apartheid's urban planners adopted the idea of the English Garden City that appears on page 120. The second is Wilfred Schärf's *The Impact of Liquor on the Working Class: The implications for the structure of the liquor industry and the role of the state in this regard* completed in 1984. The clunkiness of the titles belies the intelligence and insight of the works. Jonny Steinberg's *The Number* published in 2004 by Jonathan Ball Publishers also helped frame my thinking about the gangs, as did an unpublished piece by Superintendent Vearey entitled 'Nongoloza's legacy: From popular revolt to prison and street gangs in the Western Cape' which he kindly let me see. In addition to these sources, the quote on page 66 comes from another Pinnock piece. This one is undated and called, simply, *Elsies River*. For an account of the corruption of Irish-American cops during the prohibition era in America (and of the subsequent professionalisation of policing in the US) referred to on page 75, Fogelson's classic study, *Big City Police* (1977: Harvard University Press), is more than adequate. The quote that appears on page78 from Helen Suzman's memoirs comes from a review of the book by JM Coetzee published in a collection called *Stranger Shores: Essays 1986 –1999* (2002:Vintage Books). The others who have written about gangs and to whom I referred on page 79 are Don Pinnock and Andre Standing. The latter's most recent essay appears in a book edited by Bill Dixon and Elrena van der Spuy called *Justice Gained? Crime and Crime Control in South Africa's Transition* (2004: UCT Press). The Naipaul quote on page 86 comes from *A Turn in the South* (2003: Picador).

In chapter six, the rough-'n-ready summary of the confusing evidence about how economic cycles affect crime is drawn from a number of sources including a 2002 piece by Cambridge economists Fafchamps and Minten called 'Crime and Poverty: Evidence from a Natural Experiment', an article by Richard Freeman on 'The labor market' in a collection of essays called *Crime* edited by James Q Wilson and Joan Peterselia and published by ICS Press in 1995, as well as the similarly titled chapter in Wilson's *magnum opus* (written with Richard Herrnstein) provocatively entitled *Crime and Human Nature: The definitive study of the causes of crime*. It was published by Touchstone Books in 1985. Finally, with respect to the difficulty of disaggregating the effect of a growing economy from the effect of increased police hirings, see Steven Levitt's extremely influential article, 'Using electoral cycles on police hiring to estimate the effect of the police on crime'. It is on the National Bureau of Economic Research's website, www.nber.org.

The quote from Freud on page 129 comes from his exchange on the nature of war with Albert Einstein. It is called *Why War?* and can be found in the *Civilization, Society and Religion* volume of Freud's collected works. A 1996 piece by H Toch called 'The Violence-Prone Police Officer' and published in a collection edited by himself and WA Geller called *Police Violence: Understanding and controlling police abuse of force* by Yale University Press, discussed the relationship between police violence and countering perceived disrespect raised on page 134. The point made on page 141 about police services facing less violence when they adopt more restrictive use of force policies was taken from a 1992 manual edited by W Geller and S Scott called *Deadly Force: What we know* that was published by the Police Executive Research Foundation in Washington DC. Joan Wardop's research, referred to on page 141, was published as an essay, 'Simply the Best: the Soweto Flying Squad', in a University of Natal Press collection edited by Rob Morrel published in 2001 called *Changing Men in Southern Africa*.

For an account of the Flower Gang murders in Nieuwoudtville referred to on page 148, see chapter four of Steinberg's *The Number*. The scepticism expressed on page 157 about the efficacy of street-level enforcement on reducing the consumption of narcotics is relatively uncontroversial in serious academic work. Those interested might glance at any of the drugs and drug policy publications of the Rand Corporation, a US military-funded think-tank in California. Further evidence can be found in David Boyum and Mark Kleinman's seminal piece in the Wilson and Peterselia collection referred to earlier.

My own monograph on the detectives referred to on page 169 was published by the Institute for Security Studies in 1998 and is called *Solving Crime: The state of the SAPS Detective Service*.

The research on migrants referred to on page 181 was conducted by the Centre for Development and Enterprise in Johannesburg, while the account of why Igbo-speaking Nigerians play such a large role in the local crack market is derived primarily from Ted Leggett's marvelous book, *Rainbow Vice: The Drugs and Sex Industries in the New South Africa*, which was published by Claremont's Zed Books in 2001, as well as from various pieces by the United Nations Office For Drugs and Crime including the *World Drug Report 2004* and a paper on *West African Organised Crime*. Kurt Vonnegut's report on his experiences in Biafra was published by Jonathan Cape in 1975 in a collection of his writings called *Wampeters, Foma and Granfalloons*. It was called 'Biafra: A people betrayed'. Freud's definition of an illusion, referred to on page 197, comes from a piece called 'The future of an illusion' in the same volume referred to earlier.

On page 200, the phrase 'uniform carriers' comes from Joseph Wambaugh's novel *The Onion Field* published by Future in 1974.

The photographs described on page 218 and 219 were published in Greg Marinovich and Joao Silva's *The Bang-Bang Club: Snapshots from a Hidden War* published in 2000 by Arrow, while the quote from the TRC on page 220 comes from its report on the violence on the East Rand. Both sources provide much information on the dynamics of the conflict recounted on page 212, as does Tony Minnaar's paper 'Self-Defence Units Post-April 1994 – what role in community policing?' presented to the South African Political Studies Association in October 1996, and Sasha Gear's 2002 monograph 'Wishing Us Away: Challenges facing ex-combatants in the "new" South Africa', published by the Centre for the Study of Violence and Reconciliation. So too did Gary Kynoch's 'Crime,

Conflict and Politics: An Historical Account of Township Violence in Transition Era South Africa' which is available on the website of the Wits Institute for Social and Economic Research at Wits University.

The quote on page 231 comes from research conducted by Professor Ben Smit, and is cited in Gareth Newham's article 'Towards understanding and combating police corruption' printed in the Autumn 2000 edition of *Crime and Conflict*.

For a more extended discussion on the level of sympathy patrol officers have for the victims of domestic violence, see a paper I presented to a February 2005 conference on 10 Years of Criminal Justice in SA in Gordon's Bay. The paper is available through the Centre for the Study of Violence's website. A more extended discussion on whether South Africa is the crime capital of the world, hinted at on page 257, can be found in an article written by me in the first edition of the *SA Crime Quarterly* in 2005, while the suggestion that reporting rates for robbery have fallen comes from the *2003 Victimisation Survey* written by Burton, Du Plessis, Leggett, Louw, Mistry and Van Vuuren, and published by the Institute for Security Studies. The docket analysis referred to on page 259 was written by the Research Unit: Violent and Social Fabric Crimes in the Crime Intelligence division of the SAPS. Its data are drawn from 2001 cases, but it was written in 2004.